This book should be returned to any branch of the
Lancashire County Library on or before the date

pmo 1/3

2 5 SEP 2019

AMO
HAC

ROGER GARFITT

# The Horseman's Word

## A Memoir

VINTAGE BOOKS
London

Published by Vintage 2012

2 4 6 8 10 9 7 5 3 1

Copyright © Roger Garfitt 2011

Roger Garfitt has asserted his right under the
Copyright, Designs and Patents Act 1988 to be identified
as the author of this work

First published in Great Britain in 2011 by
Jonathan Cape

Vintage
Random House, 20 Vauxhall Bridge Road,
London SW1V 2SA

www.vintage-books.co.uk

Addresses for companies within The Random House Group Limited
can be found at: www.randomhouse.co.uk/offices.htm

The Random House Group Limited Reg. No. 954009

A CIP catalogue record for this book
is available from the British Library

ISBN 9780099571957

The Random House Group Limited supports The Forest Stewardship
Council (FSC®), the leading international forest certification
organisation. All our titles that are printed on FSC®
certified paper carry the FSC logo. FSC is the only forest certification scheme endorsed by
the leading environmental organisations, including Greenpeace.

Our paper procurement policy can be found at
www.randomhouse.co.uk/environment

Typeset in Garamon by Palimpsest Book Production Limited,
Falkirk, Stirlingshire

Printed and bound by CPI Group (UK) Ltd, Croydon CR0 4YY

For Redmond O'Hanlon

# Preface

This book has been so long in the making, and came about in such a strange way, that it really needs something the length of a preface if I am to thank everyone who had a hand in its making.

In 1988 I was living with the painter Eugenia Escobar and spending much of my time in Bogotá. The British Council created opportunities for me wherever they could but I had no work permit and in any case in a developing country like Colombia I could not expect to support myself as I had in England, by running poetry workshops in schools. I had to earn my living from my desk and that meant writing prose. A friend of mine had made a useful sum of money in a short time by writing *The Whole Hog*, a light-hearted account of the origin of some popular phrases. I thought of doing the same with place names, picking out the more intriguing place names and telling the stories behind them. I prepared some sample entries, keeping them brisk and bright, and sent them to an agent who also happened to be a good friend, Jane Turnbull. Jane said, 'Now what this needs is a short, chatty introduction so that the reader learns to trust you as an author. Why don't you tell the stories behind the names of the places where you've lived yourself?'

That was an inspired suggestion. When I first went freelance, friends used to lend me their houses while they were away and

I had a rich roster of place names to draw on. 'This is coming out well,' I thought, as I strung them together across six or seven pages. Jane sent the introduction and the sample entries to David Godwin, who was then the Editorial Director at Secker & Warburg. 'Forget the place names!' David said. 'Just write me a book about the places where you've lived.' An intuitive agent and then an intuitive editor. My luck was in.

Luck, they say, comes in threes. By the time I returned from Bogotá to sign the contract, David had left Secker and I had to hope that his successor, Dan Franklin, would honour it. Dan did more than that: when I delivered Part One of the book eighteen months later, he released the second half of the advance, which was only due upon completion, so that I could work on uninterrupted. And crucially, when I realised that I had to revamp the book, he was prepared to trust my instinct.

The book I had signed up to write was to be called *Journeys into England*. It would start with my childhood summers in Norfolk, then jump to the farmhouse in Oxfordshire where I was able to start writing seriously when the farmer rented me two rooms for two pounds a week. It would move down to North Devon, where John Moat had lent me his mill for six months and John Papworth had given me the use of a cottage rent free, and end in the farmhouse at Birdoswald, on Hadrian's Wall, which Frances Horovitz and I had rented for two winters. We could never afford it in the summer.

I wrote Part One to that plan. But as I finished it in Bogotá in the spring of 1990, I began to have misgivings. I saw the book as a reader might see it, as a succession of farmhouses in which I sat and wrote poetry. I would be creating another version of pastoral, playing to all the misconceptions people already have about the writing of poetry, because I was leaving out what had started me writing in the first place. I was leaving out the engine of difficulty that drives the work.

But to give any sense of that I would have to tell the story I had been shying away from, the story contained, if that is the word, in what is now Part Three. I took an episode and started to sketch it out, just to see how it would work. It worked all too well. I had committed myself to remaking the book, though I had an uneasy feeling that I might be putting other things at risk – not least my life in Bogotá, which the book was supposed to finance.

Dan, who had just released all the money for the old book, found himself listening to my plans for the new book the next time I was in London. But he gave me my head and he was very happy with the rough drafts I sent him the following year: the new book did cut much deeper. But it was much harder to write and I'm a slow writer at the best of times. I was running out of money and Dan, who had just moved from Secker to Cape, was in no position to help. The Authors' Foundation gave me a grant, which bought me another six months, but I finally returned from Bogotá in the spring of 1992, deep in debt. Eugenia had always taken a close interest in the book, and even lent me some money to keep me going, but we had little choice but to part good friends.

It was the autumn of 1996 before I was able to resume concentrated work on the book. I had taken on all the freelance work I could get: a writer's residency, a literature development project, two poetry commissions and three community writing projects, from which I edited three books while neglecting my own. No one, it seemed, was interested in *The Horseman's Word*, not even the Arts Council, to whom I applied five times for a Writer's Award. 'This is ridiculous!' declared my wife Margaret, whom I had been lucky enough to marry that summer. She subbed me to return to the book and gradually the manuscript began to win its way, securing the Writing Fellowship at UEA, a Creative Ambition Award from West Midlands Arts and a Royal Literary Fund Fellowship at Swansea University.

Meanwhile, the mergers in publishing were working to my advantage. Cape had already become part of Random House, which proceeded to take over Secker & Warburg. Jane had never lost faith in the book and she had been keeping Dan informed of my progress. From his eminence at Cape he was able to resume responsibility for the book and in 2008, twenty years after he signed the first contract, he came up with a refresher advance so that I could bring it to a conclusion. I have indeed been lucky in my agent and lucky in my editor.

I am also grateful to Bill Buford, who published extracts from Part One in *Granta* at a time when I had no pedigree as a prose writer, and to the editors of *Pretext* and *Raw Edge*, who published further extracts from Part One later on.

In Part Two I am uneasily aware that my own memories of attending Compline may have merged with something I read somewhere, in the work of an Irish writer, I think, probably John McGahern, from whom I learned a great deal about the handling of prose. Sadly John died before I was able to verify this and get his permission to keep whatever I needed to keep to make that passage work.

In Part Three I am grateful to D.M. Thomas for permission to use the final lines from his poem 'Lorca', taken from his *Selected Poems* (Secker & Warburg 1983). The brief quotation from James K. Baxter is taken from 'Letter from the Mountains' in his *Collected Poems* (1980) by kind permission of Oxford University Press. The brief quotations from Keith Douglas, Philip Larkin, C.A. Trypanis, Sylvia Plath, T.S. Eliot, Theodore Roethke and Ted Hughes are all identified in the text and appear by kind permission of Faber & Faber. The brief quotation from Peter Levi's *Pancakes for the Queen of Babylon* and the quotations from John Birtwhistle and Michael Hewlings appear by kind permission of Anvil Press. 'Love Without Hope' by Robert Graves and the lines from his poem 'The Starred

Coverlet' appear by kind permission of Carcanet Press (*Complete Poems in One Volume*, 2000). The concrete poem by Dom Sylvester Houédard appears by kind permission of the Prinknash Abbey Trustees. The lines from 'As I Walked Out One Evening' appear by kind permission of The Estate of W.H. Auden (Copyright © 1976, 1991). I am grateful to Nigel Wells for permission to use the poems from his first collection, *The Winter Festivals* (Bloodaxe, 1980), and the lines from his second collection, *Just Bounce* (Bloodaxe, 1988), which furnish the epigraph to Part Four. With the exception of 'In the distance', which was first published in *Ambit*, the quotations from my own poems are all taken by kind permission of Carcanet Press from my first pamphlet, *Caught on Blue* (1970)

I am deeply indebted to Mrs Ruth Hudson, my Aunt Ruth, for the family background I have drawn on for Parts One and Four. And indebted beyond measure to my wife Margaret, who gave me the chance to start work on the book again.

# PART ONE

## Norfolk

### 1944–1966

*Como pude perder aquel preciso*
*orden de humildes y queridas cosas,*
*inaccesibles hoy como las rosas*
*que dio al primer Adan el Paraiso?*

How could I lose that precise
order of humble and beloved things,
as unreachable now as the roses
Paradise gave to the first Adam?

Jorge Luis Borges, *'Adrogue'*

The long path round the back was a cinder path starred with cockleshells. Chalk stones, little flat moons of an unassailable whiteness, dust-dry and spotless as freshly blanco'd plimsolls, edged the path to the front door. The front garden was a beach garden of fine orange gravel. This was land that had once belonged to the sea, a danger removed just far enough to become a source of pride and ornament. The garden made a small, human ceremony of what happened unceremoniously with every flood tide at Titchwell, when skate's eggs and razor shells washed into the mouths of the rabbit burrows.

I think even as a small child I knew there was a measure of economy in the moonstones and the cockle-starred path. Our neighbour kept up appearances by washing her front step and pumicing it with a large chalk stone until the white rubbed off on to the step. The sea was to be used thriftily and the shrimps we hoovered into our nets as we tramped through the shallows, the cockles we picked from the sand's pockets, the samphire we unstitched from the hems of the marsh, were not just summer treats, they were free meals. But I was a child of the London suburbs for whom any seashell, even a cockleshell's nail clipping trodden into the clinker, had an edge of mystery. Part of the magic of my grandparents' house was that these small wonders were thrown out with the ashes.

The front of the house was always in sunlight, the back in shadow. The chalk stones were a broadcast of summer, the white of the beach hut or the old bowling skirt my grandmother wore for the beach. But the back had the water butt, its soaked wood black and speckled with green mould. Rainwater was always used for the wash because it was softer and saved on soap powder, an economy of which I knew nothing. To me the water butt was a presence. The shadow's core, it grew colder as you approached. A wet battery, a condenser, you could almost hear it hum. To lift the tin bowl off the plank, splaying your fingers round its thick wooden handle, and dip into the water was like dipping into a second universe, held in reserve. Specks hung there in slowly revolving constellations. Insects tracked like comets across the surface. We brought the bowl up a third full, just enough to mix a similar bowl of chicken meal. But it seemed more than water: it was a universal concentrate, a galactic tonic we were feeding the hens on.

The house had a cold tap in the scullery but no bathroom. Even this ordinary water was reserved, a kind of sacrament, to be heated in the kettle and carried up to the bedrooms. In the suburbs we were richer in convenience but poorer in ceremony. Entering the front bedroom we shared each summer with our parents was like entering a church. The door opened on to stillness and dark furniture. The water jug stood in a bowl on a white cloth on the washstand. Their very size made them ritual vessels. The china was cold to the touch. It even smelled cold, like geraniums. But our fingertips were drawn back to it, as to the marble of a tomb. First a quick dab, a furtive fascination. Then a lingering, pensive pressure.

In the morning all was warmth and benediction. We would be brought tea and biscuits, and the jug taken down to be filled. It returned with a steam fragrance, a vapour that seemed lighter and thinner and sweeter than came from the hot tap at home. Perhaps because it really was closer to steam. Washing had to be by turns, and we would hug the bed, dipping our biscuits in the tea until their half-soaked warmth merged with our half-sleep. When my mother called me up to the washstand, it was rather like taking communion, the same awkward intimacy, the same mixture of complicity and constraint. The priest wipes the chalice from the last pair of lips, as if they had proved something of an embarrassment, and then you have to concentrate on not being gross and bodily yourself. From my mother or my sister I would inherit warm, soapy water. An initial delicacy gave way to a sense of ease, as if I were still sharing my mother's blood heat, as if I were back in the womb. It was rather like climbing into my sister's bath at home. But then came the constraint of not spilling any on the white cloth or the varnished top. The wash became, of necessity, ceremonial, a slow, deliberate laving.

Mostly the sea kept us clean. But every so often we would be drummed into the ritual of Saturday night, which was bath night. A fire would be lit under the big copper, which had to be filled from the cold tap, bowl by bowl. The tin bath would be taken from its hook on the outside wall and laid on the rag rug in front of the kitchen range. Then the ladling would have to begin all over again, this time of hot water from the copper. It was never quite the occasion it could have been. I was just expanding into privilege when I would be hurried along so that my sister could take over the water. No sooner into the lukewarmth than out again, standing chilling with a towel wrapped round me, suddenly aware that the kitchen, so snug when you were dressed, was a large room with a wind rushing down from the scullery and a draught whiffling up under the door, whipping away the eiderdown of warm, moist air that would enclose me when I stepped out of the bath in the little bathroom at home. Such a rush compared to the eternity that would pass while my grandmother was having her bath and we were shut out of the kitchen. We would sit in the formality of the front room,

11

conversing in hushed tones, as if awed by the extraordinary thought that Grandma was naked in the next room.

Food was cooked in the range but prepared in the long scullery that ran down to the back door and my grandmother spent much of her time there, out of sight. If I think back to the kitchen, it is to an absorbed silence, broken only by the turning of a page. I am curled in the crook of the couch, reading one of the copies of *Radio Fun* or *Film Fun* that still come for Billy and Peter, my grown uncles. Between my fingers I am twiddling a loose strand of the couch's black horsehair. My grandfather is in his armchair, deep in the *Eastern Daily Press*. Sometimes my parents' voices wash over our heads. Sometimes my sister frets on the foot of the couch and I settle her down with one of the comics I have already read. This absorption lasts a long hour until supper. In a wet summer it can last all next morning as well, a secured pleasure, an out-of-bed lie-in. I turn the page as I might turn on the pillow, surfacing voluptuously, just for the sensation of sinking back. As the hours pass and my parents begin to discuss wet weather outings, I snuggle deeper into the crook of the couch.

If my grandmother enters this memory, it is as a pair of hands. She has arthritis and, as she brings my grandfather a cup of tea, she does not hold the cup out, she holds it in, at a slight angle to her arm. The arm has the thinness of age, the skin falling away from the wrist and the knob of the wrist bone, and rucked into little folds around the elbow. But the skin is sandy and freckled, as if it has stored every hour of sun since April. Just as her hair, once the colour of barley wine, refuses to be white. Like corn bleaching in the sun, it prints lighter and lighter tones of gold. I watch her arms as she moves about the room, almost in love with their colour. As she reaches up for the biscuit tin on the mantelshelf, the muscles, still firm in their activity, draw into a ridge along the forearm,

12

and the skin around the elbow tightens into a little whorl, almost decorative.

Sometimes, if she needed more room, if she was drawing a chicken or gutting rabbits, she worked on the end of the kitchen table. Then the fascination was to watch her fingers grope inside the chicken and draw out the string of unlaid eggs, diminishing from a shell-less egg complete in its skin to a tiny bead of yolk, an orange match-head burning inside a blood-red membrane. She used the shell-less egg for the stuffing, and almost everything else except the intestines, which were rapidly bundled into newspaper and incinerated in the range. She pulled out the gizzard, slit its little bag and cleaned away the grit the chicken used as an internal mill to grind up its corn. At this point we always tensed ourselves, expecting the grey sludge to smell like the intestines, but the little stones were clean and fresh, like rainwashed gravel. She cut off the feet, scalded them in boiling water, and scraped off the claws and scales, starting at the toes and whittling down the leg. Then boiled gizzard and feet together to make gravy. As she detached the foot and pulled the sinews out of the thigh, the chicken clenched its toes. This appalled us, and we were given the foot to see how it worked. We pulled at the dangle of sinews until we found the string that operated the toes. We had a horror from the *Ghost Train*, three cold claws that could pluck at your sleeve, or tickle an adult's neck as he read the newspaper. It became a regular game, a ghostly cock-fight in which two disembodied feet leapt and spurred at each other until it was time to give up their jelly to the gravy.

Occasionally we were useful and helped her shell peas. We would volunteer for this, remembering the way the peas pinged into the colander and the pleasure of running our fingers through their cool shot.

More often, though, my grandmother was off in the scullery and in the kitchen we sat in my grandfather's warm. This is just how

13

it felt. It warmed you simply to look at my grandfather. He was like a coal in a well-laid fire, burning in its own heat, a white steady glow. Perhaps I saw him at the age to which he was best suited. Perhaps he had really been a grandfather all his life. Already, in the earliest photo I have of him, a man still short of fifty holding me up to the camera as a babe in arms, he was well set in the mould: white toothbrush moustache, flat cap and raincoat. Summer might change the flat cap to a straw hat and the raincoat to a light grey jacket but nothing disturbed the considered movements or ruffled the voice in its slow course. He grumbled and chuckled but my Aunt Ruth only once heard him laugh outright. She was keeping watch by his last bed, as he was dying of cancer. In his delirium he was back marching with the British Legion. Suddenly he laughed and said, 'Yes, we've been married six weeks.'

We always felt immensely comfortable in his presence. Perhaps because he was companionable, talking to us over a late breakfast before he puttered off on his Autocycle to Sedgeford, where he had a shoe repairer's shop on the Heacham road, a little lean-to shed beside a petrol pump, which he minded for the garage down the bank. He had a weak stomach and great care was taken over his food. His Shredded Wheat came with warm milk. We preferred ours cold: warm milk smelled of cow's breath and udders. And we took our Shredded Wheat at a different pace, breaking into the coils with our spoons and eating at speed so that the wires of wheat in the last spoonful were still springy and unsoftened. On cold days we had porridge, made in the Scottish fashion with salt, and with the milk added afterwards, floating in a thin rim round the plate. Grandad always stirred a spoonful of Fowler's Black Treacle into his and recommended us to do the same. Good for the health, he said. We stared in disbelief as the porridge turned brown and took on a bitter taste, far too strong for us. Though it has grown on me since. When we kept horses, the handful of black molasses we threw

14

in with the oats and chaff and bran had such a dark fragrance that I began to help myself from the sack in the barn. And now I, too, stir Black Treacle into my porridge, to general disbelief.

Perhaps it was his voice that reassured us. Norfolk voices are quick and slightly sing-song, swooping up interrogatively at the end of the sentence. He was a Yorkshireman, and still left himself time for broad vowels, though he had lost their breadth over the years. His voice moved like a river in a backwater, in a slow brown swirl. And every so often would carry me on a sideways eddy, in one of his little asides. Once it was an endorsement of a speaker on *Any Questions* whom he remembered championing the rights of farm workers some twenty years earlier, during the Depression. I did not understand the details of what he said, which was based on his own experience. His letter book from 1930, when he was Branch Secretary of the British Legion, records twenty farm labourers being laid off in a single week. But the nature of it, the only political remark I ever heard in my childhood, was an education in itself. It gave me a glimpse of what I would now call independence of mind: I saw him standing back from the current of events, reflecting, remembering, and not always ready to endorse.

Perhaps that was the clue. He felt comfortable to us because he was comfortable in himself. He had secured a quiet independence. Though he might not have done if my grandmother had not been so ready to accommodate him. Rushworth he was called, Rush for short, which made the family smile. A stubborn little badger of a man, there was no hurrying him, though he was easily delayed. He took so long to persuade into a day's outing that the day was lost. Painstaking at his craft, he took pains to the point where they impoverished him, putting more time into a boot's reparation than he could possibly charge for. He rarely refused anyone credit, even if they still owed from last time. And yet to see him at his over-crowded workbench behind small dim panes of glass was to see a

15

man who had found his freedom, a man patching and piecing and perfecting in his own time.

When he had retired and came to stay with us on the farm, he spent his visit in the shed there, sorting through the extraordinary tangle of tools on the bench. The farmer had been a considerable craftsman, as well as a collector of odds and ends: a Colt 45 revolver, an ancient .22 pistol used for shooting rats, a German commando knife still wickedly sharp and nestling in the grease of its sheath. At the end of the fortnight Grandad emerged to announce that he had sorted all the loose screws and nails into sized and labelled boxes. 'I'll sort the rest out next year,' he said.

Only now, looking back, can I see that his indulgence of us, the warmth that seemed to flow from him, flowed in part from my grandmother's indulgence of him. Both of them had worked hard to raise five children through the Depression. For twenty years he did a postal round as well as his boot and shoe repairs, and attended to hardship cases for the Legion on Sundays. But the income from his small trade would never have been enough if my grandmother had not turned their front room into a fish and chip shop in winter and an ice-cream parlour in summer. Between times she dug the vegetable garden, raised rabbits and hawked fresh fish round the countryside on her bike. Once she even tried to use his motorbike: he showed her how to start it but forgot to show her how to stop and she crashed into the neighbour's gate two doors down.

By the time I knew them, the worst of their struggles was over and they had a front room full of framed photographs: Frank as one of the aircrew standing beneath the Lockheed Hudson they flew from a base in Iceland during the war; my father at the grammar school, Captain of the Hockey Team, Winner of the Fenland Mile; Ruth at her wedding to Harold; Billy standing beside the army lorry the Arabs stole from him in Egypt; Peter as a sick berth attendant in the navy. They had left Sedgeford, a closed

16

community where after twenty years they were still being treated as strangers, and moved to Heacham, a larger and friendlier village on the coast.

The front room was a light, airy room of a certain elegance. A chiffonier stood against one wall, a piano against the other. Bulrushes cut from the dyke at the back of the beach were in a jar in the corner. Hardly ever used, because that meant lighting a second fire, it was a room set apart, sacred to the household gods, to the family's pride in having come this far. Occasionally, on wet days in summer, we played draughts on the floor; and in quiet moments, when we were out, my grandmother would sit by herself and play the piano.

On Christmas Day the fire was lit and the room came alive. Everyone gathered round the piano and my grandfather sang to my grandmother's playing. We were only summer visitors and I never witnessed this scene: but it remained vivid in the mind of my cousin George, Ruth's elder son. When they moved into Caley Street, which had only one big room downstairs, he said, 'This is a funny house. It doesn't have another room for Christmas Day.'

Sometimes I would browse in the room's solitude, looking up at the photographs, at these familiar people in their strange settings: tantalised by this time I had just missed, where I could glimpse them but never join them; sensing that it was different, a foreign country, as L. P. Hartley says, just back around the corner, of which I knew all the traveller's tales but to which I could never travel. Perhaps it was a feature of growing up just after the war that I felt everyone I knew had already been through a great adventure. Or perhaps the past always seems so strange to children that we obscurely admire the adults we know, simply for having endured its oddity. Billy had a broad grin under the dark beret, as if he had already foreseen the theft of the lorry and his consequent disgrace. Whereas Frank looked shyly determined: the long RAF jacket and wide trousers gave him a peculiar stance, short-legged and square-legged, as if he were bracing himself against the camera, against history, though really it may have been against the Icelandic wind.

A similar fascination attended the books in the small bookcase, popular novels in faded cloth bindings. All books make you their contemporary but these did so in a special sense: they were novels of their own time, printed and published at the time. I took in as much from their appearance as I did from their stories. They had a kind of creaky gentility, an air of substance that could easily come to pieces in your hands. Page by page, they made modern books look thin. Blacker print was impressed into softer-laid paper: but open them and they lay broken-backed. The bindery glue had cracked along the spine and one whole section was ready to secede from the rest.

I remember a thriller I borrowed and took to Holme beach, where I read it rather gingerly, trying to keep the fine sand from lodging between the pages. The heroes were ex-officers in the years immediately following the First World War. Discharged on in-adequate pensions and unable to settle to Civvy Street, they had taken to a life of genteel crime. It was a transparent fictional device, a way of allowing them to live dangerously and still remain gentlemen. And yet it must have traded on a real unease, some disturbance that was actually in the air, or it would not have seemed credible. Here were tremors none of the official histories had regis-tered. I had a big souvenir volume, published by a newspaper for George V's Silver Jubilee, full of photographs of the signing of the Armistice, the Victory Parade, the celebrations in Trafalgar Square. But this little book that had cracked along the spine showed me a social fabric that was itself coming apart.

By the time I read this I was twelve, on my last childhood holiday and beginning to form my own taste. The thriller was not a book I would have chosen from the public library at home. Indeed, had

I found it on the shelves there, I would have felt vaguely distressed. To read it in a modern edition would be like reading it in translation. What mattered was the book as it had survived in my grandparents' bookcase, part of the world in which it had first appeared, with its brave face and its little hint of uncertainty. To find it in the front room, under the photographs, was to find it in the original.

This response, as it surfaces into words, I recognise as adult. But I suspect that beneath it lay an instinct that is childlike. It never occurred to me to take books from London to read in Norfolk. Norfolk was composed of differences and when I was there I read different things. I remember another book I was allowed to take home to finish at the end of the holidays. All year I kept it in a place of honour, apart from the other books on my shelves, and returned it religiously to the bookcase next summer. Partly because I sensed, from the contrast with my father's book-lined study, that the few books my grandparents owned had been hard to come by. But more profoundly because the book belonged to a house in which I knew every object and in which every object was charged with the difference and distinction of Norfolk.

Our sense of ancestry does not need an ancestral mansion in which to grow strong. It invests with significance whatever it finds: a beaded pin cushion, a clasp knife, a cigarette-rolling machine such as the one I inherited from my grandfather, a pocket mill housed in a sturdy silver tube, with a hinged lid, cog wheels on one end and little steel rollers inside. It can make a lot out of a little, and for most of us, throughout most of history, it has probably had to do just that. I can borrow the phrase Yeats wrought for the rather grander house he imagined his daughter marrying into and apply it to that three-up, two-down without the phrase being in the least diminished: for me it was a house where all's accustomed, cere-monious. I returned the book to the bookcase rather as I might have returned one of the stone tablets to the Ark of the Covenant. As if, by doing so, I might keep the house in place for ever.

The cinder path ran along the backs of the terrace, taking on a little shading from each household as it went. Then turned into the road itself, which was like a dried riverbed of sand and gravel, potholed and patched. This, we were told, was an unadopted road. To us its wayward, wandering surface was an immense liberation. Each year the holiday seemed to begin as the car tyres turned off the council's tarmac and scrunched across it. The engine notes changed, the wheels surged across sandbanks and wallowed down into dips, as if we were already driving along the track to the beach. Woodend Road it was called, a cul-de-sac that petered out into a vagueness of trees. We seemed to have turned off the map, left the intricate network of roads that had brought us from London and entered the width of the margin, which could prove to be salt marsh, or a shingle beach, or these potholes we were crouched over, curious to see how last year's fills of rubble, which looked as strong as houses when they first went down, had been ground into streaks of red and yellow dust, and tar's boiled black sweets sucked through in a single winter. Only the neat pats of concrete seemed unchanging from year to year: little blisters of dead skin, part of the colourless world we had left beyond the road's end, where everything was set in concrete.

All sorts of oddities persisted along Woodend Road, informal arrangements that would certainly have been breaches of the planning regulations, had they applied here. One bungalow had a builder's yard beside it, where a small contractor kept his stacks of bricks. Opposite us lived the Floods, who parked their removals van in a field behind the house. Lying awake on light summer nights, we would hear the sound of the van returning and peep through the curtains. It would be right below us, its blunt whale

20

snout up against our gate and its dark hump stranded across the road. We could see Mr Flood in the cab, white-haired and slightly flushed in the face. He would lean out of his seat, peering down at the fence on either side, while younger Floods – brothers, sons, nephews – tumbled out of the lorry and took up watchful positions fore and aft. There was a familiar tension to this manoeuvre, a near-impossibility that filled them with a kind of elation. Banter flew back and forth, mostly at the expense of Mr Flood. His head jerked back and his grin broadened with each new sally. It was his daily acclamation as patriarch. I never saw anyone else at the wheel.

He took his bearings, calculating the inches and acute angles necessary to nose round a lorry that was already wedged across the road. Then went into a frenzy of tight turns and reversings, hauling on the wheel, stamping on the clutch, tugging at the gear lever. He flung himself into it as if this time he might really bring it off, as if he could gain another inch if he saved another second and swung the lorry round before the laws of the universe caught up with him. Just before the bumper touched, an amused 'Whoa!' would come from one of his assistants. Once the shout came a fraction late and the bumper toppled our gatepost. Mr Flood descended from the cab with a slow smile and with his status, if anything, enhanced. Toppling gateposts was his prerogative.

Once he had the nose lined up, the assistants moved to the back and all the tension moved with them. Mr Flood's swings on the wheel became leisurely while their opposing shouts rose in pitch on either side. It sounded like a row breaking out. Suddenly the shouts would die away and there came an ease, an expansion that seemed to stretch the full depth of the evening sky. The lorry's whole shuddering length was tucked in behind the house.

Our eccentricity was that the front garden held the neat, brown, upright shape of the Maggot, Grandad's Austin Seven. He had hinged the front fence so that it folded back, enabling him to drive the Maggot on to the little square of gravel. Once the fence was drawn across again, the Maggot looked like a Matchbox model in its matchbox. It shone along its short brown bonnet and gleamed around its black mudguards. The radiator cap was just like the cap on the waste pipe below the sink, a plain round of metal with two uprights for spanner grips, but the Maggot wore it as proudly as a Bentley wears its winged B. Clearly it had never heard its own nickname, which may have come from the way the black hood concertina'd and stretched into a series of little ridges, like a maggot humping itself along, or may simply have come from its comically small proportions. The Maggot was like a Jack Russell or a bantam cock, undiminished in its own eyes.

But then it stood in a charmed circle. It was the first car my grandfather had ever owned, and the first car I remember riding in as a child. Our earliest visits to Heacham were made by train and I was seven or eight before we had a car of our own. Re-entering that circle now, I find successive rings of enchantment that shade into one another. It becomes hard to distinguish my sense of novelty from my grandfather's. Or to separate the affection I felt for the Maggot from the affection I felt for him. But I sense that the circle's hub, its binding spell, may be the respect with which my grandfather treated all tools and machinery, from the old foot-treadled machine with which he stitched uppers, to the electric finishing machine that burred round newly fastened soles and heels. Nothing was ever thrown away: a long boot knife that had worn thin and snapped would be sharpened up again into one of the little pointed knives he always had ready to hand. The latest machines were bought as soon as they came out and his Junker sole sewer held pride of place: but he still took the time to temper soles by running them through his old set of rollers, just as when he had sewn them by hand. Rarely with him in his workshop, I was often with him in the Maggot, spellbound by the stateliness he gave that little vehicle. Perhaps there I came closest to glimpsing the world through his eyes – if glimpse is the word for an unhurried vision in which the simplest objects, flawed as they might be, seemed to possess their own dignity.

The Maggot sat bolt upright on its chassis, rather as Great-granny Edwards, the one time I saw her, sat stiffly on her chair, all the more rigid for being a little shaky. As soon as Grandad opened the passenger door, we knew we were entering a presence. There was an emanation of warm, polished leather, a smell of decorum. Small children, clambering into the back over a tipped-down seat, we composed ourselves. Even when Grandad pressed the starter, a round plug set in the floor, and it gave an accelerating gurgle like water going down the plughole, composure was not broken. Not even when the plug ran dry and Grandad had to crank the little car so that it trembled under our feet. Gravely he descended from the driving seat and bent to the starting handle. His movements, always slow, became almost priestly in their reassurance. Give it time, he seemed to be saying, give it time.

He treated the engine rather as he treated his own delicate stomach: it was not to be unsettled. He let it steady to its beat before engaging first gear. Then moved off slowly, letting it rebuild its rhythm. It did not rattle, it shook. We could hear the small, controlled explosions, the successive rips of compression, going off like lines of caps. We watched Grandad listening, judging the moment to change up again. This was a matter of profound deliberation. As our journey unfolded, each gear had a chapter to itself, and every corner was like rounding Cape Horn. He steered rather as a bus driver steers a double-decker bus, passing the wheel from hand to hand, and the radiator cap on the little bonnet swung like a compass needle across the window-panes of the Co-op, or butted round the curve of the wall opposite the Wheatsheaf.

23

What I remember of journeys with my grandfather is that they lasted longer than other journeys. A quarter of a mile to the shops stretched in time and became an epic of small events. The High Street floated by, as clear in each detail as if it were under a magnifying glass. The effect of this, paradoxically, was to magnify the Maggot itself. I looked out over the curve of the driver's seat, past the back of my grandfather's neck, thick white hairs under the rim of a brown tweed cap, to the window frame and the sharp edges beyond, gateposts and walls and house ends, suddenly aware of this small lounge in which we were travelling through space, the leather sofa and varnished woodwork my grandfather had to steer between buildings and bring safely to rest at the kerb.

In reality the Maggot was so tiny that, when my grandparents drove us to the beach on Sundays, my parents had to follow by bus. We were wedged into the back by all the bundles and baskets necessary to sustain an English family through a day by the sea: costumes wrapped in towels, sweaters in case the wind turned cold, raincoats in case it came on to rain, and then the bulwarks of food, the slabs of sandwiches wrapped in greaseproof paper, the potatoes to boil on the primus, a lettuce to dismember into salad, half a pound of tomatoes, half a dozen hard-boiled eggs, plus everything we would be demanding by four o'clock, the tin of fruit and the cheese straws and rock cakes, which had to be preceded by two statutory rounds of plain bread and butter.

All this despite the fact that we were driving to the shelter of the Cabin, my grandparents' beach hut, which was as simple as its name suggests, a white-painted wooden hut, not much bigger than a garden shed, standing in the second row of huts at Hunstanton. It had stood in the third row, but the sea swept the first row away and reduced the sea defences to a crumbling dune. The Council countered with a sea wall, an anvil of warm stone we had to slide across to reach the beach. For a few years more, the first years of my childhood, this held the sea back. I remember a jumble of huts on a grassy flat. One was round and made from a ship's turret. There were old shepherd's lambing huts, still standing on the little iron wheels that had trundled them from field to field. There was a pair of railway carriages that had been turned into a café.

The Great Flood of 1953 washed them all away. Ruth found the Cabin scattered over the farm at the back, two miles from the sea. The first thing she saw was Grandad's straw hat lying in the middle of a ploughed field. Then the roof, a long way off to the left. Beyond that, two of the walls, still joined together but flat on the ground, like a collapsed cardboard box. All I remember of the Great Flood is being driven to Norfolk the next weekend and seeing wisps of hay caught in the treetops. But I was living in Heacham during the small flood of 1978, when the sea broke through a gap in the defences and washed along the back of the beach. What had been a caravan park was an empty field. The sea had swept all the caravans neatly up into one corner. They were heaped against the fence, buckled and bent, like a pile of old Coca-Cola tins.

The Great Flood was followed by a wave of municipal ambition. All the improvisations and adaptations that had given the huts their character were outlawed. Hunstanton Council decreed that huts must be of a standard pattern, which could be purchased only from them, at considerable expense. The result was a mass migration. Everyone collected their wreckage from the fields and rebuilt their huts on Heacham beach. Some wrecks, like the old railway carriages, were too heavy to move, and they were left to rot where they had landed. Others their owners despaired of moving and they sold them where they lay in the mud: Uncle Jack bought the hulk of a villa for next to nothing. All of us were exchanging a sandy beach for a stony one. But, one by one, most of the shapes we had known from the grassy flat reappeared on the shingle ridge of

Heacham beach. The ship's turret bobbed back up. Someone even found Jack's old shack and knocked it together again, a few doors down from his new villa.

Beach huts must have developed from bathing machines. At some point it was no longer felt necessary to draw them right into the water. Bathers changed in privacy and then braved the public gaze, the men with their chests decently covered, the women in skirts and leggings, with their hair tied up in headscarves like Mrs Mop. As minds broadened, bathing costumes shrank. What kept the huts standing was the repressive weather of the East Coast, where the skies grey over at a moment's notice and the sea retreats to the horizon at low tide. On chill, colourless days when August seems like February, the hut became a world in itself.

When we arrived, it was shuttered and slightly chill. It was like venturing into the mouth of a cave, stepping out of the wind into a fresh sea-damp that quickly dries when the sun strikes in. We could smell the sand on the beach shoes in the corner, the sheets of dampening newspaper that lined the little cupboard, a haze of paraffin from the primus, all but dispersed, like a thumbprint on the air. Grandad began to take down the shutters, unscrewing the wing nuts from the long bolts that came in through the window frame and carefully perching each nut on its washer on the sill. We were sent for water and raced to the standpipe beside the track, descending the gravel bank in a series of great two-footed leaps that cratered the gravel and threw up the black dirt below.

Once the primus was pumped up and roaring under the kettle, our small world was complete. Nothing feels safer than a thin shelter buffeted by the elements. To lie sandwiched between adult deckchairs, propped up on my elbows over a Sunday newspaper spread out on the floor, watching the grey waves turn through the open door and listening to the wind rummage under the hut, was like lying in a tent and hearing the first stipple of rain on the canvas, a primitive exultation in being warm and dry.

Once or twice during my brief first marriage, when we lived in Heacham, I took Sylvia down to the hut and we relit the primus. Playing house, I suppose, trying to re-enter as children what we could no longer believe in as adults. But everything I had anticipated as a long, secure sequence, the roar of the primus, the taste of the tea in the green bakelite cups, the packet of digestive biscuits we had brought with us, our wistful absorption in the old magazines we found in the cupboard, all the remembered pleasures were curiously abbreviated, no sooner tasted than tasteless, as they always are in depression.

The second time I lived in Heacham, I had holed up there at a moment of loss. It was midwinter, and sometimes I would walk down to the beach, closing my eyes to the spread of caravans and the new retirement homes in their gravelled estates. To come to the huts on their windy ridge was to come on an old battle line and shiver awake. A hut is a fortification against wind and weather, whereas a caravan is a bubble of complacency. Superficially a difference of materials and design – patient wood as opposed to glossy tin, Gothic angles rather than aerodynamic curves – essentially it is a difference of attitude, the difference that exists between a modern picture window and an old cottage window. A picture window frames its occupants as if they were the lords of creation, a role in which they can only appear awkward. Whereas a cottage window is no more than an embrasure in the walls that shield a vulnerable species. There was something humble in the shape of the huts, and something defiant. Often the black-tarred roof ended in a little white pinnacle that covered the join of the eaves. To walk down to the tideline and glance back at the huts was to see a silhouette from another age, a line of tents drawn up for a medieval tournament, or an army camped on the eve of battle. All they needed were pennants streaming from the pinnacles.

Fit emblems for a coast where the living was never easy. Things have improved since King's Lynn expanded to take in London's overspill, reversing the flow that took my father to London at seventeen. The coast bred emigrants, or survivors who could turn their hand to anything. When I was small, Woodend Road used to merge in my mind with the beach, both being sandy, and nothing that happened along it ever seemed entirely serious. I knew the Floods' lorry meant business but their business seemed half banter. When I grew up and worked in a canning factory in Lynn, I realised my childish perception had some truth in it. Everyone around me was improvising a living. They shifted with the seasons from the fairground to the canning factories to the field gangs, chopping sugar beet in the snow if the money was good enough. Peter, my father's youngest brother, was porter, shunter, bricklayer, lorry driver, postman and telephone engineer before discovering there was a small fortune to be made from fish and chips.

Even in the holiday trade, there was never quite enough fat on the summers to see you through the lean winters. Hunstanton is a pretty resort, with tall Edwardian boarding houses built of carrstone, a dark brown sandstone quarried at Snettisham, and a broad green sloping down to the sea. The pier lies in the crook of the green, at the focus of a natural amphitheatre. A perfect site, until you realise there is nowhere to create an esplanade. It is all elbow and no elbow room. A stratum of chalk runs diagonally across the town, rising as a shoulder of cliff, becoming the sloping arm of the green, then slipping inland to become Ringstead Down and Sandringham Heath, an old coastline that now appears as a line of hills running up to King's Lynn. Below these old cliffs is the silt and shingle of the new shoreline, a coastal fen where Snettisham and Heacham huddle behind their sea defences, and where Hunstanton, in a desperate effort to expand, has crammed the vacancy with caravans. Before cars were widespread, people used to cycle and camp. White bell tents would crop like mush-rooms overnight.

The railway used to come down from Lynn, cutting across the heath and running along the back of Snettisham and Heacham beach. In the Great Flood they tried to run rescue trains but the water over the line was so deep it put out the fire in the fireboxes. The railway gave Hunstanton its heyday, transporting entire populations from Yorkshire and Leicestershire during the Wakes Weeks, when all the mills and factories would close and the whole town would go on holiday together. Throughout the Twenties and Thirties it rolled in day trippers from Cambridge who, in a northern European lineage of hard drinkers that goes back to the Vikings and Anglo-Saxons, were the great-grandfathers of today's lager louts. Cafés had signs up saying *No Day Trippers*. On Sunday evenings the porters worked in teams of six, lifting the drunks off the platform and throwing them back on to the train through the open windows.

The millworkers from Bradford were still coming during my childhood. Hard drinkers they may have been at home, but here they were family men, paddling with their young children. Their full vowels came as dove music through the stillness of low tide, a soft incomprehensible cooing as we wandered out across the miles of ribbed sand. Behind us were all the attractions ingenuity could muster: the fairground, the boating pool, the roller-skating rink, the cockle and winkle and shrimp stalls, the sticks of candyfloss and the trays of Hunstanton Rock. Ex-army DUKWs raced out across the sand, ferrying passengers to the boats that would take them out to Seal Island, a grandly named sandbank in the Wash where a few seals basked between tides. Delivered from the clatter of the looms, they seemed content with the silence, with these long ebbs when the sea had withdrawn to the horizon and they were alone with emptiness.

Onshore, generation gaps were already opening. American hits blared across the roller-skating rink, where stability seemed to depend on having your arm round a girl's waist. Parents and children peered between the slats of the wooden fence, both equally excluded because neither were teenagers. Soon the skaters would be trying to jink to rock'n'roll. While from an island in the boating pool came the sea-sickening lurch of the electric organ, a sound as sticky as candyfloss. A signboard warned the public that Bert Bradshaw would be giving recitals on the hour. To us children, circling around him in our underpowered boats, he was boredom amplified, the sound of Sunday visits, his trills and flourishes the arabesques of wallpaper we stared at in strange houses while adult conversation droned on over our heads. To the elderly couples taking tea in the open-air café, couples like my grandparents, in exile from the music of their youth, his voluble island must have been a little piece of terra firma, a reassurance that all those emotions had not gone into the void for ever. I remember my grandparents watching *Those Were the Days* as if the television signal came out of time rather than space. For half an hour they were lost to us, singing along with the 'Lambeth Walk'.

In his younger days Bert had appeared in local concerts, performing comic songs at the piano. There he heard my grandfather, who had a fine tenor voice and sang at the Lord Mayor's Banquet in King's Lynn. The family story, imparted to me with some pride but not in my grandfather's hearing, was that Bert was eager to be his accompanist and tried to persuade him to go on the halls. For the second time in his life my grandfather said no. An aunt in Yorkshire had offered to pay for him to train professionally but then he was too shy to take the plunge. Now he had a young family to think of. I often wondered what my grandfather felt when he walked past the boating pool and saw Bert's name on the signboard. Did all the songs he hadn't sung catch in his throat? Or was he confirmed in his decision? After all, the music halls had died. Bert had got no further than the boating pool, which was hardly the organ at Blackpool Tower. Or did he envy him the recitals, the occasional mention in the local paper, the modest continuing fame? Bert, apparently, felt that the two of them could have gone right to the top. In that way, perhaps, each of them was comforted by the thought of the other. They were each other's might have beens.

The horsehair sofa in my grandparents' kitchen was the first I had ever seen. It was like a chaise longue in a nightmare, its black shiny surface cold to the touch. No sooner did it warm to your skin than stray hairs began to prickle. It might have been designed by Mrs Grundy for the express purpose of reforming the upper classes: no *grande horizontale* would have remained *horizontale* for long. In fact, it had been designed for the lower classes, as a recliner for the working man when he came home weary from the day's labours. In my father's childhood it was a standard item of cottage furniture. Horsehair was cheap and hard-wearing, and could be wiped down with a damp cloth. Ruth's dining-room chairs were upholstered in it and, all the years her sons were in short trousers, she had to spread newspapers over the prickly seats.

My grandfather needed to rest his eyes more than anything: he peered through little round spectacles, just like the old man in the long apron advertising *The Leather that Stood the Test of Time*, whose model is still occasionally to be seen, tapping away in the window of a shoe repairer's shop. In Grandad's case the horsehair was a symbol rather than a sofa: it established him as the man of the house. The front room represented my grandmother's aspirations: the kitchen was the men's clubroom, their snug, strewn with Billy's motorcycle magazines and my grandfather's trade journals. It was an atmosphere I had never known before.

Home was my mother's domain. My father was a barrister, travelling to courts all around the South-Eastern Circuit. He was often home late and always had to retire to his study to prepare the next day's briefs. It was the pattern of the Home Counties: men vanished on the train up to town. Staying with my mother's parents in King's Langley really amounted to staying with Grandma. Grandad Jaggers had an oil shop in Battersea and, by the time he came home on the Greenline bus, we were in bed. He was a man of few words anyway, like my Uncle Fred, who ran the shop with him and was married to my mother's sister Hilda. What spoke for Fred were the canaries he kept in an aviary in the backyard, and the chickens at the bottom of the garden. Sometimes there was a tray of softly chirruping day-old chicks in the airing cupboard.

Here, by contrast, was a house where men came and went at all hours. Billy worked shifts on the railway and was often in the kitchen at teatime, vesting himself for the night shift and the motorbike ride to Lynn. He was a big man, built rather like a Russian doll, with a round head and a broad stomach encircled by a broad leather belt. As he shrugged on his overalls and wriggled into his weatherproofs, the doll went into larger and larger sizes. On cold days he put on a heavy khaki canvas jacket, Grandad's ARP dispatch rider's coat from the war. On wet days he clambered into Fire Brigade surplus jacket and trousers, lined with black rubber, and waded out of the house like a deep-sea diver. An army bag dangled from one shoulder, holding his lunchbox and thermos. As a life support system it seemed hopelessly inadequate. He looked as if he should be refuelled by tanker.

Glancing back, I can see myself at my listening post, in the crook of the sofa. 'All eyes and ears' was the family's phrase for me, 'taking it all in'. Though really I took only half in, because this was a world whose workings I barely understood. Shiftwork astonished me, seeming to demand physical impossibilities. I could not imagine how Billy managed to get to sleep in broad daylight: I found it difficult enough on light summer nights. Nor how he got up at four in the morning when he was on early turn. I would look at his solid breadth, expecting to see it fraying at the edges. Or glimmering with some strange phosphorescence, the marsh light of false dawn.

I plied Billy with questions that always seemed to turn into other questions. They led to a joke or a riddle. Everywhere but to an answer. It was like having an oracle for an uncle. Questions were one of my ways of showing off. A few pert questions and everyone would declare I was 'as sharp as ninepence'. But there were older coins in circulation, double-headed pennies and trick sovereigns, and Billy had a pocketful of these. Gently he introduced me to the ancient folk art of joshing. I never knew where I was. Whatever I asked, he would pause and then give a deep chuckle, in which I recognised my grandfather's voice. Here was another backwater I seemed to skim like a mayfly.

Billy served his steam engine with the same stubborn passion as my grandfather served his craft. When King's Lynn went over to diesels, he moved to the freight depot at Billericay and drove the last steam trains on British Rail. In my childhood he was still a fireman on the Hunstanton line. This ran through the Royal Estate at Sandringham and Billy claimed to carry his shotgun in the cab. The trick was to shoot a pheasant on the way down and drop off the footplate and collect it on the way back. Over Christmas he abstained, for fear of winging an heir to the throne. Though once, pulling into Wolferton station on a foggy morning, he almost ran down the entire Royal Family. He saw them scattering up the embankment either side of the line.

Peter capped this story by nearly wrecking King George VI's funeral arrangements. When the King died at Sandringham, Peter was an undershunter in the yard at Lynn. On the Monday the Royal

Train was to convey the King's body to London. The Friday before, Peter sent the London express off down a siding. It hit the buffers and the yard gates went up in the air. It took a weekend's feverish work to repair the damage. On the Monday morning the funeral train glided through, the workers standing beside the line with their caps in their hands.

When Billy married, he moved to a house just below Ringstead Down and talked of potting the pheasants from the Hunstanton Estate when they strayed into his garden. How many he really shot, from the footplate or the bedroom window, I shall never know. Quite possibly none at all. His potshots, like his teasing replies, were humorous extensions of reality. They gave him a little elbow room, a small estate in the imagination.

Sometimes my own bookishness led me a dance. When I read Billy's motorcycle magazines, I immediately translated them into myth: a few gallant Nortons were holding off hordes of Moto-Guzzis and Gileras. To an English boy of my generation this was irresistible. It was the Battle of Britain all over again, with the Italians standing in for the Germans. What I failed to notice, because I skipped the technical columns and read only the race results, was that this time it was the Italians who had developed the Spitfire.

For two seasons Geoff Duke duelled with Masetti. Then he began to win every race and the battle seemed to be over. History had confirmed the English gift for fighting their way out of a tight corner. A glorious succession began to form in my mind: Agincourt, Waterloo, the Battle of Britain, the TT races. Until I glanced across and saw that Geoff Duke was now riding for Gilera. It was like discovering that Douglas Bader had transferred to Messerschmitt. I demanded an explanation, and Billy laughed and said the Italians had better bikes. 'If I were Geoff Duke, I'd still win on a Norton!' I declared with consummate priggishness – ignorant of the whole history of the two previous seasons, when only Geoff Duke's extraordinary skill had kept the Nortons in the race at all.

It would be a year or two before Marlon Brando rode into a small town in America at the head of a gang in black leather jackets. The motorbike had yet to sprout horns and a twin exhaust. It was still a machine, the working man's form of transport, and Geoff Duke was a working man's hero, a master craftsman, precision-engineering his victories in the TT races with as little fuss as Stanley Matthews angled his goals. Billy was in his early twenties and had a classy bike, a shaft-drive Sunbeam: but mostly it served simply to take him to work, astride its silver gills in bib-and-brace overalls and hobnailed boots.

Later he switched to a motorbike and sidecar, which was safer because the sidecar gave stability. By then I was old enough to be taken on short journeys, shut in the sidecar's stuffy box, behind blurred perspex screens, drowsy from their smell. Once we went down to the pump to fill up with petrol. It was just a single pump, outside a small hardware shop that tried to catch a passing summer trade with a display of beach balls and buckets and spades. On the doorpost hung a string of windmills: sticks topped with little plastic propellors, dark blue or red or green, that would spin if you held them into the wind. Their chittering was one of the sounds of this exposed coast: like larksong over the marshes, a constant noise in the ear. Billy had let me out of the sidecar and I was busy surveying the display when the woman came out to serve us. I glimpsed lipstick, gold earrings, a chiffon scarf in the neck of her blue overall, and turned to study her instead.

Such women fascinated me because they seemed a different species from my mother. Brown hair cut in a bob round a heart-shaped face, Mother was like a little cobnut, pretty and plain. As a girl she would have been too shy to use make-up. As a young mother she had what the hymn calls the beauty of holiness. I have a photo of her on the beach, deep brown at the end of summer and flushed with fulfilment. There she has an organic beauty that is not hers alone. She shares it with the dark, succulent green stalks of samphire in the marsh and the burnished red branches of Scots pine on the hills inland.

I never knew her to put on more than a dusting of face powder and a dash of pale lipstick when she went to a dinner dance, and that was a mistake. She looked wan under the powder and the lipstick turned her lips a purplish-blue, as if she had poor circulation. These other women pressed the moist shiny red into their lips like a second skin. They built it up, layer by layer, into a glistening surface. When it wore thin, you could see the pores outlined like courses of cement in brickwork. There was something monstrous in this. Adults were often on the point of turning into monsters. There was a woman on the rock stall in Hunstanton whose painted nails were so long they curved over like claws and clicked across the sticks of rock. I was too young to respond to sexual allure, I saw it only as social display. I had been sensitive to that ever since a lady councillor swanned into our classroom in a big hat. But something stirred in me, a curiosity, a suspicion that there were adult codes I had yet to break. Everything about my mother said simply wife and mother. These painted lips and fingernails must be sending different signals.

At this time Billy was still a bachelor and the woman must have taken a fancy to him. As soon as she spoke, I realised I was listening in on conversation of a kind I had never heard before. She teased him about me. What was this little secret that had just climbed out of the sidecar? But I could tell that I was just a joke, a ploy. Their eyes met above my head and the real conversation was going on there. Whenever the woman moved away, replacing the nozzle in the pump, going into the shop to get change, she looked back at Billy. I saw him standing there, framed in her glance. No longer

36

my grandmother's son, being sent off to work with his lunch box. No longer my uncle, the giant teddy bear I teased about his size, who would tease me in return. A young man with dark eyes and a strange, slow, white smile.

Rather than feeling excluded, I felt that I had been admitted, given a glimpse into adult life. I began to crack the code. Painted lips said more than words. They spoke around them and changed them by the way they spoke. They took up phrases and left them hanging in the air as invitations, as challenges. Their conversation seemed to be composed of laughter but I sensed that it was very different from the banter Billy kept up with me. This laughter had claws, it was a game of cat and mouse. Perhaps I did register sexual allure because I certainly registered danger. I felt as if Billy were coming under fire. He stood his ground. The more the woman glanced and glinted, the more relaxed and humorous he seemed to become. In some obscure way I felt I was learning something that might one day be of use. As if already the spark of emulation had fired in me, the ambition to grow up and stand framed in a woman's glance.

Nothing ever came of the flirtation, as far as I know. The two adults must have long forgotten and only I remember the quickening in the air. Quite different from the drowsiness of the engaged couples who came to stay for the weekend in London. My mother would always warn us when we were going to have to play gooseberry. It was difficult for them, she explained, they had nowhere they could be alone together. In those days it would have been unthinkable for young people to go away on their own. They stayed with relations, where they could be chaperoned. Families exchanged engaged couples as they exchanged elderly relatives, a weekend here, a weekend there.

We preferred the elderly relatives. They doted on us, which was what we expected of guests. Whereas the young lovers doted only on each other. They lingered in the hall, holding hands and gazing into one another's eyes. They huddled for hours on the sofa, murmuring to each other, their heads lolling on to each other's shoulders. It was like a shared illness, a flu no one else had caught. I imagined them being shipped from house to house in states of increasing debility. I imagined the family's relief when the wedding day finally came and the engagement's long fever was over.

Perhaps my view of engaged couples was darkened by jealousy. Who should arrive with a fiancé but Cousin Sylvia, Jack's elder daughter? She was sixteen and he was all of twenty-one. A little stiff, on his dignity, but doing his best to please. He sat by the fire, doing drawings for my sister. 'Huh! Look at Picasso!' I said savagely and was made to apologise. How could he know what I felt?

Sylvia was the astonishment of my childhood. I thought such creatures moved only across the silver screen, larger than life. Here she was, sitting on the beach with the rest of us, wearing a plain white blouse and a tennis skirt. Dark hair framed a heart-shaped face. My mother's classic simplicity, but raised to a higher power. Sylvia was breathtaking. Her skin was milk-white, her features perfect. I used to study the line of her lips, their long, subtle curve. I used to tell my friends about her, saying she was the most beautiful girl I had ever seen 'in real life'.

This mattered to me. I had never imagined that reality could rise to Sylvia. She transformed my sense of the possible, however briefly, unaccountably. I never expected to see her like again. In this I was a child of my class and time. We were so humble, that is how it strikes me now. In the Sixties expectations changed. People decided they had a right to be beautiful. Now every woman expects to have a touch of glamour. She dresses for it, she rinses and tints her hair, she uses rouge and mascara with no fear of scandal, no risk of being marked out as a certain sort of woman. In those days there was a drab, utility look. It was not just that clothes were rationed. People rationed themselves. They knew their place. They did not get above themselves. If someone tried to cut a dash, the verdict was swift and unanimous: 'Who does she think she is?'

Nothing Sylvia did would have allowed her to remain one of the crowd. She dressed simply and it became style. She would have caused a stir wherever she appeared, on the Boulevard des Anglais at Cannes, or on Heacham beach. Each year we smiled as the suitors presented themselves, their hair Brylcreemed and their blazer buttons shining. Mercifully, I was too young to compete. These were George's friends, an older generation who listened to Chris Barber and knew why the crowd roared when Ottilie Patterson sang 'Digging My Potatoes'. But none of them made much impression, not even Mick Herring, who had red-gold hair and played the guitar in a folk group. They were village boys and Sylvia had her choice of partners at the Hammersmith Palais. When she ran off to Gretna Green with her twenty-one-year-old and then took the boat for Australia, I realised I was not in the least surprised. Sylvia was a comet and it is in the nature of comets to vanish.

If she had lived in Heacham, rather than being a summer visitor, she might have married an American airman. The Cold War was at its most arctic. Strategic Air Command flew round the clock, one third of its bombers always in the air. Many of them were based in Norfolk, on the same airfields they had used for their massed daylight raids over Germany. The bombers were invisible, in the stratosphere, but fighters were constantly making low runs over the coast. There would be a blast of noise from behind us and silhouettes I recognised from newsreels of the Korean war would screech out over the sea. As they banked and turned on the horizon, the silence seemed to slow them into a fish-like calm. They became pure shapes, moving in their own element. Then barbs overhead and another scar of sound.

On the ground it was like living in an occupied country. When we drove from London, we seemed to cross a frontier at Newmarket. There were no large notices, like those I had seen in *The Third Man:* YOU ARE NOW ENTERING THE AMERICAN OCCUPIED ZONE. But there might as well have been. Convoys blocked the roads, lorry after lorry keeping the regulation distance, in long lines it was impossible to pass. As soon as we stopped at a transport café, I would forage for souvenirs. Nothing was more potent than an empty packet of Lucky Strike. I had a collection of English cigarette packets – Capstan, Churchman, Craven A – but they seemed to belong to the past, to the time of the bearded sailor on Player's Navy Cut. The Lucky Strike logo, a red circle ringed with black, was like the roundel on a jet fighter. I see myself smoothing out my crumpled packets, sniffing the warm tobacco smell from an empty tin, fascinated and never quite perceiving the root of my fascination: the armament, the lethal shapes the planes carried under their wings.

In Heacham every spare house was rented out to American service families. In Hunstanton USAAF police patrolled the fairground in pairs, their white anklets immaculately blanco'd, their white nightsticks managing to look purely ceremonial. As they may have remained, most nights. What I remember of the American airmen is their physical exuberance, an energy that seemed at ease with itself. There was a Test Your Strength machine in the fairground, a punchball fixed high overhead. Normally a man would hurl himself at it and swing one tremendous punch. If it connected, the bell would ring. One afternoon I heard a continuous ringing and glanced across. The punchball was a blur of movement. Below it was an American airman, tanned shoulders working under a white T-shirt. He hovered in mid-air and unleashed a small drum solo of blows. Then simply walked away. No buddies had put him up to it. There was no girlfriend standing by. It was pure male display, a marvellous bragging dance of shoulders and fists.

Another time I watched two airmen jiving with their girls in the Kit-Kat. Hardly my family's usual venue. I thought we had gone behind *The Green Door*: any moment now we would know what that teasing laughter was the song described. This must be the underworld because we were meeting Uncle Ernest, my mother's mysterious brother. Ernest had left his wife and children, and run off with a redhead called Renee. The first time they came to see us, they arrived in an old army lorry. The second time in some great humpbacked limousine.

Ernest was clever, Grandma Jaggers would mourn, he could have done anything. As a little boy he had been so entertaining, performing monologues with a penny held in his eye like a monocle. Oh! he had made them laugh! But he drank, she added darkly. Two of her brothers had gone the same way: ghostly great-uncles who shimmered into focus in her stories, then faded back into the air. I could still see the little parlour comedian in the round-faced, humorous man who met us in the Kit-Kat. Dark eyes, I noted, and a sallow skin. Just right for a black sheep.

Sure enough, he took my father off for a drink, and we were left in the room with the jukebox. It was after five and the place was almost deserted. Just two couples, jiving away the last of the afternoon. All memory of the girls has gone. What I remember is the men, the way they swung out on the girl's hand and posed for the offbeat, feet in and hips out. Or slipped the girl behind them and shimmied as she turned, their hips swaying left, right, *vroomph!*, *vroomph!*, like two notes on a slide trombone.

When Peter became engaged, I saw a different pattern of engagement: not the leisurely pattern of the suburbs, where weekends passed in a fever of unfulfilled desire, but an old country pattern, where the work and thrift of marriage began as soon as the engagement was announced. Peter and Anne bought a plot of land along the Ringstead road and began to build themselves a bungalow. Three years it took them, working every weekend and most evenings, stopping when they ran out of materials and starting again when they had saved enough to buy more. After the wedding they moved in with a bed, a table and two chairs.

Peter had worked as a bricklayer but, when we went to help at weekends, I saw that my father knew some of the tricks of the trade as well. I watched him mix cement, making a circle of sand and cement, pouring a little pool of water in the middle, and spading the mixture into the water. Later, when we moved to the farm, I helped him build new stable blocks. We would square off a piece of ground, first with pegs and string, then with a surround of boards, checking levels and verticals with the spirit level as we pegged them into place. We laid a bed of rubble and poured over the cement, tamping it down with a long plank laid across the boards.

Tamping was my job. Kneeling by the bottom board with the plank in both hands, I had to bring its edge down time and again, *chop, chop, chop*, like a kitchen knife moving across the vegetable board, until the gravel was evenly spread and the liquid cement lay across it as smooth as batter. Painstaking, repetitive work that made the forearms and the fingers ache: my apprenticeship to manual labour and the only thread I ever picked out of the whole ragbag of skills my father had learned on the farm where he worked as a boy.

Looking back, I realise that my parents were cottagers living in the city. Old patterns of thrift they had learned in their childhood helped them to survive the years of rationing after the war. They bought pig's brains and made their own brawn, ox tongues and pressed them themselves, piling Hailsham's *Statutes of England* on top of the weights from the kitchen scales. They bought eggs by the dozen in the summer, when they were cheaper, and preserved them in a pail of isinglass. My father grew potatoes on an allotment and stored them in a long earth clamp in the back garden. My mother bottled entire summers, slicing and salting runner beans into tall glass jars, stewing plums and bottling them in their own syrup.

The kitchen had its seasons, more pungent than those outside. Chutney boiling in a large saucepan gave off a steam so sharp it set your teeth on edge. Marmalade heaved like lava, exuding a heavy, resinous smell you could almost chew. Everything my generation had to learn from books, when self-sufficiency became a cult, my mother had learned at her mother's knee. A Hertfordshire girl, Grandma Jaggers had gone into service at the age of twelve and risen to be the cook to a baronet. She had great respect for her employers, all the more so because they knew when they were beaten. 'Alice,' Lady Bentley would say, 'we'll just have a cold lunch today – a little of that chicken from yesterday.' 'Oh, the chicken's gone, Ma'am – just the bones I've used to make soup.' 'What, Alice, all that enormous chicken?' Lady Bentley came down and searched the kitchen in disbelief. But the chicken had gone: Grandma had slipped home with it to feed the rest of the family.

The farm where my father worked as a boy was Hill Farm, Sedgeford. The village lies a few miles inland, in a dip behind the chalk downs of the old coastline. Hill Farm, now part of a large agricultural estate, lay to the left of the Heacham road as it climbs out of the village. The land began just below Sedgeford church and ran up to Beech Wood at the top of the rise.

Hill Farm, Beech Wood: innocent names that cannot conceive of there being another beechwood, or another farm on another hill. Names that belong to a time when travel was a rarity, when roads were muddy sloughs and the world ended at the parish boundary. Names that must have been repeated across England, in parish after parish.

Hill Farm was owned by Mr Trenowath, a commanding figure

in breeches and brown leather gaiters. He had been a cavalryman and it was from him that my father learned his love of horses. My first memory of the farm is being taken into a stable to see one of the shires they were still using alongside the tractors. I was only three or four and it towered over me, too big for my eyes to take in. What I remember is the atmosphere of the stable: a stillness I could almost touch, the gravity of that muscle and bone.

In the far corner of the yard was a dew pond, long dry but still distinct, a shallow saucer of ground where the grass was greener. My father told us how they used to lunge the horses there when they were breaking them in. Over the years I heard him describe it so often that in the end I saw him standing in the centre of the dew pond, his hands spread like the hands of a clock. The minute hand held the lunge line that ran from the heavy noseband. It kept the line taut, moving with the horse as it trotted round the dew pond. The hour hand held the whip, pointed down so that its long lash trailed across the ground. Hour hand followed minute hand but the whip never gave more than a flick over the grass, like a horse's tail brushing away flies. The control was all in the voice. *Whoa!*, breathed in an undertone like a lullaby, calmed the animal down. A click of the tongue set it trotting again.

Once a horse had learned its paces, the noseband was replaced by a bridle, a bit was slipped between its teeth and it was walked on the long reins. This sounded risky: the first thing I was told about horses was to keep away from their back legs. But long reins were long: the trainer walked where the ploughman would be if the horse were pulling a plough. We had a photo of a horse coming out of the lane, its head up, pulling and resisting the turn. My father was behind it, a lad of sixteen or seventeen, slightly crouched, his back braced against the horse, his forearms taut, fingers flexing for control. He would walk a horse for miles, trying to keep his fingers supple, a light, fluent pressure on the reins, on the bit, on the soft mouth, even as his arms stiffened and his back ached.

On Show Saturdays in summer they would groom the horses at dawn, setting out for the showground through the early morning stillness and riding home in the last of the light. You only had to hear my father talk of those days to realise they were still part of him, more vivid than his own victories as a champion miler. His voice took on the hush of concentration, the allaying tones that would settle a stammer of hooves and bring the horse back to a steady pace round the dew pond. What he recalled of his running was laying a trail for the harriers on the Boxing Day Hunt, to give everyone a good stretch at the start of the day.

He was one of three or four runners posted in the wood at the top of Eaton Farm, looking down on to the meet at Low Water. They had a haunch bone on the end of a rope and a bottle of aniseed. As soon as they saw the hounds move off, they splashed aniseed on to the bone and one of them would drag it across Eaton Farm to the bottom of Trenowath's Long Meadow. There they had built two jumps into the fence, the first of a series expressly designed to unseat the Master, who was none too steady over jumps. They would haul the bone over, splash on some more aniseed and another runner would drag it to the next jump. It was a two-mile run and they only had a four-hundred-yard start. By the time they reached Hill Farm, the hunt was on their heels. They had to be locked in a stable while the hounds cast around, yelping and sniffing for the lost scent.

Mr Trenowath had been like a second father to him; yet there was a distance, a deference that puzzled me when I was a child. My father would never drive straight into the farmyard. He parked the car in the lane and went to see if it was a good moment for us to call. Or he called on his own first and brought us later by arrangement. The lane opened into the yard, which looked homely enough.

Ducks and geese grazed the short grass. Chickens roosted in an old hearse. The gate stood open. But there was an invisible line I never crossed without feeling I had to be on my best behaviour.

Now I realise my father was paying Mr Trenowath the respect that belonged to another time. Mr Trenowath was a farmer, my father a tradesman's son, a social distinction not even his entry into a learned profession could quite overcome. The formal call, the car parked in the lane, were bows to the village hierarchy as it had existed when my father was a child.

Though he would have shown a similar courtesy if we had been calling on a smallholder. My father had tact that amounted to a sense of territory. Sharp as an animal instinct, he voiced it as human consideration. Visiting a strange farm, he would pause by the gate, looking and listening, judging whether it was a good moment to intrude. 'They're still milking,' he would say. 'We'll come back later.' In a garage or a builder's merchant he would glance around before he pressed the bell for service. If someone was clearly busy, he waited. He watched that person move about his business with a kind of tenderness, as if he knew how intimate the rhythms of work were, how his mind would not be at rest until everything was back on the shelf and he was ready to attend to the next order.

This was all the more striking because my father was not, by nature, a patient man. Perhaps it came from knowing how much of my grandfather's personality was invested in the tools on his bench. Perhaps it came from his own need to be completed by rows of runner beans climbing their sticks, or a cyclamen growing from seed in a carefully tended pot in the greenhouse. For all the hours he spent in his study, my father was in abeyance there. He did not come alive until the gold-topped Parker was laid to rest on the pile of papers and he was outside in a pair of torn overalls, digging a trench for the potato clamp.

\* \* \*

One summer, when I was still very young, we entered the farm from Beech Wood. I have no notion how we got there. Perhaps we caught the bus. Perhaps Grandad ran us out in the Maggot. All I remember is that we came into the corner of the field as they were cutting the last of the corn. Most of the field was bare, the sheaves already pitched on to the wagons. The tractor had stopped in front of a final small wedge of stalks. I looked up at the big wheel of the reaper, the red spokes that would cut the corn and sweep it into the binder. It was like looking up at a windmill, the triangular scoops of white canvas set like sails against the sky. I followed my father up the field. Something was happening. The men were coming down off the wagons. They were spacing out, forming a horseshoe round that last crest of corn. They made a gap and my father took his place in the line. One of them cocked a shotgun. My father reached down, I felt the touch of his hand on my chest: *Stay back!*

I was just outside the curve of the horseshoe. The tractor started up and I peered between the men's legs. A rabbit broke from the corn. It ran straight towards us, flat out, ears laid along its back. Came to the line of men and turned, only to find itself running into the curve. Tried to slew round, almost on its side now, skidding and scrambling for footholds in the dust. The men glanced along their line, like fielders signalling a catch. A black-haired man in a flat cap drew himself up and threw out his chest. As the rabbit ran in front of him, he fell forward. He came down on it like a plank.

He bounced back on to his feet, picked up his cap, and tossed the rabbit behind him. The men roared, as for a brilliant catch, and he allowed himself a quiet smile. A fall so neat it might have been executed by a gymnast. That was what shocked me. One moment I had been watching an animal scrabbling to make a tight turn. I had glimpsed the white fur of its underbelly as its hind legs slipped in the dust. The next moment it had been hammered flat. The man drew himself up. He fell full length. His chest banged to the ground. I pictured it again, daring myself to look.

I could not repress my admiration. But there was something there I feared: that quiet smile, the man's pleasure in his deft blow. I might as well have feared the decision with which an Inuit harpooned a seal. What I was seeing was a skill bred of hardship. There had been a series of agricultural depressions, the last of them ending only with the Second World War. For decades the only meat a labourer and his family ate was bacon on a Sunday, from the pig they kept in the back garden. The rest of the week he took bread and onion to the field, with a smear of bacon fat. The woods and fields abounded with game but the gentry owned everything that ran or flew or swam. Poachers snared and lamped at night, and sold their catch in the pubs. Otherwise farm labourers learned to keep their eyes open, to dive on a hare if they passed one crouched in a field, to drop on a rabbit if it ran under their feet. When I think of that smile now, I feel he had a right to it. He had learned that trick in a hard world.

Rabbits were a plague until another plague was inflicted on them: myxomatosis. Every cornfield was thinned and pitted at the edge. They flattened corners quicker than a thunderstorm. I heard of whole fields eaten down to a few wisps. Cutting the last of the corn was a chance to even the odds. Whatever had retreated deeper into the corn when the reaper first circled the field was trapped there. Foxes, hares, rabbits, rats all huddled together in the remaining stalks. Half the village turned out to watch or to take their place in the line.

Every year my father borrowed a shotgun from Mr Trenowath. One morning, looking over our teacups and seeing an empty pillow on the double bed, we would be told he had gone shooting. This sudden absence was tantalising. Imagine rising in the dark and slipping out of the house while everyone else slept . . . I woke to find I had missed an adventure.

By mid-morning he had returned with a shoulder bag full of rabbits. Once he brought home a mallard drake, a strange creature, completely of water, its green neck shimmering like the surface of a pond. The sun was out and a gold light seemed to float over it. The sun went in and it turned to a cold silver. The sleek keel, we discovered, was all waterproofing, a tight thatch of feathers, inches thick. It was like trying to pluck velvet, our fingers ached as the layers diminished to a fine, stubborn down.

I watched my father skinning and gutting rabbits so often that, years later, I found I could do it from memory. By now I had recovered from my shock. I was only too anxious to be taken shooting. 'When you are older' I was told: the inevitable reply. I had heard it so often I had lost any sense of its meaning.

To my surprise, when I was ten, my father decided I was old enough. I could walk behind with the game bag, as long as I was careful to keep behind. The next morning he woke me at four, one of those hours I had always imagined must be like outer space. They were habitable, it seemed. There was oxygen, though perhaps not quite enough. I felt a little dizzy: still prickling from the numbness of sleep.

The sky was just beginning to lighten as we drove towards Sedgeford. The dark bulk of Beech Wood rose on our right.

'There's the gateway!'

My father drove straight on.

'Someone's just gone through the gate on the other side. I think it's the gamekeeper from the estate.'

'But we've got permission from Mr Trenowath.'

'Yes, but the keeper doesn't know us. If he sees us parking, he'll only worry what we're up to. Much better to wait a few minutes and let him go peacefully on his rounds.' My father's tact. We drove down into Sedgeford and sat for ten minutes outside Grandad's shop.

By the time we returned to Beech Wood, the sky was a thunder-head blue, with black hanging in heavy streaks like rain. There was a thin grey light under the trees. We seemed to be moving through a primitive world, only half evolved. I searched the tangle of tree-tops for the silhouettes of pigeons. I thought I saw one and my father aimed into the primeval light. Before he could fire, a pigeon clattered down from a lower branch and sank into the grey.

We came out of the wood into daylight, the grass shining between long patches of shadow. My father advanced into the meadow and I kept a careful six paces behind. We were walking so slowly a rabbit sat up to watch. I should have said, 'Over to your left!' but now I was hesitant, afraid to break my father's concentration. By the time I spoke, the rabbit was running along the edge of the field. My father fired after it into the hedge.

Then our luck turned. There were rabbits in a patch of sunlight. As they scattered, my father fired and the shot rolled one right over. We repeated this in the next field, and the next. The game bag filled and the strap began to pull under my shoulder. I carried it uncomplaining, too proud to fidget under the weight. That ache was my investiture.

We came out on to the slope of a cornfield they had cut the day before. Bales glinted across the stubble's white haze. The reaper and binder had just been replaced by a combine and these building blocks of straw were new to me. There were small stacks of them, fours and sixes, along the slope above us. As we started downhill, I heard a faint drumming, like an echo in the ground. Something was running on the slope. My father turned and fired between the stacks. He had seen a flash of yellow fur, the size of a fox.

It was a hare, so big we had to lift it by the feet and carry it between us. The body hung down, long and heavy and rank. The men looked up in surprise as we entered the farmyard. They gathered around us. They held the hare up by the hind legs and measured its length. They passed it to each other and weighed it in their hands. Later, in the kitchen, Grandma would grumble that it was a doe in kindle. The meat would be scraggy, hardly worth the trouble. But for that moment nothing soured our triumph. We felt like two hunters home from the hill, the carcass of a deer slung between us.

That morning was the only time I saw the inside of the farmhouse, which was set back on a terrace of lawn above a low stone wall, just where the lane broadened out into the yard. The sun was hot and we had been in the fields since dawn. Mr Trenowath invited us in and immediately I felt my father's eye upon me. As we went through the gate, his whole body seemed to stoop over me, saying, *Best behaviour now!* The house itself, a long frontage of weathered brick with tall casement windows, had a robust dignity. The terrace gave it an added reserve, a gentlemanly detachment that seemed to match Mr Trenowath's own.

Two or three low stone steps took us on to the terrace, an ascent so gradual I hardly noticed it in the drowse of sunlight. The door opened into a flagstoned hall, cool and whitewashed. A lance hung on the far wall, over saddles and harness. The floor was the colour of history. It was like entering a castle and finding it still garrisoned: a washstand in the corner, a kitchen table against one wall, almost hidden by a wooden screen.

I walked in the echo of the men's footsteps as they crossed the hall and turned into the sitting room. I saw the fireplace and remembered my father telling me how, in the days before Mabel came as housekeeper, he would cook a rabbit in a bucket over the open fire, making a rough stew with swedes and turnips.

51

Now we were in a gentler epoch. Mabel appeared from her kitchen at the other end of the house and Mr Trenowath asked her to make some coffee, and bring a glass of lemonade for me. I perched myself in the window seat and fixed my gaze on the hall, on the stones' armoured gleam that seemed to stretch back seven or eight hundred years.

As we stood in the doorway, saying goodbye, sunlight slanted in, warming and softening the flagstones. Mr Trenowath was at his ease, framed in the door with the saddles on the wall behind him, the bridles looped on their pegs. A pair of riding boots stood to attention against the wainscot, braced by their trees to a stiff shine. He was smiling, for a moment almost like an uncle or a grandfather, looking down at me out of a life in which he was clearly content. But when I caught sight of the washstand, tucked into its corner below the saddles, I felt a chill under the sunlight. For the first time in my life I had witnessed solitude.

When I thought of Trenowath's after that, I found that my memories of it had changed. The farm had become an interior, a silence. I could taste it on my tongue, as cold and clear as spring water. Nothing could have been plainer or more distinct from everything I knew. This made me thoughtful. Until then Norfolk had been mine for the imagining, a world of differences where I could never be a stranger. I had moved in and out of my grandparents' lives, absorbing them into mine. Elusive as the past was, that other country I glimpsed in the front-room photographs, my own studio portrait stood on the piano, a small boy with crinkly ears and a toothy smile, his cheeks tinted by the photographer an embarrassing shade of pink, and that gave me right of entry. Now I began to wonder how far I had really seen into these lives that so intrigued me. There was no absorbing the silence of Trenowath's, no diminishing its strangeness.

Years later, watching the film of *Far from the Madding Crowd*,

I saw the farm again. Mr Boldwood was sitting alone at a mahogany table, eating a meal prepared by his housekeeper. Bare flagstones resonated with the tock of a carriage clock. It was the same atmosphere as Trenowath's: austerity and high polish, the solitude of a kept house – and Bathsheba's Valentine bewitching him from the mantelpiece.

The morning we shot the hare was the last time I saw Mr Trenowath. He died suddenly the following year, early in May. We were still in London, our thoughts not even turned towards summer, and the news came like a message from another world. My father described the funeral to me, how the coffin was carried from the church on the hand bier, under the falling rain. They should have carried it up the lane, he said, past the house and through the farmyard. They would have come out opposite the cemetery on the Heacham road. As it was, they took the usual route, down Utting's Lane – named after the farmer before Mr Trenowath – up Bunkle's Hill – named after Uncle Bunkle, the keeper of the Buck Inn, who was also the blacksmith and had his shop at the top of the rise – and on to the Heacham road that way. It was strange to listen to these names in our large Victorian house in Surbiton – Chiswick Lodge, it was called, we had no idea why – and be carried back to the village, where every twist and turn had its story, its familiar ghost.

What I did not know then was that the two worlds were about to fuse. Within a few years we would have bought a farm in the suburbs, a stray patch of land between a housing estate, a dual carriageway and the main railway line to Waterloo. My father began to break and train his own horses, realising an ambition that must have formed in the intent hush of the dew pond. My own apprenticeship began, a curious, intermittent apprenticeship that would leave me half-bonded to the land, just intimate enough to know how much I remain a stranger.

I returned to Trenowath's when I began to write this book, walking the lane from memory, up past the church. It still opens out with an air of enclosure, an undeclared threshold: a formal apron of short grass in front of the low stone wall, the house set back on its terrace. Beyond is the farmyard, the beaten earth almost reclaimed by grass. The fields have been sold off but goats are penned in the stable yard and a squad of ducks forms at your heels. The dew pond still spreads like a ripple from a stone, the grass green and thick as a fairy ring.

Now the lane is simply called Church Lane. Farmer Utting must have been forgotten by the time the Council came to set up the road sign. I would have had to keep to it, glancing discreetly at the house, if Ruth had not told me that the present owner, Mrs Hammond, is an historian and would certainly be sympathetic to my project. Besides which, the years had furnished me with a visiting card: I could present myself as the son of Judge Garfitt.

Sitting in what had been Mabel's kitchen, with a mug of coffee in my hand, I reflected that I had finally crossed that invisible line. Mrs Hammond was so friendly that really I needed no credentials. The fact was that I had them all and that probably helped. My father had left Sedgeford at seventeen to join the Metropolitan Police. Too young to go straight into uniform, he had become a typist in Brixton police station. What had transformed his expectations was the Second World War. In the last years of the war, the armed forces had become a crucible of social change. Discussion groups formed and adult education classes: there was a determination to construct a new society. It was the servicemen, writing home to their wives to tell them to vote Labour, who brought in the Attlee government of 1945.

I don't think my father ever had my grandfather's political awareness but all this talk of change had an effect on him: he raised his sights. He took a correspondence course from London University and studied on the end of his air force bed. He stayed on as an education instructor, rehabilitating other airmen, as it was called, for civilian life. By the time he was demobbed in 1946, he had an LL B and had passed his Bar exams. Now I sat conversing with Mrs Hammond, matching her stories of Cambridge with my reminiscences of Oxford, all too aware that my father's midnight oil had given me what he never had: a cultured ease.

It was Mrs Hammond who told me that Mabel was still alive, in a nursing home in Hunstanton. The next day Ruth and I went and found her. In her late eighties, she might just have bustled out of the kitchen with a tray full of scones, an apron tied round her full figure. Grey hair, loosely caught up into a bun, fell over cheeks whose skin was as clear as it must have been when she was a girl. The only signs of age were a bandaged leg, resting on a stool, and the walking frame by her chair.

I asked her about the Lady's Well, the pool that flowed from a spring below the church, and she remembered the watercress that used to grow there. Ruth asked her about the wild flowers, the violets in Beech Wood and the primroses in the Long Meadow, so thick, Mabel said, 'they were like a carpet, you couldn't walk without treading on primroses'. When she spoke of the flowers, her voice changed. She forgot the discreet whisper of visiting time, the sibilances of the old ladies around her rustling like dried everlastings, and spoke in her full contralto. 'Oh, the violets, the violets were lovely!' she said, and I heard the long Norfolk 'i' in violets and all the energy, the stride of a woman in her forties and fifties, whatever age she had been when she kept house for Mr Trenowath and walked over the fields to Beech Wood. The body was incapacitated but the voice rose out of the chair, impatient to walk the paths again.

My memories of the house had suffered a shock when Mrs Hammond showed me round. I saw the hall again and could hardly believe it was the same room, dusty and shrunk under the stairs. Now, as I listened to Mabel and looked through her photographs, Mr Trenowath began to emerge from its sunlit silence. I saw him on a light summer evening, riding over Snettisham Marsh, where he ran a flock of sheep. In the early dark of winter, pitching hay to the bullocks in a muddy gateway. Five hundred cattle he had at one time, she said, and nearly wore himself to the bone.

To my surprise, I saw him with other summer visitors: the Kneales, who drove over from Melton Mowbray in a coach and four, their arrival chronicled every year by the local paper; the Dutch family who came in a chauffeur-driven car and camped beside the Lady's Well. Here was a coltish young girl, balanced nervously, feet apart, on a home-made raft, floating across the grassy shallows.

Enough high days and holidays to fill the box on Mabel's lap. As she sorted through them, recognising a face, remembering a story, Hill Farm came to life. I began to hear laughter round the kitchen table. The hall and the big sitting room stayed empty: as soon as Mabel let slip that Mr Trenowath went visiting every evening, I knew that the silence I had heard as a boy was real. But now I could hear the voices from the kitchen, Mabel, and her husband, and Mr Trenowath, sitting around after supper, talking over the day.

Nothing was ever the same, Mabel's husband used to say, after Mr Trenowath died. They moved to a cottage in the village and he found work for another farmer. They lived out their lives as the village changed around them, families dying out and holiday cottagers moving in. They looked back to Hill Farm and her husband would repeat, like an article of faith, 'The years with Mr Trenowath were the best.'

As we drove away from the nursing home, I felt as if I had laid a ghost.

* * *

My grandfather's workshop still stood then on the Heacham road, converted into a greengrocer's stall. Outside, a display stand covered the window, but inside, under boxes stacked for the freezer, I could just see the workbench. I imagined the hammer dents, the nicks and scorings of the knife, the screw holes where the machines used to stand. I knew my grandfather mended bikes as well as shoes but Colin, the greengrocer, told me of another little sideline: people brought him their radios to have the accumulators charged. He showed me behind the door: there was a flat white sink, like a small fishmonger's slab. 'He used to charge the radios there,' he said, 'three ha'pence a time.'

When Colin sent me over the road to meet Gertie, who had taught my father in the village school, I began to wonder if everyone in Sedgeford lived into their nineties. Gertie must have been little more than a girl when she taught my father. Later she married another local runner and remembered my father beating him in the Sedgeford Race. Now she was a shrewd, sharp-eyed old lady, sitting on her sofa in front of an electric fire. My father had been one of her star pupils: she drilled him for the scholarship to the grammar school in Lynn. But when she came to talk of the younger boys, of Billy and Peter, she glanced down, indented her cheek with three pointed fingers and fixed her gaze on the fire's single bar. 'Didn't they get into trouble?' she said. 'Something to do with some shoes?' She would say no more and I asked Ruth when I returned to Heacham that evening. It was like innocently tapping a rock sample from the side of a volcano: the air hissed and steamed. If I had laid a ghost with Mabel, I had raised one with Gertie.

It seems that the family's last home in Sedgeford was opposite the village school. A new schoolmaster arrived with new ideas, one of which was that the children should make themselves a pair of indoor shoes out of felt. Over half-term the sack of shoes disappeared. Burnt, it transpired, on the bonfire. The caretaker had probably thrown the sack on, thinking it was rubbish, but suspicion fell on Billy and Peter because they lived so close. The schoolmaster took them to court.

The trial before the local magistrates lasted two days. Twenty or thirty witnesses appeared to testify that Billy and Peter had been nowhere near the school. Ruth herself had been in charge of them and they had never been out of her sight for long enough to commit the crime. The magistrates were in a dilemma: they should have dismissed the case but that would have made the schoolmaster look foolish. In the feudal society of the village as it was then, his position had to be preserved. They compromised by finding the boys guilty but giving them an absolute discharge.

The verdict was shame enough and the family never forgave it. They felt they had been offered as scapegoats because, after twenty years in the village, they were still regarded as strangers. Everyone else belonged to one of the tight-knit family groups. 'Got no uncles! Got no aunts!' the other children would shout after Ruth in the street and she would shout back, 'When my uncle comes to visit, he'll come on a train – yours won't!' Everything my grandparents had done in the village, the time they had put into the British Legion, the football team, the Mothers' Union, counted for nothing beside the simple fact of not belonging. Now I knew why they had decided to leave. I had met for myself the stubbornness of old Sedgeford, where mud still stuck after fifty years.

One of the squires of Sedgeford, Sir Holcombe Ingleby, wrote an affectionate little book called *The Charm of a Village*: but the charm rather depended on where you stood in the social scale. Ruth remembers another member of the squire's family calling at the house and asking, 'Is this Garfitt's cottage?' Frank answered her with the courtesy she expected, 'Yes, Ma'am,' but Ruth thought, 'Why can't she say, "Mr Garfitt"? We have to show her respect. Why can't she do the same for my father?'

Ted Bradfield, a local gamekeeper, put the point very sharply when he said in his memoirs, 'Gentlemen don't give a damn about our class of people. I've been with them so long I know just what they are.' The gentry lived in another world. However well-meaning their descents into village life, their good works and acts of charity, they were haphazard and often arbitrary. One man's patronage could be another man's disappointment. When a shoe repairer in Hunstanton fell ill, my grandfather took on his repairs and kept the shop open for him. Eventually the man died and my grandfather expected to be offered the shop, which, being in the town, had a better trade. In stepped a local major and ensured that it was offered to another man. The other man was lame and the major undoubtedly thought he was doing him a kindness. Which he was, but at my grandfather's expense.

Later my grandfather helped out another tradesman in Lynn and would not apply for the lease when he died. He was too disheartened even to ask. My grandparents never had much luck when they tried to better themselves. When the fish and chip shop in the front room proved a success, the landlord tried to sell it over their heads. They stopped him by pulling out the fish kettles, which they had installed at their own expense. That way they kept the house – but they lost the income.

My father had all the luck. When he applied for the Metropolitan Police, he was one of hundreds of bright country boys who had written away to London. The police was a coveted job in those days because it carried a pension. For a long time there was no reply. My grandfather mentioned the problem to Lord Fermoy, whom he knew through the British Legion, and Lord Fermoy said he would put in a good word. Within a fortnight the papers had arrived from Scotland Yard.

My grandfather had great respect for Lord Fermoy and agonised over whether he should vote for him when he stood for Parliament.

He knew he was a good man, he said, but he was not of his party. In the end he held to his beliefs: one good man could not right the wrongs of a system.

Among the characters of Sedgeford was a man who was always known as Funny Drury. Funny worked for Shanks, the master builder in Hunstanton. In those days labourers were taken on or laid off at a moment's notice, according to the work in hand. Peter's bricklaying came to an abrupt end one Friday night and he had to spend Saturday cycling round to find himself another job. But Funny had evolved a strategy for these occasions. Whenever Shanks tried to give him his cards, he would take off his cap and produce a photo of his wife and children. Once Shanks hardened his heart and sacked him anyway. Next morning Funny was back on the job. 'I thought I'd given you the sack,' said Shanks. 'Yes,' said Funny, 'but if you can't tell when you've got a good man, I can tell when I've got a good master.'

Who would think of saying 'master' and 'man' now? They seem phrases from another century. And yet they encapsulate the world in which my father grew up, a world of fixed social positions, where people rarely moved far from their birthplace. The more I compare my father's Sedgeford with the village I have known since childhood, the more I realise that they only appear to be the same place. The fields are much the same. My grandfather's workshop stood until recently on the same worn patch of sand and gravel. Church Lane begins between the same flint cottages, edged with brick. But I never had to while away the weeks, waiting for a letter from London. Never walked a horse up on to the shoulder of the downs, watching the fields rise around me to their near horizons, and felt as if I were drowning, horse and man, in their steady swell.

My summers in Norfolk ended with childhood. As if from instinct, I broke the pattern when I was thirteen and booked myself into a

Christian Holiday Centre in the Lake District. This looked like a declaration of faith but really, I suspect, it was a declaration of independence. Then my father bought the farm and the pattern reversed itself anyway: my grandparents came to stay with us.

If I was responding to an instinct, it was a wise one. Norfolk has kept its innocence. I remember it through a child's eyes. For my sister, even for my parents, I imagine, it kept a special quality, the one place where we still pictured ourselves as a family. Children lend a marriage their childhood and our parents separated once we were adults. None of us would ever be so simple again.

Though we fell back into simplicity when my grandparents came to visit. Something shone out of them, an expectation it would have been hard to disappoint. Contentment seems too secure, too passive a word. They were still vulnerable: you could see that in the little silent mumble, a sideways movement of the jaw, with which my grandmother swallowed any small rebuff. And they were still thrifty, still anxious to contribute: while my grandfather sorted and salvaged in the toolshed, my grandmother hobbled out over the back field, rocking awkwardly, on one fallen arch, over the hoofpitted grass, and gleaned bowls full of blackberries from the tattered hedge. But they felt they had survived, they had outlived all their troubles, and this gave them a modest claim on happiness. So modest that it hardly registered as a claim: it was a kind of trust.

We, in turn, felt protective. We kept them in a frame, two grandparents in a photograph. Forgetting that their eyes were alive and taking in, perhaps, more than we realised. Forgetting, in my case, how odd some of the transitions were that I went through in adolescence.

There was my evangelism, for instance, which began when I was 'born again' at the age of twelve. It was the early 1950s, when respectable families still sent their children to Sunday School. My parents packed us off every week, thereby absolving themselves from going to church except at Christmas and Easter. If they had attended more often, they might have realised they were playing with hellfire. Our local church was the sort that held revivalist meetings outside the swimming baths on a Sunday morning. As the good people of Surbiton queued up with their towels under their arms, we pointed out their strong resemblance to the population of Sodom and Gomorrah, forgetting the Lord's Day and abandoning themselves to the delights of the flesh. Then I would be called upon to give my testimony. I seem to have my grandfather's gift as a performer, but in reverse. He would stumble over the introduction to a song and then bring tears to the eyes as he sang it. I can't sing a note in tune but I can move an audience. So I would lift up my child's voice and tell of the darkness and waste of my first twelve years, and of the joy I had found when I accepted Christ as my Saviour.

That much was true. I had cycled home from the Bible Class in an extraordinary state of joy and told my parents that my life had changed for good. The next morning, of course, I woke up the same as ever. But I took my new allegiance seriously and throughout my early adolescence it dominated my life.

I gathered other boys around me at school, talking to them at lunchtime and taking them off to an empty classroom to pray. I distributed tracts on my bicycle, overtaking unwary cyclists and holding the tract across their handlebars. As the two of us wobbled together in the middle of the road, they had little choice but to accept.

I must have been a public nuisance, as one of my friends later put it, 'a God-botherer': but I was even more of a nuisance to myself. I did not want to be accosting strangers in this way. I would much rather have cycled home with my friends. But, in my self-imprisoning logic, the very fact that I did not want to evangelise meant that I had to. Reluctance was the voice of the Devil, trying to disarm me.

I was like a figure in a medieval morality play, the evil angel whispering in one ear and the good angel in the other. Between them they gave me no peace. Once, when I was sitting among the old men in the hairdresser's, just about to submerge myself in *The Dandy*, the good angel stripped away my sense of ease. 'Give your testimony,' it whispered, 'NOW!'

That was the last thing I wanted to do. Men's hairdressers in those days were like transport cafés or the snugs of northern pubs, secure male havens. For an hour you were absolved of all responsibility except getting a haircut. You perched yourself on one of the upright wooden chairs with cracked leather seats and settled into the warmth of the heater, the exploits of Desperate Dan, and the background chat of the Home Service. I generally entered just as *Mrs Dale's Diary* was finishing. With any luck I could hear the whole of *Children's Hour* before the barber turned to me and said, 'Next!'

Ease always attracted the good angel. I had only to relax and he would hand me a whip or a hairshirt. If I had finished my homework and was looking forward to an hour's reading, he would insist that I said my prayers first, 'while my mind was fresh'. Then make me repeat them, 'because my mind had wandered', over and over again. But this startling suggestion in the hairdresser's was the furthest he had ever gone.

It was like a dare. Once the thought had formed, there was no backing down. I tried to forget it, to lose myself in *The Dandy*. But the mood of innocent absorption had gone. There was nothing for it. I waited for an interval in the barber's chat, crouched behind my cheekbones, bunched just above my voice, like someone poised at the top of a long slide. Then heard my childish treble rise above the radio and the shuffles and grunts of the old men: 'I would like to tell you of a wonderful change that has come over my life . . .'

It was as if I had confessed to incest. There was an ice-locked silence. No one spoke. No one so much as moved in his chair. All you could hear was the radio and the click of the scissors. Finally an old man stirred, as if in protest. 'What are you going to do now, then?' he asked. A good question. I thought for a moment and the answer came pat: 'I am going to become a missionary.' 'Well, good for you,' he said, as if he had seen through me then and there. But even he could not break the cold spell. Everyone sat frozen to their seats until I was called up to the big chair and began chatting brightly to the barber. Then I heard the room relax around me.

There's no telling what form my adolescence might have taken if I had not been converted. All I know is that I spent some of my formative years behind bars: hearing voices and laughter outside but resolutely keeping to my monkish cell because those voices were the world, the flesh and the Devil. One of my friends asked me to go with him to see the film of *Look Back in Anger* and I refused because the cinema poster was too alluring: Mary Ure was shown in her slip. When the ripples of Existentialism reached England and everyone else was reading Camus and Sartre, I was reading seventeenth-century Puritan divines.

I don't think my grandfather ever quite realised the full extent of my oddity. He left me his bible when he died, which suggests that he took my religion on trust. But he once saw me in an odd state. I had just hitched back from Provence, where I had been teaching English to the children of a French family. The journey took two full days and almost didn't begin at all. I had sat by the roadside for hours, thumbing hopelessly at a continuous stream of cars. Perhaps people were put off by my great cardboard box full of books. It was the summer before I went up to Oxford and I had sat under a pine tree, reading Cicero. Or perhaps it was simply difficult for cars to stop. In the end I was rescued by an English couple who spotted my little Union Jack and reversed against the traffic.

At the roadside I had slumped into a kind of trance, mesmerised by the succession of cars. My eyes fell on the string tied round the box and I began to improvise, inspired, I imagine, by the monologues in *Beyond the Fringe*, several of which I knew off by heart. Three days later, back at the farm, I saw the dinner table crowded with a potential audience: my parents, my grandparents, the new Danish au pair girl and half a dozen stable girls. I slipped away and fetched the string from the box. As soon as the meal was over, I rose to my feet:

'Ladies and Gentlemen, let me introduce you to our revolutionary new product: Pre-Knotted String. At £3 a foot it may seem a little expensive. But it took some developing, I can tell you. Years of work in our Nottingham laboratories. And it will save you hours of time. Have you ever thought how much of your life you have tied up in knots? How much free time you could have at your fingertips? Let me express it for you in a simple equation: $S = T = M$. String takes up Time which is Money. Now we will take your money and give you our Pre-Knotted String. Take away M, do away with S and you are left with T. But Time, Ladies and Gentlemen, *is* Money, $T = M$, so you get it all back. In fact, the more Pre-Knotted String you buy, the more Time you save and the more Money you make. It's a snip at only £3 a foot. Do yourselves a favour, Ladies and Gentlemen, and buy as much as you can. Just think of that well-known saying: it's money for old rope.'

Well, it was an improvement on my testimony. There was some startled laughter and the table cleared. I was carrying my plates to the sink when I saw my grandfather making his way towards me. He gave me a strange look: amused, appraising and anxious. 'Does funny things to you, doesn't it, lad, being on your own too long?' We stood together for a moment while everyone dodged around us. Then he moved away. I was not sure whether he had been re-assuring me or reassuring himself about me. But he had touched on a nerve. The comic monologue *was* an improvement on the testimony. I was much happier at nineteen than I had been at twelve. But still trapped in an intense solitude.

It was poetry that finally led me out of the labyrinth. I had chosen to read Classics, as a preparation for Theology, but could not bear to give up English. In the weeks before my A-levels, when I should have been revising Latin and Greek set books, I would open *The Prelude*, on the pretext that I had to revise English as well, and be held by it all evening. I went up to Oxford and duly read Classics. Towards the end of my second term it dawned on me that the elaborate and time-consuming structure of my religious life, the daily prayers, the weekly services, the repeated cycles of sin, repentance and confession, no longer contained me. I was elsewhere, responding more vividly to a poem by D. H. Lawrence, a painting by Egon Schiele or a solo by Miles Davis than to anything I read in my daily bible study. That realisation set me free. I stood upright and the whole weight of observance rolled off my back, as suddenly and completely as Pilgrim's burden.

It took me much longer to emerge from my inner isolation. I had become so used to that monk's cell I did not know how to leave, I could only refurnish it. The poet replaced the evangelist and the cell became a garret. The poet was more sociable and no longer had any qualms about chastity. Otherwise, he was much the same: immured in himself, even as a lover.

Perhaps his saving grace was that occasionally he was aware of it. One of my early love poems, written when I was twenty, goes like this:

> From inside my eyes, looking out,
> I see your eyes, black from the doorlight,

quiver to silver
as they follow your fingertip trace
my cheekbone visor.

From inside my eyes, looking in,
I can see that my head is a wedge
splitting your breastbone.
You may trace embroideries down its grey edge
and not mist the iron.

If you stop, your gaze coming to meet me,
I will hide my eyes, turn them aside
to the air:
and yet you, refusing my desire,
felt unfair;
as if my eyes, tactful in their redoubt,
seemed gentle to you,
from inside yourself, looking out.

In some ways, I suppose, it's a period piece, rooted in the calculation we had to use then to get girls into bed. Those were the days of separate women's colleges, when they had to be back inside the college gate by midnight. St Giles was furtive with amorous shadows, girls being walked back to Somerville and St Anne's, and stopping for a last embrace in a shop doorway. Saying goodbye at the college gate was an art form in itself. You choreographed your farewell so that, as the chimes began to strike, the two of you were locked in a passionate, parting glance, like the final frame of a Hollywood film.

It was the light coming through the postern of the college gate and glancing off the girl's dark eyes that gave me the initial image of the poem. I am not sure how well I handled it. 'Quiver to silver' seems to me now to have come too easily to the ear. But the second stanza still works: that's just how I was then, an armoured head, predatory and impervious.

Or almost impervious. I courted that girl assiduously all one autumn term and wrote to her every single day of the Christmas vacation. Then appeared in her room on the first day back to confess that I did not really love her after all. I was trying to be honest. But honesty had become a storm in my head that broke regardless of her feelings.

Give me a real storm and I would add lightning flashes of my own. A year later I learned that my grandfather was dying. Unknown to me, he had been seriously ill for eighteen months. A sore place he had had on his tongue for years, and always thought of as a recurring abscess, had proved to be cancer. By the time he went to the doctor, it had spread to his throat. Like Dick Darby, the cobbler in the folk song, where every line is punctuated by a spit and a tap, he always held the tingles, the cobbler's small nails, in his mouth. The cancer may have grown from there, from the little pit they wore in the tongue.

One day towards the end of the Christmas vacation, while we were all sitting round the big farmhouse table for lunch, the phone rang in the hall. It was Ruth, letting us know that my grandfather was nearing his end. My father had a case in court the next day. My mother was running the farm. I volunteered to go instead.

It started almost as an adventure. I put some clothes in a rucksack and my father added a chicken, a jar of honey and a jar of cream. I caught the train from Liverpool Street, changed at King's Lynn, and came down on the diesel to Heacham. As I walked up from the station, the village was a huddle of lights under a dark winter sky. I had not been there for nine years and no longer knew my way around. Ruth had moved into Collins' Lane, into a house I had never seen, and my grandparents had moved into her old house in Caley Street. I knocked on a door in the first street I came to and was directed round the corner to Collins' Lane. Harold was home and walked me up to Caley Street.

When I was a child, it had always been down to Caley Street. Left out of Woodend Road, past the village school where my grandfather was caretaker in his latter years. Long grass grew in the shade of six tall trees where I imagined myself mooching through long summer lunch hours. On the brown carrstone wall of the school itself, some benign headmaster had painted a big white circle with a bull's-eye. I thought of the generations who must have bounced a ball off that wall: fathers, uncles, elder brothers. For one moment every year, as I stood and looked between the railings, I was ready to forgo all the advantages of London.

Right into Broadway, past the prefabs where the American service families used to live. Once I saw one of their great cars pulling away from the kerb, the hood down and the radio playing, as crowded with heads as a Thames pleasure steamer.

Down to the High Street past the butcher's shop on the corner. A fresh smell of sawdust came through the open door and I would glance into the cavernous interior. Men moved in a hanging forest of meat, ducking between swaying white lengths of pig.

Cross the High Street and vanish down Joyce's Lane, a gravelled dip that ran through Joyce's yard, past his stacks of bricks, his sand heaps, and the little wooden shed that served as his office. Joyce's Lane breached Caley Street like the floodpath of some old watercourse, a broad, sandy gap between houses. Ruth's was on the left, the end house of a small carrstone terrace.

That night, as I was led round to the back gate, I felt the scrunch of gravel under my feet and the old elation rose, the release of walking down a road that felt like a beach.

There was a new back door. An extension with a flush toilet had replaced the backyard privy I had dreaded on my visits to Ruth's, where flies buzzed over the stinking pit. Harold ushered me through a strange hall and I was back in my grandmother's kitchen. She sat at a small, square table in front of a huge black range. There was the green chenille tablecloth, worn through in places to the backing's rusty brown; the ship under full canvas sailing round the curve of the biscuit tin, whose steely sky had clouded with copper; the Friesian cow on the lid of the butter dish, still spick and span, neatly curled on its lick of grass, expecting rain.

Ruth came through from the front room, where she had been sitting by my grandfather's bed. His mind was clear and he had asked for a cup of tea. The day before, in his delirium, he had kept saying, 'Bring me that red teapot!' They had never had a red teapot, only the old brown earthenware. Ruth was wondering if he had wandered back to his childhood in Yorkshire. Then she noticed the red teapot in the pattern of the kitchen wallpaper.

Another time he had asked her to clear the animals off the end of the bed. When he swung his arms and chatted, she knew he was marching with the British Legion. She had sat up with him every night for three weeks and told these stories with a wry affection. Her face was so white it seemed to be powdering away. Once he had even asked her when Ruth was coming. She replied quietly, 'She'll be along shortly.'

I don't know what I had been expecting. I had no experience of a deathbed, no idea what would be asked of me. I had come to the house fresh-faced, full of news from the farm. Now I found myself lifting my grandfather, rolling his tubby body in striped pyjamas first to one side of the bed, then to the other, while Ruth remade it under him. The odd thing was that he looked just the same. All I could see was a scar down the side of his neck where the glands had been removed.

Ruth asked me to sit up with her so that my grandmother could get some sleep. It would take two of us to change the bed and two of us to get Grandad back into it if he set off in the middle of the

70

night to open up the shop. She took the chair in the corner and left me the one at the foot of the bed. I settled myself down with a blanket and a pillow, and my copy of Blake. Blake was a talisman. I imagined wandering with my grandfather across strange landscapes, hearing half-phrases swept away by the wind. Or saw the two of us huddled at the bottom of a trench in the First World War, enduring the bombardment before a dawn offensive.

But the night was quiet. In the morning he said, 'You didn't get much sleep either, did you, lad?' and I realised he had been watching over me quite as much as I had watched over him. I had sat in my chair fighting ghostly battles. Reliving old defeats and returning to the scenes of past humiliations. At Oxford I had campaigned for Robert Lowell as Professor of Poetry and been reprimanded by my tutor during Warden's Collections, a public assessment in front of the Warden and Fellows, for daring to canvass my 'elders and betters'. I'd had to bow my head and keep silence. Such was the convention. That night in Heacham I delivered my reply, a rapid string of aphorisms, modelled, no doubt, on Blake's *Proverbs of Hell*. Once or twice I giggled aloud.

I was succumbing to the hero myth, dreaming that out of this ordeal I would be reborn, invulnerable and invincible. And yet I no longer cared for my life, I wanted to throw it away. On the train from Liverpool Street, I had picked up a discarded newspaper and read a shocked report of beatniks living in the Matlock Caves. At weekends, according to the paper, the caves filled with orgiastic teenagers and schoolgirl prostitutes sold themselves for half a crown. Enticing as that was, what really drew me was the thought of the permanent community, a handful of beatniks living without purpose or belief, wintering in the caves. As the dawn light came through the curtains, I reread the report and thought of catching the train to Matlock. I had a vision of myself arriving to join them, a silent, enigmatic figure, bearing a jar of honey.

That day I didn't know what to do with myself. My grand-mother sent me for some bread and I leaned against the display counter, afraid that I was going to faint. The woman said, 'Can't you stand up straight even for a moment?' I threw back my head and told her, 'I've been sitting up all night with a dying man.' She looked down at the counter, wrapped the bread and said, 'Four o'clock in the morning is the worst time.'

I went down Collins' Lane to Peter and Anne's, another house I had never seen, and was introduced to their children. Stephen liked writing, they said. Out came my copy of Blake and I read him 'The Garden of Love'. He listened eagerly to the poem. But when I reread the last two lines,

> And priests in black gowns were walking their rounds
> And binding with briars my joys and desires.

and started to expatiate on Blake's use of internal rhyme, his little forehead went tight with strain. He was only eight.

I was seasick with energy, swaying from one adrenalin surge to the next. But not wise enough to rest. I believed what my mania told me, that I had been reborn into this brittle twenty-four-hour light. From now on, it said, consciousness would be constant and unremitting. It was godhead, of a kind. But felt more like damnation, the fate of the Flying Dutchman or the Wandering Jew. I assuaged it by buying twenty Senior Service and starting to smoke. What had a vampire to fear from coffin nails? My grandfather noticed and said, 'Don't start the fire, lad! You'll never be able to put it out.' He was blaming his cancer on the pipe he had given up thirty years before.

The second night was easier. I listened to my grandfather murmuring in the bed, to Ruth shifting in the corner, almost at ease in this strange companionship: but I was too weary to face the dawn when it came. I could not bear another day as long as the last.

After breakfast, I tried to sleep in the spare room. Winter sunlight was bright on the ceiling. A thin panel of warmth extended from the airing cupboard but the room seemed cold and bare. I put my head on the pillow and listened to the pulse in my temples. Suddenly I had an illumination: if I left now, I could reach my girlfriend's home in Wiltshire by the end of the day.

I raced downstairs, full of fresh energy. My grandmother was perturbed. Where was I rushing off to? Wouldn't I at least wait until she had made me some sandwiches? Ruth took one look at me and said, 'If he says he wants to go now, Mother, I think you'd better let him go.'

The decision carried me into the front room before I had time to think. I said goodbye to my grandfather, promising to see him again soon. Everyone was keeping up this bright pretence. Even as I said it, I could see how lonely the lie left him. He said to himself, 'It's breaking already' and turned to the wall. I had no need to ask him what it was that was breaking: I knew.

And I was running for comfort. Running to the dark-eyed girl of the poem, whose security I had shattered the previous January when I appeared in her room to confess, after a string of love letters, that I did not love her. My scruples had lasted all of six weeks. If it was not love that drew me back, it was a compound of fair substitutes: desire, tenderness, affection. We had been improvising an affair ever since, risking nights in my college room, or creeping out of the farmhouse with armfuls of bedding while everyone else slept and making love in the caravan in the garden.

But that was no preparation for the whirlwind of grief, anger and exhaustion that was heading her way. The house stood by itself down a lane on the outskirts of the village. I reached it in late afternoon, only to discover that she was still at her holiday job in the local factory. I had not thought of that. I had imagined walking the lanes with her while she showed me where a fox slipped through the hedge or a wren nested between the spikes of the blackthorn. I had imagined standing on the edge of a wood, staring into rainwashed distances, and hearing the first percolation of birdsong as the rain stopped.

Instead, I found myself in the kitchen, trying to explain my sudden arrival to her mother. 'How long are you planning to stay?' she asked. She had never liked me. Small, dark and good-looking, a tigress compressed into a tabby cat, she saw me as a threat to the domestic virtues.

'I don't know,' I replied loftily. 'I don't make plans any longer.' It was Rimbaud talking. I had been in the shadow of his vagabond genius all day. The mother and teenage daughter whose compartment I had shared from Lynn to London were intrigued. 'We met a fascinating character on the train,' I heard the mother exclaim to the friend who was waiting for them at Liverpool Street. 'I can't begin to imagine what nationality he is.'

'Well, that's just not practical.' Rimbaud wasn't cutting any ice in this kitchen. 'Other people have their lives to lead too.' I took that to mean I was imposing on them, which I was rather. 'There's all my money!' I said, and flung my wallet across the floor.

After that the reel breaks. The memories come in flashes. I am trying to bury my head in my girlfriend's shoulder and she says, 'I can't help you.' Her father looks at me and asks, 'Were you very close to your grandfather?' He is driving me up to Oxford and she is sitting in the front. The entire length of the journey, her eyes pulse with tears. We reach the city and her father asks, 'Have you any friends you can go and see?'

I went to Christina's. She was older than us, in her late twenties. One of us had met her when she was working in a coffee bar in Hampstead. She had just come out of hospital after a suicide attempt and we regarded her with a strange mixture of awe and disdain. None of us had known anything but success. That was why I was homing in on her now.

She had been drawn to Oxford by the aura of learning and was living with a postgraduate. They took me in without a word. Christina warmed up some food. She played me a blues record. She gave me one of her tranquillisers and I went to sleep on the cushions on the floor. In the morning I was steady enough to go back to my own flat.

I had left Heacham on the Friday morning. My grandfather died on the Saturday night. In those last two days, Ruth said, the flesh simply melted off him. As she watched, he wasted away. Though I shall always regret not having the strength to stay to the end, I had left at the right moment.

That first sleepless night, when I imagined myself crouching beside my grandfather in the trenches, had a strange sequel. The following October I went down to the Cheltenham Festival to sell copies of *New Measure*, an Oxford poetry magazine. By then I was almost lost in ghostly battles. I was wearing an old French army jacket. I had an air pistol tucked into my belt, under my shirt. Later I would use it to hold up an American poet who had refused, rather churlishly, it seemed to me, even to look at the magazine. But first I saw the hunched, grey-haired figure of Edmund Blunden. I went over to present him with a copy of the magazine, to which he had contributed a poem. Blunden thanked me and glanced at the contents. Then he glanced at my jacket and confided, 'You know, I have the feeling that there is always a war going on somewhere. But I don't always know where it is.'

# PART TWO

## The Farm, Surrey

### 1960–1963

*e il trapianto felice al nuovo sole,*
*te inconscia si compì*

and the happy graft in the new sun
knit without your knowing

Eugenio Montale, '*Il giglio rosso*'
'The Red Lily'
translated by Jonathan Galassi

There was one place where the farm was still complete, one turn of the lane where trees screened you from the council estate and the railway station. You picked your way around a muddy corner, which an elm kept always in shadow, and for some thirty yards the lane opened out into a green ride, a slowly curving width of grass with the bushes of a ditch bank on one side and the trees of a grown-out hedge on the other. Not that much grew there other than grass. I looked for a rarity every time I walked through, feeling that here, if anywhere, I should find one. But no, not so much as a primrose on the ditch bank in spring. All the place had was itself, its uninterrupted self.

Everywhere else on the farm you could feel the twentieth century rushing past. A main road ran along one side and the main line to Waterloo along another. Between the road and the railway was the council estate, source of the rusting tricycles and improvised goalposts we had to clear out of the back fields each summer before we could cut them for hay. These fields belonged to the Greater London Council, which had started to build on them just before the war, putting in the first service road at the back of Hersham station. The kerb was still there in the grass. You would trip over it and look down to see what was under your feet: the small, blue-grey, knuckled grids of the paving stones, that must have promised hard wear in 1939, and the flats of concrete where the houses were to go. It was a strange sensation to walk across them, as if you were trespassing on the lives that might have been lived there.

After the war the Green Belt was drawn round London, preserving the farm as an anomaly. Not all of its land could have been built on anyway: along the third side flowed the River Mole, a wayward small river that tunnels underground and floods overland. The house had a shallow moat round it that filled when the fields turned to silver and swans drifted past the hayrack. It had been the home farm to Esher Palace, which had stood on the wooded hill across the river, and the footings of a bridge were still in the mud of the riverbank. When we led horses down to graze by the river or fetched the cows up for milking, we would use the track the farm carts had taken, a finger of grassed-over stone that crooked itself over a field drain in a culvert. Sometimes I used to walk down there just to feel the stones of the track carry me over. They were the simplest form of inheritance, provision made for me whoever I was.

Across the river were the houses of a private estate, each with its frontage screened by trees, each with its long lawn sloping down to the riverbank. The daydreams, I used to call them, each one pretending the others weren't there. I would walk along until I could look across at the Wayneflete Tower, which was a true dream. Built as a hunting lodge for Hampton Court Palace, it had a magical lightness, a diamond mesh of white bricks in the red that lifted away all the weight.

The track down to the river was the first place I would take visitors, the track and the Wayneflete Tower. But I never took anyone to the turn of the lane. There was nothing to see. Only the slow bend, still held to the curve of a wagon swing, and the trees cupped over the path so that for a few yards you heard ditch-seepings rather than the sounds of traffic. It was a subtler survival than the stones of the track, a stillness nothing had dispersed, where you could sense the fields stretched on their river silt, on the screed of the flood plain.

The house was Elizabethan, built of thin red bricks that dipped over the back door, clambering back to a horizontal above the long kitchen window. I was quick to point out the dip to visitors as showing the age of the house but it did more than that: it put us at ease with the past, it made us family as we went in and out of the back door. I used to glance up at it every time I walked up the path from the yard. That was my private devotion, to glance up before I reached down for the doorknob and stepped down into the concourse of the back hall, into the ranks of riding boots and wellingtons, and the coats humped on their pegs.

The barn must have been built at the same time, an L-shaped building with walls of whitewashed brick and a roof so long it enclosed the yard like a second sky. The tiles were the same soft red as the bricks of the house but some had been blown out in the war when a stick of bombs fell on the field by the river, destroying the old bridge. The blast had ripped across the front of the house, demolishing a conservatory, and punched a hole in the barn roof, just short of the high opposing doors designed to create a draught across the threshing floor. Two ragged patches of yellow tiles, all the farmer could get in wartime, were still there in the roof, the entry wound and the exit wound.

Sometimes the roof looked as if it had absorbed them into its flow, two muddy swirls. It rocked over a couple of rafters and stretched to its high ridge, reflecting the weather down into the yard. Cloud shadows streamed off the gable as you passed, head and shoulders in the race of an April sky. You felt a lightness as you walked through the barn, an elevation between the two high doors.

Sometimes the creases of those rafters filled me with solicitude.

81

I would stand in the yard, looking up. Follow the undulations with my eyes and traverse from them to the old tiles on the ridge, water-smooth and glossed with light. As if the ridge could brace the rafters. Or I could fix my attention in a brace.

The other roof of the barn, the short roof, came steeply down over bull pen and stallion box before rising to an arch high as a haycart, the arch of the wagon house. There was a dell in this roof too, a dell so long and deep it looked like a scree slope running down into a corrie. The tiles hung in a near vertical, half the depth of the roof, before they bellied up to the guttering. But I never feared for the dell as I did for the long roof, perhaps because visitors were always astonished by it and always predicting its collapse. I felt proud of the dell, proud and reassured. To me it was like the hollow in the thigh where the Angel of the Lord had touched Jacob after they had wrestled all night, a sign of strength.

House and barn stood at opposite diagonals of a long yard. In the days when George III, the Farmer King, came here to practise his ploughing, they must have been the two halves of a handsome farm. But the barn had sprouted a concrete lean-to: turkey shed, milking parlour, and cattle shed. An open tractor shed ran up the other side of the yard, creosoted wooden posts marking out the bays under a slope of corrugated iron. The blue breezeblocks of the farrowing house sealed off the top of the yard and either side of the gate to the fields was a pair of low brick pigsties. If you saw royal patronage in the size of the barn, at the top of the yard you saw struggle: all the makeshifts and approximations of a small mixed farm.

The only time the farmer had made any money was during the war when he had to plough up the fields, forcing winter wheat and then spring wheat and then winter again out of the sandy soil. He was left with the ghost of a farm and just one possible crop: the gravel under the fields. Every few years he would apply for planning permission to extract it and every few years he would be refused.

My father represented him in his last application and came to get the lie of the land. As he edged round the potholes in the long drive, tacking from one fence post to the next, he saw why the farmer was applying. When he came to the house in its semicircle of trees and the yard in the elbow of the barn, he understood why he had held on for so long.

My father had bought his first horses by then, a family of part-bred Arabs he was planning to break and train. He was keeping them on patches of waste ground while he looked for a house with a paddock. But this was a two-hundred-acre farm: a hundred acres between the road and the river he would have to buy outright and another hundred at the back, between the council estate and the railway line, he would have to take over on a lease from the GLC.

Too much, my mother explained, for us to take on. That was the first I was to hear of the farm and apparently the last. It was already in retrospect, already bathed in the serenity of regret, a tone that came naturally to my mother, as it did to most of her generation.

But not to my father, who could not bury his sense of loss. He went back to the farmer the day before he was to sell the place for a Field Studies Centre and was given just twenty-four hours to complete the purchase ahead of the local council.

One reason the farmer preferred to sell to us was that we had promised to keep on his dog Stevie, a Welsh collie. Farmers are not sentimental about animals but Stevie had saved his life and he was loath to have him put down. A bull had knocked the farmer down in the field and broken his leg. The bull was just lowering his head for the kill when Stevie clamped his teeth on to the nose and clung on until the farmer had crawled out of the field.

Stevie had a strong protective instinct, as we discovered when we began to farm for ourselves. If a sow was farrowing down, he would lie all day close to the wall of the farrowing house. If there was a newborn calf, he would mount guard over the pen. Even when a hen went broody and had to spend days in the broody hutch, you would find him there, his nose resting on his paws and his brown eyes watchful under the broad white dome of his forehead.

A rose bush climbed up over the back door and was trained along under the kitchen window. If there was nothing in need of his immediate protection, that was where Stevie would lie, under the wing of the rose bush. The long stems had intertwined as they were bent to the window, creating a patch of dry no rain seemed to penetrate. Sprawled against the wall, his head raised to look down the path and the smoothly dividing snow flurries of his chest glistening between the chestnut of his shoulders, Stevie had a sovereign ease on which it was unwise to presume. If he came up to you, he would accept a stroke of the head, but if you bent down to him, he would snap at you.

I never quite lost my fear of him, which was the other part of the sensation I felt as I walked up the path. I would look up at the dip over the door, always aware that there was a doorkeeper I had to pass, a tutelary spirit that belonged to the farm and not to us.

In the end bay of the tractor shed stood the hay cutter, the blade drawn up so that it showed as a flight of arrows. The outline used to catch me unawares, a moment's flare along the nerves. I felt just as I had at the age of eleven or twelve, catching sight of a blade in a junk shop window: a Gurkha kukri, a Japanese officer's sword, once even a bayonet from the Franco-Prussian War. Junk shops were awash then with the debris of war and it was surprising what pocket money could buy.

Thrill would turn to disappointment as I read the arrowheads again: steel tips to separate the grass and flanges to slide it back on to the blade. But they were still intriguing, sigils of a craft I had yet to learn. I had listened to my parents talking and knew how uncertain haymaking was, how you had to choose the right moment to cut and the right moment to bale. The grass lost its goodness if the weather broke and it had to be dried all over again. Bale it too green and it would smoulder in the barn and catch fire.

We were lucky that first year. We moved in at Easter and a window of fine weather came just before Whitsun. As soon as my father was home from court, he would start up the old tractor and lower the cutter blade into the grass, laying it in flat green swathes that we had to open up to the wind and sun, tossing them on pitchforks until our wrists ached. I would come home from school to see my mother silently labouring away, a lone figure in a twenty-five-acre field. We cut a hundred and fifty acres that year and would never have managed if Gibbs, the agricultural contractors, had not found us a second-hand tedder. It was extraordinary the difference that machine made, a difference we felt in our very bones. The tractor chirred along the rows in third gear and smoothly revolving tines flung the drying skeins up to glint against the light.

Though that was as nothing to the offhand grace of the contractor rowing up for the baler. He raced past our careful rows in top gear, lowering a long arm with four sets of spokes. They spun to a shimmer, an eye of light that opened and closed as he swerved away again, leaving a new row, neat and thick as a hedge.

We had started baling in the big field by the river, where the grass was so thick it still had some green in it, and looked greener still for the thin reedy spikes of bent grass pressed into the bales. They were packed so tight I could hardly get my fingers under the strings, dead weights I had to snatch with a quick intake of breath, as if I were back in boxing training, and throw on to the trailer with a gasp. I was beginning to doubt myself when I heard a little

85

cry from Mr Davy and the thump of another bale slotting into place. 'Phew, Rog,' he said, 'don't want too many of those.'

Mr Davy was a small, thin man, in a flat cap and the brown overalls of the Water Board, for whom he drove a caterpillar tractor during the week. On my way to school I used to cycle past the reservoirs, three great stone baths built into the bank of the river at Thames Ditton. One was always drained for cleaning and I would glimpse Mr Davy in miniature, sitting motionless at the head of a line of trucks while brown figures shovelled black streaks off the orange sand.

I don't know whether five days' confinement to the tractor seat left him with pent-up energy, or it was simply that he needed the money he earned gardening for us and was anxious to please, but Mr Davy worked as if he were driven by compressed air. Keep him standing and he would vibrate like a road drill.

Loading on the other side of the trailer were two lads from the council estate, Dennis and Doug, a year or two older than me. They had turned up in the yard one evening and explained that they used to help out the farmer in return for permission to shoot over the land. They became familiar figures after that. Doug would emerge out of the dusk with a .22 air rifle but Dennis would rather be feeding and watering the horses. A tall, dark, slim lad, he had a gentleness animals trusted.

He had found his vocation, though he had only the haziest idea of how to pursue it and nothing in his background to help him. Every day he caught the bus out to Weybridge where he was taking an agricultural course at the technical college, a milkman's son sitting with the farmers' sons. And every evening he would appear in our yard, a dependable presence, who had come to embody the memory of the place. We were forever asking him where the various tools were kept or how a particular job had been done.

My father stacked, tying each pair of bales in with a cross bale, and my mother drove the tractor, letting the clutch up slowly so as not to jerk him off his feet and topple our hard-won load. We fell into a rhythm, catching our breath from one bale as we paced to the next, and the layers rose until I was hoisting bales over my head and propping them against the top of the load, waiting face down in a shower of specks for the thump of the bale hook as my father drew them into place. By the time he had a locking row along the top and was ready to rope the load down, I was blinking hay out of my eyes, spitting it out of my mouth, shaking it out of the collar of my shirt.

Doug grinned and flexed his shoulders, as if he were just warming up, Mr Davy took off his cap and wiped away the sweat with a handkerchief, and Dennis knelt at the front of the trailer, tying the rope under one corner. He threw it diagonally over the load, a long, falling line that my father took a little wider, tucking the rope over the corner bale. Dennis ran round and swung on it with all his weight, scuttling into the side of the trailer to draw it tight to the fixing ring.

The tractor moved off, so slowly that the engine sounded absent-minded, each eddy of exhaust from the upright pipe coming as an afterthought. We leaned back as we walked, looking up at the cuttle-fish bones of cirrus in the sky. Though it was not the eyes that drew back our heads but our vertebrae. They stretched after stooping from bale to bale and we could be bipeds once more, delighting in our spines.

We had loaded the trailer so high that the tyres waddled into every little dip in the ground and the bales we had inset in such careful steps, layer by layer, wavered against the skyline. We watched anxiously as they came up to the field gateway. The tractor recollected itself, the exhaust chopped out two or three notes and the trailer rocked on to the hard standing at the top of the drive, the bales swaying under their ropes past the farmer's last haystack.

A loft ran the full length of the barn, the timber floor laid above the crossbeams so that you seemed to step from the long ladder into a building in the act of ascension, a lattice of light through the tiles. For a moment you had the sensation of movement, a riffling on the skin of your face as the outside air entered with the light. You were afloat, as if, in stepping from the ladder, you had stepped off from earth's shore. Sky you had always known as distance was all around you as depth, as the element the barn was moving through, the pressure of its tides against the ribs of the roof. You looked up at the cross-struts, at the hundreds of laths of wood on which the tiles rested, each so thin that the eye ran along it protectively, each with an individual break in the grain where it had sheared off against the saw, and you were caught up into the roof's first raising, into the voyage of its four hundred years.

There were lofts under the short roof too, either side of the wagon house. You could back the last load of the day in under there and leave it for the morning. But the first loads we drove round to the far side of the barn, angling the trailer back into the high door, where the ladder ran up into the loft space. My father stood on the top of the load, throwing the bales up at forty-five degrees so that they came tumbling across the frame of the loft. I stood just back from the square of space, catching the bales as they landed and swinging them round to Doug, who sent them skidding across the floor for Dennis to stack.

There was no let-up, no pace from bale to bale in which to catch your breath. My father had Mr Davy on the trailer, feeding the bales to him. He turned and threw, turned and threw, and I had to catch and swing, catch and swing, clearing each bale before the next bounced back off it. My breath became a wall I was leaning against, taking deeper and deeper gasps. I could hardly stand, I was about to slide down it. Then the brain reconfigured and adrenalin went to the lungs. I became a gasp with a guidance system.

We worked all evening, bringing the last load home in the gradual midsummer dark. Backed it under the wagon house and turned across the yard towards the light from the kitchen. No spine-stretching now, no leaning back to look up at the night sky. We leaned forward, almost falling from step to step, as if we had been stunned but were still walking on.

Tea. Mugs of hot tea. Plates of eggs and bacon and sausages. Rounds of bread to mop up the last smears of HP Sauce. And then a wordless well-being, a moment when we just sat round the long table, listening to the brimming of the teapot as it was refilled and the sudden fierce intake of breath, like an inward spit, as Mr Davy drew on his roll-up.

We had a milking parlour, the floor properly sloped so that it could be hosed down and swept clean. There was even a makeshift dairy, a curious little oblong that had been built to house a pump at a moment of confident expansion, when the barn itself was turned into one long milking parlour. It stood in the yard, just past the entrance to the barn, and looked like the wheelhouse off a tug or a trawler. You slid back the green door, on which the paint was cracking, and there was just room to step between the pump and the tiled shelf that ran round to a sink.

These simple arrangements were enough to secure us a licence to sell cream from unpasteurised milk, which was possible then. We bought a Guernsey cow, bigger than a Jersey and surprisingly handsome, the gold of her coat deepening to ginger and spreading in patches over the white. I used to walk her up from the river and had my first lesson in the otherness of cows. She would wander up at her own pace. The one and only time I tapped her with the stick, she gave a swing of the head, looking at me from under a bony ridge that ended in two stumps of horn.

The cream separator was a nest of funnels. Seven funnels,

descending in size from one you could pour petrol through to one you might use for icing a cake. Twice a day you had to take them all apart and wash them, a conical washing-up that looked as if it had been painted by Léger, and twice a day you had to fit them all back together again. Each had a thin slit to let the skimmed milk pass and the separation was achieved by centrifugal force. You poured the milk into a big bowl at the top and slowly turned a handle in the round, heavy base, which had two opposing spouts, a bucket under one and a jar under the other.

For the first few turns nothing seemed to happen. Then the handle juddered and a buzzing came from the base, a buzzing that steadied and deepened to the tread of a turbine. Skimmed milk began to splash into the bucket. If you could keep patience, a thin beading of cream would begin to run into the jar.

If you were drawn into the sound of the turbine, as I was the first time, and turned the handle faster to hear it whirr, the cream would run out too thin. Keep patience, look out of the dairy window at the life of the yard and turn the handle as if you were turning it in your sleep, and the cream would come out so thick the spoon would stand up in the jar.

Though the cream was as nothing to the butter my mother made from it when we had a surplus. Cream separated invisibly as it was whirled through the funnels but you could watch butter happen. The paddles of the hand churn wound through cream until suddenly there were yellow clods on them and they were slapping through buttermilk. My mother emptied the clods on to a wooden board, batting them back and forth with the butter pats until they had shed their last drops of milk. Gradually they formed into a solid block of colour, a deep, glistening yellow that I was astonished to recognise. It was the yellow of a buttercup.

We raised pigs on the skimmed milk. When our first Large White sow came to farrow down, I was sent to join Stevie in his watch at the pen. Sows have large litters and they can lie on them or start to eat them as they clean them up. I sat all evening until there was a double row of snouts fastened to the double row of teats and the runt of the litter scrambling for a place.

It was Charlie Chambers who found us the sow and bought the piglets to sell on as weaners. Charlie was a dealer. He had a little land but kept no stock of his own. What he had was the knowledge and the knowledge had bought him a white Jaguar and a smart brown lorry. He knew the Surrey hinterland, all the small-holdings that persisted down back lanes, all the pockets of farmland, like ours, that had been cut off by the suburbs and needed to get their stock to Chertsey market. Charlie would always offer you slightly less than you expected, twenty-eight shillings and sixpence, say, when you had been hoping for thirty shillings a head. But if that came to an odd amount, as it often did, he never bothered with the odd ten shillings, he would toss you for the difference. You were left feeling that luck had been with you after all, or that it might have been.

Ours was not the only patch of hinterland in Hersham. There was Mr Maskell, who kept pigs in a backyard off the High Street. We used to take our sow to his boar, towing her behind the Land Rover in an old wooden trailer that was really no more than a pig crate on wheels. By the time we reached the High Street, the sow would have her nose under the tarpaulin of the roof and emerge head and shoulders to startle the shoppers. Once she looked ready to jump and I had to climb out on to the tow bar to push her back down. Pig and boy, we wrestled the length of the High Street like a float from a village carnival or an interlude in a Mystery Play.

It was chancing on the hinterland that had reawoken my father's boyhood dream of breaking and training his own horses. That ambition had lain dormant until my sister reached the age of twelve and demanded riding lessons. No chance of those in Surbiton. An advert in the *Surrey Comet* took us out to the West Ewell Riding Stables, which sounded ordinary enough until we turned off the bypass and found ourselves in Shep's yard.

The stables were on the right, a block of half a dozen stalls, airy and high-roofed, built for the coach horses from the old manor house. On the left was a hut, the size of a garden shed, and there sat Shep. He must have been in his fifties then, his black hair swept over a bald patch. The balding gave a certain roundness but something in the face stopped you from seeing it as round: a firmness, I think, in the line of the mouth, and broken blood vessels in the cheeks, which were strangely weatherbeaten for the suburbs. Just as something in the way he dressed, the tie with a horseshoe tiepin, the tweed jacket with a watchchain on the waistcoat, meant that you were slow to notice the flap of his riding breeches, neatly folded back over the stump of his right leg. The left leg stretched to a gleaming brown riding boot.

Shep had lost his leg as a boy, in an accident when he was out shooting with his brother. We knew no more than that: only that his brother had gone to live abroad and Shep had stayed in Devon and become a shepherd, faster across the ground on a crutch and one leg than most people on two legs. When he came to a fence, he would just swing his crutch over it and vault over. He had moved up to Surrey during the war when every scrap of ground had to produce food and they ran sheep on Wimbledon Common.

His speech was still pure Devonshire, his turns of phrase pungent and unexpected, which added to the impression that we had turned off the bypass into an independent kingdom. Usually he would take his crutch from where it leaned against the wall of the hut, pull himself out of his chair and supervise the departure of the hourly ride, gripping the crutch under his right shoulder as he moved between the horses so that he had both hands free to tighten a girth or adjust the length of a stirrup. Sometimes he led a ride himself, long practice in the way he moved alongside the horse, put his foot into the stirrup and pushed on the crutch, handing it away as he rose into the saddle. But he had bookings to take and the yard to watch over, and mostly he sat straight-backed in his chair, the door of the hut open in all weathers.

Shep's business depended on a back road on the other side of the bypass. In the 1950s there were still gaps in the traffic and his experienced riders would file round the roundabout and take the back road up on to the downs. Beginners like us would be taken up on to the verge along a side road and cross over into Nonsuch Park, where we would file past the remains of the palace, lines of foundations that were no more remarkable than the roofs of old air-raid shelters further along.

But first there was the embarrassment of being taken down West Ewell High Street on the leading rein, our own reins knotted into a loop so that we could hold on to the front of the saddle. Almost as soon as we turned out of the yard, the road began to slope downhill. There was barely time to feel the seam of my jeans cut into my knee before the horse's hooves seemed to slip away, carrying my centre of gravity with them. Old ladies looked up from their shopping as we clattered past but I was too dismayed to care. I was seated on an eddy that might swirl me away at any moment.

Gradually I learned to sit, to lean back as the horse walked downhill and to rise to the trot once we had turned past the pub on the corner. I acquired a pair of second-hand jodhpurs that cushioned the knee and a hacking jacket with a cut in the flap at the back. I began to imagine the glances of quiet admiration as my bottom rose in the line of rising bottoms. I might have thought myself a rider had my father not gone to the horse sales at the Elephant and

Castle, another curious survival, right in the heart of London, and bought Pinocchio, a fine-boned Irish hunter.

There was one pace I had yet to experience, the smooth flow of the gallop that lay beyond the steady buck of the canter. A hunter should be able to gallop, I thought, and took Pinocchio through the park to the edge of the playing fields. By now I was allowed out on my own. I had graduated to breeches and boots so that I even looked the part.

I kicked him into a canter, which just shows how much I knew, and kicked again. The air became a wind. The ground flowed under us. And so did the startled faces of the people along the path. The blackberry pickers shrinking into the bushes. The man running to haul his dog out of the way. I pulled on the reins and Pinky pulled back. It wasn't a gallop I'd sent him into, it was a state of alarm.

I was becoming alarmed myself. We were coming to the end of the field. Ahead of us was the gap in the bushes, the twist in the path that led down on to the bypass. I reined in again, as hard as I could, and the tension in my fingers was more than physical: I was holding on to the sense of things as I knew them, the common sense that said Pinky had to stop before we ran into the traffic.

But it wasn't common sense I was riding, it was a frightened animal, separated from the rest of the herd, an animal whose response to fear is flight. I did rein him back, but only to a slow canter. The harder I pulled, the more the fear in him seemed to compress. It bunched against my fingers like a muscle, a dogged panic.

I saw the shine of the path, the darkness of an overhanging branch, and ducked down on to Pinky's neck. Then the tree at the bottom of the dip, the jut of its roots and Pinky's hooves going down into a fingernail's gleam of flat.

We sprang out on to the verge of the bypass and a man on his afternoon walk stepped sharply back, a horn-rimmed stare of concern. Over his head I could see the first lamp post. That had been my last hope, to steer Pinky inside it, keeping him to the narrow grass of the verge.

As it was, we had to go wide, over the kerb on to the carriageway, and I heard the sound I knew I should never have heard, the sound of a horse cantering on concrete, the steady beat of laming shocks to the bone.

Cars slowed as they came up behind us. No one overtook. Ahead of us, like film projected from another afternoon, afternoon as it should have been, a bus held to its steady pace along the kerb. Crouched almost like a jockey now, hands halfway up Pinky's neck and fingers numbing as I tried to twist back another half inch of rein, I felt a separation, a gap opening in the hushing of the tyres, in the engines easing back. I was exposed to the unforeseen as the watching drivers were not.

The bus was signalling. There was a stop just before the round-about and it pulled in, the broad green of its metal blocking most of the inside lane. Neck drawn back like a warhorse, charging inside his short straps of rein, Pinky shouldered past the rear window, the rows of seats, the driver's face in the wing mirror. I looked up, hoping for a sympathetic glance, but the eyes that met mine were oddly detached.

We were thirty yards from the roundabout and in the middle of the road. I felt a helpless grief for Pinky, for the narrow chest and the fine legs in their chestnut skin. With the deep fear of someone who had never so much as broken a bone, I imagined myself in hospital, having to miss months of school. But luck was with us, luck and the mid-afternoon lull in the traffic. One slip as Pinky shied from a braking car and we were cantering down the road to Shep's, the hooves resuming their echo in my head, *This is Wrong! This is Wrong! This is Wrong!*

＊　＊　＊

Pinky was kept at Shep's on half-livery, which meant that Shep could use him for lessons to offset the cost of his care. My father had bought him on impulse and I don't think he ever quite knew why. It was a prompting he had yet to recognise, the surfacing of a dream he could only half recall.

A few weeks later, reading the *King's Lynn News & Advertiser*, the local paper my grandmother used to roll into a tight tube and post us each week, he came on a small ad, *Horses for Sale: Arab-Hackney cross*, and the dream came into sharp focus. Mr Trenowath's mare had been an Arab-Hackney cross: Beauty, the mare my father used to ride as a boy when he was shacking the pigs, herding them out to graze on the stubble or clean up the tops from the sugar beet; Beauty, the mare they put in the tumbril and drove in the dogcart. A good cross, my father had thought: the spark of the Arab with the endurance of the Hackney.

On his next free day he drove to Norfolk and took Shep with him. On a later visit my father took me but I wish I had been there that first time, listening at his elbow, because Shep and the old man were two of a kind. In the lean years after the war, before the hill-farming subsidies came in, the old man and his wife had set out from Wales in a horse and cart. They had wandered the width of the country until they came on the remains of an old army camp at Beeston, just outside Swaffham, and set up a smallholding, raising ducks and hens. They had to find a use for the mare that had drawn them from Wales and decided to breed from her. Horses are expensive to keep and all too often a snobbery attaches to them. But there can be a freemasonry, too, among horse owners, and this was an example. The old man put his humble mare to Jalis, an Arab stallion belonging to Miss Coulson, a redoubtable lady who had left a farm in South Africa to become the doyenne of the local Pony Club.

My father had settled for what he thought was a fair price. 'No,' said Shep, 'that's too much' and turned back to the Nissen hut to haggle the old man down. The bargain struck, the two of them were free to talk the afternoon away. The old man sat in his blue overalls, plucking a chicken between his knees. Shep leaned on his crutch, small feathers settling in a fine haze on his tweed jacket and blurring the gleam of his boot. My father kept glancing at his watch, thinking of the rush-hour traffic building up on the North Circular, but the others were far away, back on the byroads of chance that had led a Devon shepherd to run his flock on Wimbledon Common and a Welshman to walk over to Norfolk.

In all, the Hackney mare was to have five foals by Jalis and we were to buy all five. On that first trip my father bought the eldest, a three-year-old, and the third foal, a yearling. The three-year old, a strong bay filly, reminded him of Beauty and that's what he called her, Beeston Beauty.

These were unbroken horses that had always lived in the open. My father knew that he could not hand over their care to Shep, as he had with Pinky. We had to take care of them ourselves. That was the heart of the dream, the exchange of trust he remembered from his boyhood. Breaking the horses did not begin with strapping a saddle on their backs. It began with a look of recognition, with them coming over to feed from your hand and allowing you to brush the mud from their coats.

We kept them on a patch of rough grass behind a chain-link fence, an empty slope among trim suburban houses. This was where, when the first avenues were laid out beyond the bypass, the planners had pencilled in a church. Then the war came. Then the Green Belt tightened and there were no more avenues. The Methodists were still trying to raise the money to build on it.

So much began with our renting of that paddock that remembering how I was at the outset is like glimpsing someone else, some town cousin who was only too anxious to lend a hand but comically inept. My father gave me what he called 'a hook' and asked me to cut down the nettles. I looked at the half-circle of blade and realised that I was holding a sickle. All I could think was, *This is half of the hammer and sickle*. It seemed almost seditious to have it in my hand.

By mid-morning I was wishing it was a scythe. I crouched in front of thick ranks of nettles, swiping them at the base of the stems, and the leaves fell stinging across my hand. 'Hold them back with a stick!' my father said but the odd one still caught me and my wrist burned for days.

By late afternoon we had cleared the ground and walked it foot by foot, looking for nails, broken glass, twists of wire, anything that could catch in a hoof. The next day I went with my father to collect the horses, arriving in the car ahead of the horsebox so that we could help load them up. The old man had accustomed Beauty to the head collar but it took a lunge line drawn tight round her hindquarters to drive her up the ramp.

The family started to spend every Saturday out at the paddock, calling in at Shep's at the end of the afternoon. I had been so involved in the preparations that my father must have hoped I would join them. Some part of me must have wanted to because, every Saturday when the family came home, I would ask about the day's work with the horses. But these were the years of my religious fervour, years when I was my own prisoner. Sunday was the Lord's Day and my observance of it was strict. Which meant that Saturdays had to be given over to homework.

I was at the grammar school by then, a regime of study I had espoused as if it were a priesthood in itself. My father's old brief-case, presented to me when I passed the eleven-plus, was becoming a beast of burden, the ripples of the pigskin seamed with dirt and the stitches strained to bursting. My mother had bought it for my father when he passed his Bar exams and it grieved her to see it now. It was a good briefcase, she used to tell me, I should look after it. But what was I to do? By the time I strapped it on to the carrier of my bike on a Friday afternoon, it was a solid block of books, buckled on the last hole of its straps.

'You must be like young monks,' our old English master used to say, 'wholly given over to the life of the mind' and there was a satisfaction in the weight of the bag, a sense that Saturday was already marked out: so long for English, so long for Greek, so long for Latin, so long for Ancient History. Sunday I kept just as if I were a monk, constant in the back pew from Early Communion to Evensong.

In the face of this, there was little my father could do. Every so often he would mumble some hopeless phrase: 'There's an old saying, you know, everything in moderation.' But he was in the grip of his own passion and what he gave me was a training in immoderation. He bought two more horses, the two-year-old from Beeston and a pony for my sister, and rented another field from an old horseman out beyond the bypass.

Every Saturday for the next two years the family went off and left me to myself in the big house in Surbiton. The day was not entirely monastic. If I finished the morning's work in good time, I could catch the last of the *Hit Parade* on the radio while I made myself cheese on toast. If the afternoon went well, I could fry myself some sausages and settle down to watch *6.5 Special*, the BBC's first showing of rock'n'roll, with Pete Murray and Jo Douglas looking like two youth club leaders in their cashmere sweaters. But I used to look forward to the work itself, its sequence of demand and reward: the intentness of ten in the morning, the sharpness of hunger as I worked towards lunch, the easing at four as I moved towards the last of the series of completions. Those long Saturdays gave me a taste for solitude, for the passage of hours I had come to know pitch by pitch, as if they were a practice climb.

\* \* \*

At the farm my bedroom was just over the back door and I worked with one ear on the comings and goings below. That was not easy as the place awoke from the long spell of disuse. Every week there would be the rhythmic scrape of shovels as cement was mixed on a board or the hammering of nails as old stalls were made ready for new stock. My imagination would follow the sounds until I was poised between beginnings, between the first stride of a long Latin sentence, a Ciceronian period I was constructing from a speech of Edmund Burke, and the burgeoning hubbub below me, all the changes I was going to find when, the last subclause in place, the final phrases in balance, I was free to close the exercise book and walk downstairs. I was forever appearing in the yard at the end of a job, offering to help.

Dennis came to work for us when he left college and the runt from the first litter of pigs used to follow him around the yard like a dog. We bought a second sow and the two sows would lean over the front wall of the pigsties with their arms crossed like two old gossips chatting over the fence. One reason so many families came up the drive to buy eggs and cream was that walking around the yard was like turning the pages of a child's first reading book. C was for the calf suckling from a bucket and P for the piglets rushing to the trough.

Feeding and watering the pigs on a Saturday was my job. One afternoon I closed the sty door and turned to see two strangers crossing the yard. One was an English squire, tall and spare with a military moustache. The other looked like the attaché of some foreign power. Small and dark, he wore breeches and boots, a battle-dress jacket with no insignia and a plain fawn cap.

The squire had the slow stroll characteristic of his caste, an unassertive ease that bespoke a kind of ownership. Which proved to be the case: he was to become my father's business partner, though not for long.

The small man saw me watching them. He looked down, but with a glance that left a dark line on the air. He was the Hereditary Riding Master to the Kings of Portugal and not used to lowering his eyes.

That afternoon was the only time I saw Antonio at a disadvantage. Once the partnership had been agreed and we started to build a riding school under his direction, he became the focus of the yard, so sharply drawn that everyone else seemed to be pencilled in around him. Antonio was not flamboyant: he had a contained quality, the physical concentration of a fencer or a dancer, and that gave him definition, the look of being inked-in when everyone around him was sketchy.

He always appeared in the fawn cap and battledress jacket, a uniform he had adopted in Portugal, where he had been a civilian instructor in the cavalry. Short and tightly fitted round the waist, the battledress jacket was perfect for riding and he had a new one made in brown serge, the closest the local tailor could get to khaki. But there was more to it, I suspect, than convenience.

Once in his office, a whitewashed room in the end of the barn that faced on to the lane, Antonio would take off the cap, unbutton the jacket and lean back in his chair to smoke a cigarette, his gestures becoming more expansive as he relaxed. He was in his late thirties, the first creases marked in a forehead that was rounding as the black hair receded. Round as it might, the face was dark with more than five o'clock shadow. You could hear the edge in his voice before he spoke.

On the wall hung a large framed photo of Antonio taking a horse over a jump. He was in army uniform, an officer's cap and a long jacket with a Sam Browne belt, and there was a crowd in the background. The horse was in mid-flight, front legs drawn up like an equestrian statue, and Antonio was poised over the shoulder, hands, knees and heels all on a perfect diagonal. Next to the photo

101

hung a certificate. It was in Portuguese and difficult to read through the flourishes of calligraphy but it had the full roll-call of Antonio's Christian names, his surname, Menendes, and one final phrase that looked like a title.

The title had gone, together with the royal household where he had his place. The cavalry must have offered him a place in another hierarchy. But Antonio was a cultivated man who had grown bored with the officers' mess. He was left with only the sense of himself, the inheritance he carried forward into a world where there was no way of marking it. Which is why he would never leave the office without buttoning up his battledress and putting on his cap. He was reassuming his dignity as Riding Master.

My father rode with a long stirrup, leaning back in the saddle like a tipsy farmer in a hunting print. Antonio taught the Continental or forward seat, which was just becoming accepted then. You measured the stirrup under your arm, fingers folded back as if you were about to make a fist, first joint against the top of the leather strap and the metal bar stretched into your armpit. That length set you upright over the horse's centre of gravity, just behind the shoulders.

But a stirrup was a concession. Antonio had us riding without reins or stirrups, going over jumps with our hands on our heads, or swinging ourselves out of the saddle like Cossacks, touching our feet to the ground on one stride of the canter and springing back into the saddle with the next. He began without stirrups, sitting us on a horse as if we had never ridden before and walking us round him on the lunge line. With an impersonal rigour, as if we were life models who had slackened in the pose, he turned our knees in and tugged our heels down until we were deep in the saddle, thighs clothes-pegged to the horse's back. We spent several weeks on the lunge line, learning to absorb the horse's movements until sitting to the trot felt as natural as rising to it. Sitting to the canter was the purest ease, like leaning back on a swing and letting it take you.

They were widening the road at the bottom of the drive, turning it into a dual carriageway. My father did a deal with the ganger, an old Scotsman who had built everything from ships to bridges, and in the course of a single weekend he and four of his muckers erected a large, steel-framed building on an old rick yard the far side of the barn, just before the bend in the lane. We put down three feet of sand, salt and sawdust, lined it with protective boards and leather padding, and Antonio had his covered school, the riding master's equivalent of the ballet studio. There was even a huge mirror on one wall so that riders could check their position as they rode round.

You felt spotlit the moment you entered, the horse's hooves so quiet on the soft floor you could hear the creak of the saddle underneath you, the shift of the stirrup straps. You gave a long rein, let the horse settle to the oval of the track as the others filed in behind you. I used to hate the beginning of lessons, everyone so self-conscious and everyone trying to give their horse the most casual saunter.

Once the high wooden doors were dragged shut and Antonio pronounced his distinctive *Ta-rrrot!* you were caught up in the movement, the changing paces, the increasing tempo as Antonio built from exercise to exercise, dispensing with the stirrups, which you crossed over the front of the saddle, and then with the reins, which you knotted into a loop. The horses started to move as one flowing line, taking their stride from the lead horse. You brought your leg over the back of the saddle and leaned on the front, hands gripping the saddle-bow and legs together. Secure in the rhythm of the canter, you swung your feet forward as the horse's shoulders dipped into the next stride, touched ground, and let the surge of the stride pull you back into the saddle.

\*　　\*　　\*

'Antonio doesn't talk to the horses,' my father would complain. He had always worked from reassurance, gentling a horse with his voice as he approached. Antonio believed in command. When he walked down the line of loose boxes, the horses would lift their heads from the half-doors and shrink back in fear.

But my father knew mastery when he saw it, even though it was born of a different tradition. The cobbler's son and the aristocrat got on surprisingly well. The squire departed, declaring that he could not work with my father, but Antonio stayed and my father found other backers. He laid the concrete for two rows of loose boxes between the barn and the covered school, then added a third row. Ponies were stalled in the barn and others loosed in the fields. The old pump house was knocked down and more loose boxes built under the eaves of the barn.

As the yard filled, so did the house. There was a third floor of large attic rooms, reached by a narrow, twisting, wooden staircase. In the days when farm labourers worked for bed and board, receiving their wages in a lump sum at the end of the year, these must have held milkmaids and wagoners, packed in under the eaves. Now they filled with grooms and trainee riding instructors, 'working pupils' who paid a premium to be prepared for the British Horse Society exams. Mostly they were girls who had just left school but there always seemed to be one man, some thoughtful young man in his late twenties or early thirties who had started out as a solicitor or a chartered accountant, only to despair of the life he saw stretching before him.

I might almost have been one of them, split as I was at seventeen. At my grammar school we took our A-levels early so that we could spend an extra year preparing for the Oxford and Cambridge scholarship exams. It was the ideal of a university, that first year in the Upper Sixth. Your chosen subject lay before you like a Promised Land, the great names you could enter like ancient walled

104

towns and others you would chance on as unfrequented paths, every turn taking you deeper in, each new rise yielding the glimpse of another horizon.

I had chosen Classics, which by then was becoming rather esoteric. I would descend to the basement of second-hand bookshops and crouch on one knee in front of the end shelves. Once I found an edition of all the surviving comedies of Aristophanes in two volumes, the maroon cloth of the binding faded to a russet brown but the title embossed in Greek, delicate curves and cross strokes still clear in their gilt. The notes were in Latin and I felt that I was listening in to a conversation that was centuries old, to a time when Latin was the lingua franca of Europe.

I had a similar sensation when I attended Compline, the old monastic service for the end of the day, which was said on weekday evenings at the church in Esher. There might only be three of us, the curate, myself and an old lady whose name I did not know, but, as we knelt in the half-light of the side chapel, and said, *Protect us from all perils and dangers of this night*, I would imagine other voices murmuring in Paris, in Athens, in Prague, other altar lamps and candles forming a chain of light across the hemisphere as it moved into darkness.

At moments like that my boyish determination to enter the Church felt like a true vocation and my path lay clear before me. I would read Classics at Oxford and go on to read Theology. It was not until my first morning in the Upper Sixth that I realised I had another allegiance. I was standing in the dinner queue, looking at my new timetable. Free periods stretched either side of Latin and Greek with George Worth, the Head of Classics. Most of my timetable was free. I should have felt elated: I was out of bondage, I had crossed over into the Promised Land. Instead, I felt only desolation. There was no English on the timetable. I was no longer doing English.

The preachers at the Hall, the Christian holiday centre I booked myself into, used to speak of the gift of the Holy Spirit. This was an extra blessing, a state of grace that descended on you and kept you from sin. Sometimes it sounded almost like a form of divine possession, as if Christ simply took you over. I could see no point in that. Then we would all be the same whereas we were all supposed to be different. I preferred to imagine a kind of companionship, a voice inside you. I had prayed and prayed for this blessing, only to find that I was still alone with my striving self.

What I realised as I stood in the dinner queue was that I had companions after all, companions I was loath to lose. The first was Keats, whom I had been surprised into liking when we had to study him for O-level. I was as innocent as the Nightingale of 'the weariness, the fever and the fret' but the music of that ode had enabled me to imagine what it might be to 'fade far away, dissolve and quite forget', to understand, even from my rapid tempo at thirteen, how he had come to be 'half in love with easeful Death'.

I might not have heard the music so clearly if we had not had to learn the poem off by heart. I can still remember how strange it felt, standing in the kitchen and going over the lines so that my mother could test me, to make myself form the words and say them out loud:

> My heart aches, and a drowsy numbness pains
> My sense, as though of hemlock I had drunk,
> Or emptied some dull opiate to the drains
> One minute past, and Lethe-wards had sunk:

This was different from the language of prayer, which I had learned to manipulate expertly, like a boy playing with a set of Jacobean dominoes. The words were just as charged but they were more intimate, more particular, more down-to-earth. *My heart*, that unimaginable cavity, passage of so much ghostly traffic in my prayers, was made so real by the addition of the simple word *aches* that I could never start the poem without a sympathetic shiver, the fear that I might feel a pang in the chest.

Once past that perilous phrase, I found myself making a kind of mouth music. I came to relish the hum of *a drowsy numbness* and the murmur of the 'm's as they built through *hemlock* and *emptied*, and I was fascinated by the dark 'a' of *opiate*, which sounded more narcotic than opium. A quick breath at the pause on *One minute past* and I would let myself sink into the long 'e's of *Lethe*, into their endless desolation, that one word more haunting in its place in the line than all the descriptions of the underworld I was to read in Homer or Virgil or Dante.

Then came a surprise, a change of pulse. The voice speeded up, taking on an eagerness that felt very natural to me at thirteen:

> 'Tis not through envy of thy happy lot,
>   But being too happy in thine happiness,
>     That thou, light-winged Dryad of the trees,
>       In some melodious plot
>   Of beechen green, and shadows numberless,
>     Singest of summer in full-throated ease.

That was the moment when I felt most confidence in my delivery. My voice would rise at *being too happy in thine happiness* and give the line a boyish impetus. I had never felt that before, that moment of identification. All the poems we had read seemed to be composed of drumbeats, hoofbeats and drumbeats. What I could hear in Keats was the onrush of feelings I was just becoming aware of in myself. He became like an elder brother: from him I gleaned what I could of sensations I was curious about, the intent lover on the Grecian Urn,

> never, never canst thou kiss,
>   Though winning near the goal –

possessed by forces I could only imagine.

The second was Hopkins, whom I had studied for A-level. I understood some, at least, of the forces at work in him. My Evangelical rigour had softened a little since I had moved to the church at Esher and come across the devotional tradition. But my religious affinity was almost incidental. What astonished me was the physical power of the language. In common, I imagine, with schoolboys all over the country, I used to recite those lines from 'The Windhover',

> then off, off forth on swing,
>   As a skate's heel sweeps smooth on a bow-bend

in a little half-dance of delight, arms braced as if I were heading into a turn on the ice.

We had a new English teacher, Jack Dalglish, who was himself a poet. In an exasperated postscript to a letter to Robert Bridges, Hopkins points out that to do his work 'any kind of justice you must not slovenly read it with the eyes but with your ears, as if the paper were declaiming it at you.' Jack was the voice of the paper, reading the intricate stanzas of 'The Wreck of the Deutschland' so clearly that we heard every word fall into place. The *hurl and gliding* of 'The Windhover' lived in my head: but so did one of the quiet passages from 'The Deutschland', the two balancing images of the hourglass and the well.

Those were, I knew, Metaphysical conceits. My friends in the English scholarship set were going on to study the Metaphysical Poets. I had only to change from Classics and I could join them.

But that *only* was deep. That *only* was a chasm. Not because it meant questioning my vocation. Or sensing that I might have another. But because I was the only scholarship candidate George had. I was the only one in the set.

There had only been one the year before. He would emerge from the gloom of George's cubbyhole with a look of vivid abstraction, the light of the sky swimming over his round spectacles. I was already familiar with the occasions when George broke off from whatever we were reading, leaned back in his chair, straightened the folds of his black gown over his knee and allowed a thought to develop. There would be more of those, I thought, more of those.

Classics at Oxford culminated in Greats, the rigorous course in Philosophy and Ancient History that had led generations of colonial administrators to believe they were running the second Roman Empire. George held himself as if he still represented that tradition, a one-man Encaenia as he walked through the school grounds with the long black gown flowing behind him. As first-formers playing tig we had hushed as he passed by. Now that his dignity, in some sense, depended on me, I felt oddly protective of him.

I stood silent as the others made plans. Someone had already been to the library and found Eliot's essay on the Metaphysicals. And then it dawned on me: free periods were free. There was nothing to stop me sitting in with the English set when I wasn't closeted with George.

As if two masters were not enough, I took on a third. I arranged to spend my games afternoon having a lesson with Antonio. Permission was given because I had chosen horse riding as my sport for the Duke of Edinburgh's Award. The Award did not matter to me that much. Nor did the riding, not in itself. What mattered was that hour spent under Antonio's exacting eye. It was like having a weekly piano lesson with Sviatoslav Richter.

Perhaps what I really needed was a weekly lesson with Fats Waller. Some break from my own earnestness. One Saturday I closed my books to find that the reading did not stop. A weariness behind my eyes kept trying to focus on the next phrase. I sat blurred through dinner at the long kitchen table and joined the sprawl in front of the television. But, when I went to bed, the reader in the brain was still awake. Queasily, like someone enduring a long ferry crossing.

The crossing took four days. I found myself held at sea. I have a memory of standing on the kerb on the Monday morning, braced against a gale at my back. But the gale is inside me. I am standing there in my prefect's crimson half-gown, one of a squad directing traffic as the school walks over to the chapel for Morning Assembly. A master comes to stand alongside me, a young master I do not really know, and I look into his eyes as if we were comrades, each of us risen from the night's wrack to present a calm surface, a figure in a blazer with a Windsor knot in his tie. We step off the kerb together as if swept forward in a great pulse, a unison to which I have only just awoken.

But there is also a memory of myself seated behind the desk in the Prefects' Room. A small boy stands in front of me, waiting to be punished for playing on the air-raid shelters. I have warned him once before but that does not excuse the melodrama of my opening remarks, at which my fellow prefects turn quickly away, like actors about to corpse. There is an awkward silence in which the boy stands there puzzled and I sit shivering in my chair like an SS officer on the brink of an atrocity. I give him three with the slipper. As he leaves, one of the older prefects stops him at the door to reassure him and to explain that I am ill.

My concentration had gone. In my free periods I would lie on the sofa in the Prefects' Room. If anyone asked, I would say that I was resting my brain. 'Why come to school?' someone said. 'Why not stay at home?' But all through the small hours I had longed for the bustle of school. Just six more hours, I would tell myself, and I shall be in the corridor, the bell for Assembly will follow hard on the bell for Registration and time will pass without my noticing.

The next night I took two bottles of brown ale from the fridge, slipped out of the back door, and climbed a ladder to the loft over the coal shed where I knew that Bill would be stretched on a mattress in his long coat, contemplating the ragged fire of his roll-up as it died between his fingers. Bill hadn't slept since the war. Or not as most of us know sleep. Nights of watching were engraved either side of his nose, in lines cut so deep the long face had folded over them. There was still a little curl, a little black in the greying hair brushed back and receding over the temples; enough for you to glimpse the man he must have been, with that Latin look the Welsh can have. But the head was bowed, a living pietà: you were drawn back to the lines slashed down the face, to the brimming dark of the eyes in their wells of skin.

Bill had been foreman in an aircraft factory, building a plane for the Fleet Air Arm. The flaps on the tail were lifting as the plane came in to land and met the sudden updraught from the carrier. Five pilots had been killed in training. Asked to solve the problem, Bill devised a counteraction, a second control wire, if I remember rightly, that took an hour and a half to fit. But the men were on piecework, being paid by the completed plane. They refused to put in the extra time.

Bill reasoned with them. He pleaded with them. And then he spoke his mind, with such force that the men declared they would strike if he were not sacked on the spot. Strikes were illegal in wartime and the management took fright. Bill walked away without deigning to collect his cards.

Forced into the black market, he had lived a fugitive life ever since. My father came across him when he went to buy timber from the demolition of Walton Studios, part of the declining British film industry. Bill was selling off the doors and windows while he waited for a buyer for the sound stage, on which he had gambled all his capital. No buyer appeared and Bill came to work for us, dossing

111

down in the loft while his wages went to preserve the rare woods and perfect dovetails he had been obliged to put into storage.

Bill was more than a fine carpenter. He was inspired, someone who in another age would have had the secret of a cathedral roof revealed to him by an angel in a dream. He took the dell out of the barn roof, crouching in the loft over the stallion box and rebuilding it from underneath. He even replaced one of the main beams in the long roof, jacking up the roof and raising the new beam into position on a rope made of binder twine strung over a pulley. I would like to think that he found solace in renewing the work of the Elizabethan carpenters but I am not sure that the possibility of any such feeling had not been worn out of him. Once we did a stretch of fencing together, banging in the posts with a drive-all, a weighted iron tube that fitted over them and served as a manual piledriver. We had to lift it by the handles and thump it down, lift and thump, lift and thump. We drew the wire taut with a monkey strainer, a pair of claws on a ratchet that closed over the barbs and hauled the wire back, claw over claw, as we worked the handle. 'Well, Bill,' I said brightly, 'another good job done.' 'Yes,' he replied, 'thank the Good Lord and he'll give you a bit more to do.'

Two nights I sat up with Bill, listening to stories from the war: accounts of extraordinary sexual excesses that, like today's urban myths, he had only ever witnessed at second hand. There was a Christmas Eve orgy, I remember, at an RAF station on a remote Scottish island, mysteriously sanctioned when a massive steel door between the men's sleeping quarters and the women's was left unlocked. And a tale of men with commando training being recruited from the pubs of a garrison town to pleasure the wives of officers who were overseas. Bill's own marriage had broken up during the war and he regarded women with a melancholy fascination, as feral creatures who were only waiting to slip the leash of convention.

By the Wednesday I felt like a ghost, attaching myself for warmth to the company of the living. At lunchtime, when I should have been heading home for my lesson with Antonio, I found myself lingering with my friends from the English set, strolling over to the church hall where they played badminton and knocking up for the first game. As the shuttlecock rose and hung in the air, their easy banter felt like shelter.

By the time I came puttering up the drive to the farm on my moped, the high doors of the covered school were closed, the lesson already begun. One of the stable girls was waiting for me, holding my horse. I think that's what broke me, the sight of the animal all tacked-up, the stirrups gleaming below the polished saddle, the buckle on the bridle bright against the dark leather. It was the perfect turn-out Antonio expected, the due order of a tradition I was dishonouring by arriving late.

Up rose the bitter energy of those days and I rushed into the house to change. But as I took the reins, reached up to the saddle and bent to put my foot in the stirrup, I was shaken by tears: sudden, overwhelming, undeniable tears.

Sent to bed like a small child with the mumps or the whooping cough, I drifted in and out of half-sleep, a warm, absolved half-sleep, quite different from the tense vigil I had been keeping. And something was lulled awake, something at the back of my mind I had been saving for when I had time. Phrase by phrase, I began to try out lines for a poem.

One of the farm cats was an accomplished thief. On a Friday, when my mother was cooking fish, it would crouch by the garden shed, watching her movements through the kitchen window. If she went to the pantry, or into the hall to answer the phone, it would be in and out through the fanlight, leaving a flurry of paw marks up the windowpane as the only evidence. The idea for the poem had come when I thought of merging that cat with one I used to

113

watch out of the corner of my eye during English lessons. Our prefab overlooked its backyard and, as Jack took us through the intricacies of 'A Valediction: forbidding mourning',

> If they be two, they are two so
> As stiffe twin compasses are two,

it would be disposing itself in the sun, regal on its coal bunker.

I cannot remember much of the poem itself. Only that it opened with a colloquial flourish, a trick I had learned from e. e. cummings,

> That there cat
>    's a darn nuisance
> filches fish

and that the cat on the coal bunker came into focus later, sat upright with its tail neatly encircling its feet,

> a pert, proletarian beauty.

What I remember is how the cluster of words grew each time I surfaced. I began to drift purposefully, waiting for the pull of the next phrase.

One Saturday, a couple of years before, I had awoken on the morning of a school cross-country match and tried to describe the feeling of butterflies in the stomach:

> Mind hovering,
>    Never 'lighting,
> Nervous sickness
>    Not relaxing . . .

I would never have thought of doing that if some older boys had not started a magazine and asked for poems. That simple request had come to me with the force of a revelation: 'So you can *write* them too!' I thought all the poems had already been written, by an elect company known as poets. Our place was merely to read them.

That first effort never went beyond light verse. I had yet to read anything written later than the nineteenth century, which accounts for the archaisms:

> Friends are rivals,
>> Opponents devils,
> Spirit 'gainst such
>> Half-sport cavils.

But there was a rhythm there: the discovery of that rhythm created such a resonance in me that I felt like a loose string that had suddenly been tuned.

As the cat poem began to take shape, the last four days seemed to re-form around it. The insomnia, the mania, the embarrassments, they all fell away. I was intent on my compressions, on making the cat scramble through the lines so fast they rattled in their frame. It was like being given another life.

Film companies sometimes used the farm as a location because it was so near London. The white horse that rears out of the darkness at the start of Joseph Losey's *Accident* is one of ours. The shot that establishes Humbert Humbert's arrival at Camp Climax in Stanley Kubrick's *Lolita*, the rather misty shot of a line of girls on horseback, was taken on our drive. Sue Lyon, the sixteen-year-old they had flown over from Hollywood to play the part of Lolita, used to ride with us in her breaks from filming.

Not that you would have known from the wall chart in the

office, where she was booked in as Sue Day. Nor even from the discreet, chauffeur-driven Mercedes Sue and her mother, who always accompanied her, preferred to the studio's Rolls-Royce. They liked to glide through the Thames Valley like two genteel spies out of Agatha Christie, drawing up unremarked at a riverside pub. The farm was a safe house – the studio had promised publicity later if we kept the secret – and they would linger after Sue's lesson, the mother setting a chair against the whitewashed office wall and leafing through her newspaper in the afternoon sun while Sue wandered down the lines of loose boxes or smoked a cigarette with Dennis in the shadows of the barn. 'They've got her so worked up,' he confided, and for once I hated his calming gift, whatever it was in him that caused cows to yield their milk or pigs to dog his heels or girls to seek out his company.

One Saturday afternoon I did manage to appear at the door of the farrowing shed, filling a bucket of water for the pigs, just as Sue rode her horse round to its box in the elbow of the barn. I bent my head over the tap and was rewarded by seeing her glance across the yard, with that instinctive curiosity young people have for someone of their own age. I began to imagine myself seated in the front of the Mercedes, acting as guide as the chauffeur drove us to Hampton Court. 'Has anyone', I asked in the kitchen at tea break, 'taken Sue Lyon and her mother down to the river to show them the Wayneflete Tower? They might be interested.' 'She's a film star,' they said. 'She'll be interested in nightclubs, not in old buildings.'

I felt just as I had at fourteen when the tomboy from primary school reappeared at bible class with her brown crop turned blond and curling to the collar of a white satin blouse, a creature of such astonishing delicacy that we circled hopelessly round her, feeling clumsy and ill-fitted in the coarse tweed of our sports jackets and our best grey flannels. We kept butting in to talk to her, the lips

116

with which we had traded insults three years before so subtle in their new shapings that we simply wanted to watch them move. The cut of her hair where it fell against the collar, even the cut of the collar itself, which had its own soft shine: nothing about her seemed ordinary any longer. She had come into a power none of us could match.

One Games afternoon, when I was still condemned to desultory cricket out at Grist's, the school sports ground, and had to walk into Kingston to catch the bus, I had found myself on the narrow pavement behind two young women in hoop skirts. They were processing in single file, skirts sprung out so wide on their hoops that I had little choice but to follow them, watching the legs move like antelopes in a glade of gingham. There was the filtered light, the green cotton check as taut as glass; there was the neat arc of a pair of panties, cut high over slender buttocks and so adult in the lightness of their green, so skimpy that I pondered them as something quite new to me; and there was the back of the thigh, the long, inward curve that became the tapering calf, the ankle's arch under its strap, the pounce of the foot on its high heel. Some thirty yards that revelation lasted before the first girl stopped at the tobacconist's, her skirt bobbing against the open door, and pitched her voice inside. I edged past the laughter on the pavement as the man brought her cigarettes. But I saw the girls again as they began their progress up the High Street. They were two walking flowers, the stretched bell of the corolla nodding over slim white pistils.

Much earlier, and more potent still, had been the glimpse one summer at the Hall, while I was roaming with another boy over the hills above Morecambe, of a naked leg on the next hill, flexing and stretching into the air. It was the whiteness that had caught my eye, the whiteness and the movement, like the movement of river weed on the bed of a stream as it splays out in the current. Then the shape came into focus and I felt a sense of shock, informed by all the wet Sundays I had spent poring over the *News of the World* on the floor of the beach hut. 'We'd better go over there,' I gasped. 'That could be rape.'

Had I been a little older, I might have read the exposure differently. Something in the luxuriance of that movement might have suggested to me that it was not rape. As it was, we rushed across, full of Christian zeal, and came on a couple in the advanced stages of foreplay.

'That's the kind of thing Billy Graham was complaining about,' I said to my friend as we moved on to the brow of the hill. The evangelist had been in the headlines, inveighing against acts of immorality in the London parks. But already I was regretting our trespass. Deep down, under the pronouncements of the little judge that I was at thirteen or fourteen, I knew that I had seen something rare, a woman moving at her pleasure as grass might flow in the wind.

I kept her languorous high kicks like secrets, not allowing myself to glance at them too often. Just knowing they were there, so complete in themselves they seemed to move in another plane, made it easier to wait out the years of adolescence. They were a calming sign, a pagan blessing sketched on the air.

We were supposed to wait. Not just to wait but to keep to the cloister of a boys' grammar school. When posters began to appear for weekly stomps to trad jazz at the Coronation Hall, the Headmaster took to the pulpit at Morning Assembly, Monty moustache bristling on his upper lip. He had returned from the war as a brigadier, a rank that had blossomed into a persona. He wore a monocle, attached on two swaying cords of black silk to the waistcoat of his black pinstripe suit, and his thinning hair was primped into black and grey curls behind a head the wide cheekbones gave a sculpted look, as if he had become a bust of himself.

His warning on the dangers of 'this developing teenage nightlife' was not as memorable as his survey of Western civilisation on the day some unfortunate boy was found to have carved his initials into a desk. That had started with 'man hauling himself up from the primeval slime' and ended with the observation that 'everything we hold today has been' – Churchillian pause, monocle in hand – 'most hardly won'. But he need not have troubled: the only time most of us met girls was on the evening of the school fête, when a jazz band played in a huge marquee.

The licensed bar put it out of bounds and I remember the first time I slipped through the entrance into the composted air. There were the smells familiar from Scout camp, hot canvas and trampled grass. There was the unfamiliar, sour, heavy smell of beer. And there, waiting diffidently by the bandstand, was my female equivalent, a slim, dark-haired girl whose white blouse and dark skirt were not school uniform but might as well have been. I felt the springy touch of her hand as we leaned back into our elementary jive. I stood with her in the crowd, watching the closing fireworks. I asked her out and received the expected reply, 'I have exams.' And then I felt the moth-touch of her lips, a gentle pressure, warm and with just the first silkiness of wet, that I mulled over for the next year.

There was an intimation of the complexities to come. When we moved to the farm, my mother took on an au pair, a girl from West Berlin who was perfecting her English to become an air hostess. Ute was older than me and I felt rather as I had with my Cousin Sylvia, helplessly attuned to her physical presence but only as an incidental audience.

On her first Sunday with us, Ute asked to be taken to the local Methodist church. She had been told by another au pair that a church youth club was the best place to make friends. It fell to me, as the family's only churchgoer, to accompany her. I put on my best

119

shirt and went down to the sitting room, where she was waiting for me. It was a warm evening and she was wearing a light-blue summer dress. As she came across the room, the dress flowed back and the light from the windows turned it to a blue dust. For a moment her silhouette surfaced, the rounded hips and long thighs swimming towards me like a figure in a cave painting.

I was vividly aware, as I escorted her down the drive towards the Sunday traffic, of the lightness of the dress, the flow of next-to-nothing that left her body so unprotected and so potent. It was like an erotic dream that had suddenly turned into a dream of exposure. I was grateful for the parapet, briefly shading in the dress as we crossed the bridge over the river. But then I had to walk her up the hill into Esher, step by step on the narrow strip of pavement, keeping my eyes down as a bus went past and wondering if we would be arrested before we reached the church. She's just come over from Berlin, I was going to say, imagining the streets there as so many daydreams by Paul Delvaux, all the women entranced in the transparency of their summer dresses.

We must have startled the Methodists, who proved to be rather an elderly congregation. Ute never went there again. Next day she met Dennis and began to spend all her free time in the yard, a stylish figure in a white blouse and three-quarter-length slacks. 'It's so funny,' my mother said when I came home from school. 'I sent her over this morning to call Dennis for coffee and I've hardly seen her since.'

I felt no jealousy then. And when, a few weeks later, a sadness came over them, I even felt slightly affronted and asked Dennis why. They had, it seemed, come to the realisation that their lives could never mesh. Lufthansa did not fly out of London. And what would a cowman do in Berlin? Better to draw back before they became too involved. I listened to these words, *draw back, too involved*, rather as I listened to my father explaining that he was

120

selling off the front two fields to reduce the size of the mortgage. Serious words, adult words, they had yet to encompass me.

But when my friend Colin came to work for us the following summer and I caught a glimpse of Ute in his arms in the back of a loose box, oh that did, that encompassed me. It told me how clueless I was and how unfathomable this power was. Scholar and prefect, deliverer of the Latin Speech on Speech Day, I was a boy after the Headmaster's own heart: but Colin was the one with Ute in his arms.

I had watched him grow in confidence as he grew taller and his hussar's chest filled out. Slightly pigeon-toed, as if bred for spurs, he had an unusually upright stance, the small of the back curved in so that you noticed the spring of the spine, the branching width of the shoulders. As I bent over my Puritan divines, Colin had acquired a motorbike and become a teenage heart-throb. And yet, for reasons of his own, he kept in touch. I was never quite sure how he saw me, whether I was *idiot* or *savant*. Sometimes it seemed to be his mission to instruct me in how the world actually worked. But when, in our final year in the Sixth, he applied to Oxford and was offered a place, I realised that I had been a talisman all along.

What astonished me was his physical command. A year of sharing the house with Ute had only served to domesticate my adoration. I could have told you all about her, from the cut of her light-brown hair, the Hessian's mitre of loose curls that, after a year in the hands of an English hairdresser, still looked distinctively un-English, to the modest swell of her calf below the three-quarter-length slacks, the long line of the foot going down into the flat shoes she wore for work. I knew nothing of pheromones then but I knew how the air of the kitchen could change around her, how it could be filled with alacrity at coffee time and mysteriously allayed on her afternoon off when she mooched in her dressing gown, wet hair wrapped in a towel. I was aware of something tremulous about her, as if

121

that delicate skin were a meniscus. But could I have reached out and touched her? Could I have taken her in my arms?

First I had to move into my own body, to become fingertips, hands and shoulders, rather than this headlong reader of the world.

It must have begun with glances across the long kitchen table. With my noticing the gloss of dark curls over the collar of a check shirt. Or the blood in her cheeks as she came in from the yard, the vividness of colour that seemed a kind of imagination. She was always about to break into a run, all the lines of her body drawn up to a point just ahead of her, at breast height.

The other girls had certainly noticed. When it came to the Christmas party, an innocent affair in which we played games like Flip the Kipper across the sitting-room floor, one of them held up the mistletoe and the others pushed us together. Only somebody piled in at the last moment, bumping us together so that one of us had a nosebleed and the other a bruised lip.

Next thing, we were huddled together in the downstairs bathroom, ministering to each other with cold water and a flannel. And then we were kissing each other in a tender frenzy, a delirium of discovery.

Our timing could not have been better. I had just left school, having secured my Oxford scholarship. Koki had just come to train as a riding instructor. And for the next six months I was going to be working in the stables, earning enough money to hitchhike round Greece.

It was the winter of 1963. The high doorway to the barn was a vault of deep cold, the standpipe frozen, for all its lagging. Morning after morning I had to stand over the tap with the kitchen kettle, drenching the brass until it steamed and shone, and the ice inside cracked. Once we had watered the horses, we had to fill a great tub for the cattle and haul it on a sledge over the frozen fields, two of us pulling on the rope and another pushing on the tub when the runners stuck.

There was an exhilaration in working outside in hard weather, a transfiguration of the muscles as the blood raced against the cold and aches became shimmers of sensation. In my head I had Charlie Parker's 'Kim', the hurtle of hard notes I had found slipped in among the pop singles in a second-hand shop. I had stared down at the small neat print on the label: Charlie Parker Quartet, unable to believe my luck. People spoke of Charlie Parker as they spoke of Samuel Beckett or Albert Camus. Yet the name sounded so colloquial, so everyday. I felt as if it had been left for me by the angel of chance, as if, simply by finding it in that box of 45s, I had been linked into some vital circuit.

Koki was a modern-jazz fan. I offered her the record, knowing how impressed she would be. 'No,' she said, 'it's yours. You found it.' And so I played it on the machine my aunt had passed on to me, an old disc recorder with a heavy head and fierce amplification. What I heard left me stunned in its wake. It was faster than I could listen. But I worked at listening to it, playing it over and over again. Partly out of allegiance to Koki and partly because, even as it slipped my hearing, I caught the glimmer of something I respected, elusive but hard-edged.

Other music left me no choice. I had only to hear the sway of strings on the radio and I would listen for a chord on the piano and the parched cry of 'Georgia, Georgia', remembering the song as I had first heard it, sitting next to Koki in the upper circle of the Odeon Hammersmith, our two consciousnesses suspended in an expectation several thousand deep. No strings, just the muted brass and the chord so resonant under the fingers of the jerking figure we had seen huddled to the piano between two strong men, one at each elbow, that we seemed to hang in the pause.

The frost was still deep, the nights still dark when my mother

123

announced that the daughter of one of her old school friends was coming to stay. It was Koki's weekend off and my mother had asked whether we had any plans. She was expecting me to play host. We came to a tactful arrangement: on the Friday Koki's parents invited me over for a meal and on the Saturday I waited for the guest to arrive. It was not certain that she would even be able to travel: trains were being cancelled because of ice on the line. But arrive she did, a pleasant girl of my own age. I showed her round the farm, willingly enough, and wondered what to do next. 'Why don't you take her skating?' my mother suggested.

Skating was one of the things I had learned to do with Koki. We would catch a string of buses in to Richmond ice rink and eat fish and chips on the way home. I'm not sure that the real excitement didn't lie there, in the two of us hopping from bus to bus, moving as easily across our stretch of suburb as two chimpanzees swinging through the tree canopy. Certainly there was more of an onrush, if the timetables fell right, in the next bus drawing up than in our shaky circuits of the ice on hired blades, two of the humble crowd cleared off at intervals to make way for the speed skaters.

I was only too happy to show off my newfound savvy, telling the girl to be sure to lay a shilling on the counter with her ticket so that the attendant would give her a good pair of skates. And I was careful only to hold her hand when I helped her off the ice. But not savvy enough to foresee what Koki's reaction would be: 'You took her to Richmond! That's our place.' After long afternoons in the tack room, Koki grimly scrubbing at a bit or working leather to a steely shine while I pleaded that I had only been acting under orders, it emerged that a person with any feeling would have taken the girl skating at Battersea. As if, the moment she had come down on the train from London, I was supposed to take her straight back up again.

The next time I asked Koki out, she was unavailable. She had met someone at the jazz club in Richmond. Immediately I began to feel inferior. Richmond had an air of bohemia, more Chelsea than Surrey. But I had only glimpsed those fabled streets from the bus. I could only imagine what it must be to sit in the Auberge, drinking coffee and listening to blues. All I knew was the ice rink.

There was worse to come. This sophisticate was called Damien. And he was Irish. What could I say in the face of such otherness? I just felt helplessly ordinary.

We still went out together but only as friends. After a while I noticed that there had been no mention of the intimidating Damien. I asked after him, somewhat to Koki's surprise. 'Oh,' she said, 'he's gone back to Ireland.' But that miserable proviso remained: only as friends.

Outwardly it made little difference. For all that heedlessness in the bathroom, Koki had come to resent the goodnight clinch. She resented the expectation of it, rather as she disliked having anyone's arms round her at the Gladys Dare School of Dance, which she quit before I had learned to waltz.

But it robbed me of what I had valued most, the fascination of being close to something so mercurial as another person. Or, at any rate, as this other person. What I had loved in her were the knight's moves of feeling, the suddenness and completeness of her emotions.

It was not until we met again, some years later, that Koki confessed to me that Damien was an invention, devised to punish me. Which accounted for his cunning blend of the hip and the otherworldly. And it was not until another girlfriend, years later still, alerted me to my mother's interventions that it occurred to me to wonder why anyone's daughter should have been invited for the weekend when the fields were sheets of ice, when the whole country was deep under frost. Though she came in all innocence, that girl was herself a device, a trap set for Koki, who was not my mother's idea of a daughter-in-law. Koki was not biddable. She was a Catholic. And worst of all, she was a stable girl. It had always been understood that the stables would be my sister's one day.

Fewer clients came in the hard weather. We had to ride in the lessons ourselves, just to keep the horses exercised. By nine o'clock at night, when the last lesson was over, there were echoes along my spine. As I moved down the lines of loose boxes, refilling the water buckets and tying up the hay nets, I could still feel the slow, rocking stride of Fidus, the heaviest of the horses, who launched himself into the canter like a swingboat. But at least I had the chance to ride Brummel every day.

The fourth of the Arab-Hackney crosses, Brummel had almost brought disaster on us when my father went to collect him from the field at Beeston. Caught by one of the local lads who used to help the old Welshman out, he was nervous and shying from the head collar. My father tried an old trick, putting his arms round the horse's neck so that he could slide the collar up unawares, and Brummel took off. My father could only cling on as he was dragged across the ground, the hooves coming down either side of him and reducing his riding mac to thin strips. Three circuits of the field Brummel made before he sank to his knees. 'Well,' said a gypsy who was watching, 'I've never seen anything like that afore.'

My father was barely able to drive the Land Rover and trailer back, the bruises stiffening as he sat in traffic and each change of gear bringing him fresh pain. But Brummel went into his loose box quietly enough and proved to be the gentlest of animals. He was more lightly built than Beauty, a liver chestnut with a gloss to his coat and a natural elegance that earned him his name, Beeston Beau Brummel.

Officially he was my horse. I knew that was a polite fiction, a way of keeping the balance in the family. But for the months I was working in the stables it almost felt true. Brummel was so finely paced he was effortless to ride. There was no sense of weight, only what the manuals call impulsion, the spring of the horse under you. Sometimes I would still feel that as I walked through the yard afterwards, an energy at the base of the spine, impelling me forwards.

One evening towards the end of winter Antonio started to send us over the *cavalletti*. These were white poles fixed to 'x's of wood. First he would turn the 'x's down so that the pole lay flat on the ground, just enough of an obstacle for the horses to break their stride and pop over. Then he would turn them up to form a low jump. And then, if all the horses in the line were jumping freely, he would put two *cavalletti* together and rest a third on top. That was still not very high but, as the pole rose, there was another progression: first we would be told to ride without stirrups, then without stirrups or reins. Finally would come the order to put our hands on our heads.

That order was crucial because it brought your head up. You could not look down, which meant that you could not anticipate the jump. You had to rise to it as the horse rose.

I remember looking into the strip lights at the far end of the school, a grid of glare under the roof, and feeling a moment's lightness as I rose towards them, a sensation almost of flight.

Three or four times Antonio sent us over the jump. Each time Brummel took it with the same easy stride and each time I felt the same easy lift, the upward flicker of a swallow on the wing.

Afterwards Bridget, the head stable girl, came up to me: 'Antonio has just been raving about you in the office. *"What I could do with that boy! He's a natural. Perfect timing. I could take him right to the top."*'

Everyone had hushed Antonio up. Horses were my sister's province, which in all conscience she needed. I had been an insufferable success at school. But the obverse of that was that at home I was under a curious kind of shadow, as Bridget must have noticed.

127

I felt that I had completed my apprenticeship to Antonio. And I knew that if I wanted to follow in my father's tradition, I would have to do it quietly, on my own.

Among the horses in my care was an Anglo-Arab, Nefertiti, a delicate blue-grey dapple. Her owner kept her with us on full livery and came to ride her two or three times a week. On the other days I would school her on the lunge line. Often two of us would be working at the same time, one at the bottom of the school and the other at the top, and Nefertiti would keep to her sand-sifting trot while the other horse bucketed into its canter.

One afternoon, when I knew that we would have the school to ourselves, I closed the high doors and loosed her without a lunge line.

'Walk on!' I said, quietly walking myself to the centre of the schooling ring and picking up the long whip, a ritual gesture, casually done so as not to alarm her. I drove her with my voice, hardening the tone until she stretched her neck and lengthened her stride and I heard the four muffled beats of a horse walking full out on the sand and sawdust. For the next half-hour, as I put her through her paces, there was no constricting line, no weighted noseband. Only tones and glances, her reading of my stance, my reading of her action. At one point, as she was taking off into a canter, she flung a kick at me. Only it was not a kick, it was foreplay, a fling of the heel as if we were two horses racing together in a field. I laughed, surprise taking on just enough of an edge to make her canter at full stretch, out on the edge of the ring.

To my surprise, I had a letter from Koki's mother, the handwriting's flourishes on the Basildon Bond of the same severe elegance as the dark hair pulled back into a French roll and the long mouth's shade of scarlet. Koki's mother was Franco-Spanish, one of the second generation of an immigrant family, and spoke perfect English. 'Pushy,' said my mother, who had only to be pulled in my father's wake.

The letter was asking me to be patient if Koki was not as responsive to me as she might be. They had been concerned to bring her up as a Catholic and the parish priest had insisted on her being sent to a convent school. Inevitably, this had left her with certain complexes and inhibitions. Like many modern Catholics, they were trying to allay these by creating a more generous atmosphere at home. She was sure of the depth of her daughter's feelings for me and sure that, given time and understanding, she would be able to express them.

The letter breathed such good sense that my surprise only deepened. Why hand your daughter over to the nuns if you knew the damage they would do?

But what was breathing there? A mother's intuition or a mother's ambition? Whatever Koki's feelings might have been, she had become fascinated with her own power. She had discovered that she could toy with me, keep me on tenterhooks. Ever since I had pleaded and pleaded my innocence over that skating trip, I had been pleading in vain.

By the spring I was weary of it, and only too glad to go to Greece. But whom should I go with? Such friends as I had were still at school. And then I thought of Frances Henry, in whose house we gathered every Sunday after Evensong.

Her mother, who had been a theatre director, was the alternative mother every teenager should have, tumultuous, scatty and wise. Frances herself was quiet, a thoughtful girl with the look of a Victorian heroine: a strong, straight nose and a mass of golden-brown hair that, as fast as she pinned it up, sprang out again in fine curls. We were rather wary of each other as friends. There was no attraction between us, only a baffled sense of difference. But Frances was in the same position as me, waiting to go up to Oxford.

I rang her mother, only to be told that Frances was on a boat somewhere on the upper reaches of the Thames. I asked Terry, the son of well-to-do clients who had his own Triumph Herald, to take me on a search of the riverside towns and found myself acting as chauffeur to his summer romance, driving through the suspended sunlight of a June evening while he canoodled in the back with Lindy, a Canadian girl who was working in the stables to pay her way round Europe.

We were on the night train to Athens after a sunstruck day in Belgrade. There should never have been such a day. Frontiers should have flowed past the windows of a compartment that pulled into couchettes, days changing to nights around us as we sped on like Yuri Gagarin in his Vostok. But we had ignored all the calls on the ferry for the Paris train, thinking of ourselves as passengers on the Athens train, and only realised our mistake as we came to the rank of silent trains at Calais, none of them ours.

We had to follow on humbler trains, sleeping in our seats through France and Switzerland and chugging in sunlight across the top of Italy, two dishevelled figures who delved into their rucksacks for bottles of bitter lemon and ageing ham rolls. 'Now you must be students,' said a dapper little man in the seat opposite. 'Where do you study?' 'Oxford,' I said proudly, laying claim to an identity we had yet to possess. 'But Oxford!' He threw up his hands. 'Top hat! Tail coat! And you!'

By the time we drew into Belgrade on the second morning, we were a full twelve hours behind the departed express. And then we came to the blank in the timetable. There was a local train to Skopje. Otherwise nothing till that night, when the next express passed through.

The station was already returning to stillness, to the long roof's shadow across the yard, the curve of its wall lined with empty hand-carts, tipped up so that they rested on the handlebar at the end of the shaft. One of these high-wheeled carts had gone bowling out

130

of the yard with goods from our train, cardboard boxes of what we guessed to be office stationery, one man running with the shaft at chest height, another with his hand on the back, and both of them taking such long strides that it looked as if the delivery were being made by corps de ballet.

The streets behind the station seemed to cross epochs. There were Sixties tower blocks marooned in an almost total absence of traffic. There was an open-air market on a bleak raft of concrete where a man in Turkish trousers and curly slippers was hanging a haunch of goat on the scales. But it was the stillness of the station itself that told us we had come to the edge of Europe as we knew it. When we returned in the afternoon, the owners of the hand-carts were lying on them, sleeping at 45 degrees.

Row upon row of curious eyes scanned us as the express pulled up. The only passengers to board, we found seats next to a Swede who spoke to us in German, thinking we must be stranded hitchhikers.

'Nobody', he said, 'gets on at Belgrade.'

A travel agent in a lightweight suit, he was on his way to Mykonos, where he spent a month every summer. Listening to him talk, I realised that this was the focus of his life, a yearly gathering of friends from all over Europe who seemed, as he described them, to be the illuminati of pleasure.

Once we had crossed the border, the lights were dimmed and the Swede drew the blinds on the corridor. The compartment settled down to sleep, Frances leaning back into her window seat, as did the man opposite her, a Greek with an aquiline nose and a thick black moustache. I had no one facing me, which meant that I could put my feet up on the seat.

I woke because something was wriggling under the small of my back. Then I felt fingers gently close over my hipbone. The Swede had put his arm round me.

What rose in me then was neither excitement nor shock: it

was curiosity. *What do they do?* I shifted a little closer, in order to find out.

Needlecord, so worn that it had become like a second skin, lifted from the skin of my belly. Fingers probed for the zip. As they drew it down, slowly enough to mask any sound, I thought how odd it was that my old grey jeans, worn for haymaking, worn on Saturdays for feeding and watering the pigs, should be party to this.

I held still, determinedly still, keeping my eyes on the face of the Greek, who was sleeping with his head back and breathing through his nose. It looked strangely thin and inconsequential now, two sallow rims of nostril above the broomhead of the moustache. I was watching them narrow and flare with each inhalation, watching every twitch of every fold of the eyelids to be sure that he really was asleep and not just pretending.

Stealthily, so as not to wake the man opposite him, the Swede unfolded a plastic mac into its first stiff panels, laid them across my lap and ducked his head beneath. So far I had been his partner in stealth, keeping watch like a schoolboy in an adventure story, ready to whisper *Cave!* With the first touch of his lips on the head of my cock, the first pressure of moistened membrane to the stretching membrane beneath, that pretence vanished. This was adult and sexual, a sliding grip that drew sensation out of me ahead of the shock.

'No one will ever know,' I told myself as the shock followed, the realisation that I was permitting one of the mysterious acts of gross indecency the *News of the World* was unable to describe. One of my father's lawyer friends, a thin, gentle man I had known as Uncle Stanley, had been disbarred because, in the underworld into which homosexuals were driven then, he had signed a passport form for someone he did not know. It was easy to see the shades of that underworld in the yellowy green of the nightlight, easy to feel a sadness in the relentless motion of the train, to imagine it carrying

132

me into a distance from which I would never return. And yet I held still, clamped into place like a piece of apparatus, an experiment I had just set up. The Swede was rotating his head around my cock, creating an extraordinary oscillation in which he seemed to be all mouth and no teeth. I was wondering how that was done when I felt a confusion, half-numbness, half-pain, and tried to push his head away.

He kept it there, hahing with his breath so that my startled cock was soothed and left warm and dry, lulled back to sleep. This seemed to me a most delicate attention, a point of etiquette, no doubt, among the illuminati, but bordering on tenderness.

'Now,' he said, 'I go into the corridor and smoke a cigarette.' Those were the only words spoken that night. I spent the next morning out of the compartment, rushing up and down the corridor in the black fur hat I had bought in Belgrade and looking more and more incongruous as the train sweltered south. Only after we had glided into the station at Athens, and the Swede had lifted down his streamlined suitcase and gone, did Frances tell me that he had opened it to show her his perfume, a dark, aromatic scent whose particular qualities he had taken great care to describe to her, giving her a dab on the back of the hand. She was astonished by the encounter, astonished and rather moved by it, and I left her astonishment intact.

Forty minutes I had waited before I went in to breakfast! Forty minutes of feeling so conspicuous at the foot of the girls' stairs that I tried to lose myself among the little groups at reception, only to become such a continual subject of enquiry from the staff and such a frequent cause of collision with the big packs being shouldered for departure that in the end the manager sent me outside to wait in the street.

But forty minutes seemed nothing to Frances, who had been

caught in the queue for a shower cubicle. What dismayed her was the greeting with which I had emerged from the cafeteria when she finally came down the stairs.

'Hi! I've just had my breakfast. I'll wait outside while you have yours.'

I was anxious to get to the Parthenon before the heat rose. She had half a mind to go straight home.

We sat in the street outside the youth hostel, we who had been so companionable on the train, while Frances tried to explain to me what had brought us to this impasse.

'It's just that, when I'm with my friends, I expect us to have breakfast together. It's one of the things we look forward to, talking to each other, starting the day in each other's company.'

I listened to this as if I were eavesdropping on another species. All I knew at home was the speed with which the long table filled as people came in from the yard, the muttered veterinary reports: 'Fidus was coughing again.' 'Frosty's still lame.' And before that, the waking to bible study and prayer, the ironside putting on his armour.

'What do you talk about?' I asked, rather as an android might enquire into human behaviour. But it was an honest enquiry: I had no idea what it was to sit two or three at a table, no experience of conversation over a leisurely breakfast.

Night over the Aegean was so large and still that the ship seemed to sleepwalk through the water, the bow wave a breath of the Hesperides, a lulling of warm air against the rails. Just to sit in the bows was to find yourself in a kind of trance. But my eyes were half closed because I was trying out phrases. Were we *cradled in a calm? Guests of air and water?*

The others sat further down the deck, talking. All except one of the girls from the Beaux Arts in Paris, the gamine with short, dark hair, who was sitting at the foot of the foremast, reading in the light of a lamp.

Frances and I had been making our way to ancient sites, hitching lifts on battered old lorries that would simply pull on to the roadside when darkness fell and set off again at dawn. On the back roads of the Peloponnese we had been touched by the traditional hospitality accorded to strangers: stop at an outlying house to ask directions and we would be seated in the shade of a tree and brought the simplest of refreshments, a glass of retsina and slices of bread and tomato.

Now we were back in our own time, on the night boat to Mykonos and within a side glance of free love.

There had been a beach party the night before where, rumour had it, the other girl from the Beaux Arts had bestowed herself on an English boy. Judging by his look of bewildered good fortune, the rumour was well founded. I had been watching them on the bus out to the port at Piraeus and thinking that no one would grudge him the experience, he had such an open face, such unassuming physical presence. Like a young Harry Ploughman, *as a beechbole firm*.

The girl had caught Frances's eye when we first returned to the youth hostel. 'Look over there!' she said. 'That girl's got a really good figure.' 'Too buxom,' I said. 'Like a ship's figurehead.' 'No, watch when she turns!' And I saw the inward curve of the small of the back, the spine taut as a Scythian bow. That was what Frances admired: the stance, the self-possession.

We had had to stand on the bus. The lovers had found a double seat at the back, as if all luck were theirs, and the gamine a single seat on the aisle, only a couple of rows from where we swayed and held on to the overhead rail. Looking down at her brush cut, I had noticed how it offset the fullness of the eyes, the softness of the skin over the cheekbones, making them clues to a femininity you had to detect. I was already imagining the texture of a skin that would be like pear skin and yield to the touch when Frances leaned closer and breathed in my ear, 'Just in case you're harbouring any illusions, she also slept with somebody last night.'

I felt as if I were ten again and someone in the playground had just whispered to me the facts of life. *She'd done it!* The girl sitting in front of me had done this sensational thing. Then I felt a little older and began to wonder how she could sit there so composed in her black T-shirt and jeans when the night before she had engaged in fornication. All the voices of my upbringing denounced her: not just the voices raised in church but the voices lowered round the kitchen table, the mistresses of implication, of the meaningful pause. I remembered my mother coming home one night from a dinner party and talking of a woman who had looked sultry. Was that what happened to a woman if she did it too often? Would she become sultry? I looked again at the face I had studied so carefully as if there on the forehead, under the spray of the brush cut, I should see BABYLON.

By the time we were on the boat, I had forgiven her. I was nineteen once more and afloat on the night like a swimmer on his back. I wanted just to float wordlessly, letting the warm air lap against me. But how would I ever become a poet if I let an experience like this slip? And so there I was, sat on my own, a little self-consciously, in the bows.

Every so often I would become aware of the gamine, sitting reading under the lamp. I liked the presence of another solitary, the implicit company. Sometimes I would imagine myself in the lamplight, talking to her. And sometimes her absorption seemed so complete that I would look away, shy of breaking it.

When I've finished the poem, I told myself, when I've finished the poem. But the dawn came up without the poem moving beyond the obvious. And I laboured on fruitlessly because I was afraid to give up.

It never occurred to me that there might be a better poem to be found by talking to her.

I took out Koki's letter to read under the pine tree. There were plantations of pine all around the old farmhouse in Provence where I was staying as English tutor, ranks of timber-bearing trees open to the light. But one bent a branch over the sandy path at the back of the house, wresting just enough shade to hold off the sun.

I had been away from home for almost three months: a month in Greece, a month tutoring the young Coutagnes at their chalet in the Alps and these weeks at Le Défends, which felt more like a rock formation than a house, its corridors rambling between thick stone walls. In Athens I had come across an American paperback by Carl Sandburg, one of Koki's heroes, and all my letters home had been addressed to her. Which must have been why, for all my mother's determination not to have her as a daughter-in-law, it had been left to Koki to break the news of Antonio's death.

He had been found lying in the field with a fractured skull, his horse grazing nearby. The horse was Fidalgo ('nobleman' in Portuguese), a difficult horse he was schooling for an important client. But, though Fidalgo was put down, it was by no means certain that he had thrown Antonio. There was a grass stain on the saddle, which suggests that he may have stumbled. And the post-mortem revealed that Antonio had a very bad heart. Only a couple of weeks before, he had blacked out for a moment on a hack and had no idea where he was when he came round.

The only certainty was that Antonio would not have fractured his skull if he had been wearing a hard hat. No one else was allowed to ride without wearing a black hunting cap. Antonio was strict about that with his young son, who was following in the family tradition and already a good horseman. But just as strict in keeping to his own personal uniform, the fawn cap that complemented the battledress jacket.

It was a long time before I went back into the house. I sat in that crook of shadow, remembering what Antonio had said when I asked him if he missed his days as an international showjumper: 'Your ambitions change as you get older. What I care about now is my wife and children, making a good life for them. I'm no longer so concerned with myself.' And yet there were the dark looks, the scarifying turns of phrase, the furious cigarettes. There was the inheritance he carried into a diminished world, using the skills that should have been shown in the levade and the piaffe so that a line of children could ride to Duane Eddy's 'Pepe'.

The letter told of another death, just as unexpected. Terry, the friend I had chauffeured on his summer romance, had come to Greece on holiday with his parents. We had met them for a drink at their hotel, putting on our best shirts to sit at the silver ring of the cocktail bar. They had gone on to Yugoslavia, where Terry contracted appendicitis. The appendix had ruptured before they could operate and he died in hospital.

I had been finding it difficult to sleep at Le Défends. Partly it was the heat, even in late September. But mostly it was the sense that I was on a threshold. A box of books had been sent from home so that I could do some belated reading for Oxford. The sense was all the more acute because the house around me felt as old as the earth.

The presence of M. Coutagne's parents, who had ended their days there, was still so strong that even the family must have felt like guests when they came each autumn for the grape harvest. The grandfather's books, some works of French literature and many works of Catholic piety, still stood on the shelves in the sitting room, their bindings as worn as a priest's old suit. The room was always dark and cool, the curtains drawn to keep out the sun. As we sat there in the evenings, in the hush of long lives brought to their close, I felt provisional by comparison: no more than a manuscript conjecture, a possible reading in the classical text I was studying, which had yet to win acceptance.

The room I slept in could have been the cave of a Desert Father, the corner over my head rounded as if it had been hollowed out of rock, with a broad stone sill where I put my book and my carafe of water. As the warm air lay against my skin, I would shift on my pillow and begin to conjure girls out of the night, or rather, parts of girls: the thigh of the gamine as she changed under her towel on the beach on Mykonos – *ça vous excite?* she had said when she noticed a couple of us watching her and made a little moue of amusement – or the thin olive shoulder of the neighbours' nanny I had begun to flirt with in the Alps until M. Coutagne nipped the scandal in the bud. Sometimes my imagining of their scent and skin texture was so intense, my hunger to touch them so fierce that I felt like an incautious Anthony who had invited his demons in. And sometimes the sense of possession fell away and I would just be aware of myself, of the energy of my nineteen years pressing out of this cradle of rock like an imago against the walls of its chrysalis.

It was very strange to think that Terry, whom I had heard just over my shoulder, canoodling with Lindy in the back of the car, no longer felt these hungers. He had crossed out of all imagining.

I reached home late on a Friday evening. The elderly couple who had spotted me slumped on the kerb outside Aix-en-Provence, the little Union Jack stuck into my box of books streaming in the draught of cars, had given me a lift all the way to London. Overnight in northern France, while they were installed in their hotel, I had found two drainage pipes waiting to be installed at the roadside, two massive tubes of concrete almost my height, and wormed my sleeping bag into the gap between them, out of the sight of passing traffic.

Koki had just gone to bed but I was allowed to run upstairs and announce my return. Oddly enough, she was in my old room, which had been transformed in my absence, just as I seemed to have been. 'Roger!' she exclaimed and surged out of a top bunk, face to face with me in the light from the door and greeting me as if I were just home from the Crusades.

A lamp was switched on. A head looked up at us from the bed that used to be mine, the short, tousled hair so blond that it was almost white.

'This is Anna,' Koki said. 'She's come as au pair in place of Ute.'

Anna was younger than Ute, as I was to discover next day: only seventeen and still in the first flood of adolescence, her face a little sulky in its puppy fat, her breasts hoisted like storm cones in a navy-blue fisherman's sweater. She was part of the audience at lunchtime when I delivered my sales pitch for pre-knotted string, the monologue I had worked out at the roadside. And before that she brought me a plaster when I was so busy talking I cut myself on the cheese knife.

'You're trembling!' she said as she bent the plaster over my finger. At that age I was in a constant tremor. I could hardly, in the phrase Jimmy Edwards was always using on the radio, contain myself. But she was right: I had felt her like a charged cloud, an atmosphere so close I jumped at the touch of the fingers, firm and practical.

We were curious about each other anyway. It was Saturday and Koki, who already had a date, had fixed us up: 'Why don't you take Anna to the pictures?'

I borrowed my mother's little Austin van so that we could drive there in style. The back row was almost empty and, the moment the lights went down, we were engulfed in a kiss, our tongues mating like two eels that had found their Sargasso.

140

My hand took a risk and slipped under her sweater. And then came the shock: there was no wire and cotton, no bra. Bare skin over the ribs led up to skin so smooth that touch felt like speed, an acceleration under the fingertips. The palm opened to the contour and all the nerve endings of its soft, inner skin sang out the shape. I ran my hand over her breast as though I would never recover from its nakedness. And then more slowly to learn the weight, the supple fall under my fingers.

I was still imagining the whiteness of Anna's skin under the navy-blue sweater, the raised arm as the distant curve of the galaxy and her breast as a fall of light, when she twisted out of the embrace, bent over my lap and reached for my zip. I felt a surge of alarm, imagining us caught in the thin beam of the usherette's torch. 'Let's go!' I whispered and, ten minutes into the film, we rose from our seats.

I drove to a parking place off the A3, a picnic area on the sandy heath we used to ride across. The back of the van, spare wheel clamped to one side, was too short to lie in. I knelt there naked, wondering how to proceed, but Anna was in no doubt. Stripped off, she climbed over the gear lever and straddled me. I felt a fierce drive, with all the compression I could have wished for, but it was not mine: I was a piston driven by a wheel.

'Was it the first time for you?' she asked. 'Yes.' 'For me too,' she said, though that clearly wasn't true. The pretence held us in silence for a while. 'And when you go up to the altar tomorrow' – she must have heard all about me from Koki – 'will you thank God for this experience?'

'Yes,' I promised, though I disliked the weight of the question and the motherly tone. I much preferred the way we had been before, the wordless drive of the wheel.

It was quite a promise, though. The words of the Prayer of Humble Access, 'We do not presume to come to this thy Table, O merciful

Lord, trusting in our own righteousness, but in thy manifold and great mercies', were the most intimate in the Communion service, the approach to God so simple and direct. Could I really take my sin up to the altar rail and thank him for it?

But then it did not feel like sin. When I woke the next morning and washed and dressed for Early Communion, my skin was no longer the familiar, neutral integument, feeling the warmth of the water in the washbasin, the softness of my flannel shirt, the stiff cloth of the green tweeds in which I looked like a sprig of the squirearchy, a cadet colonel: it had its own song and moved with the body in a kind of descant.

They were warm voices, though, voices that rose from the body's ground bass and sank back again, and that's what I felt as I knelt in the chancel, such a warmth wrapping me round that it would have been impossible not to give thanks.

It was several days before the descant faded, the sense of procession, as if I were being initiated into the Mysteries.

Beneath it, I was in an unholy mess. Koki had finished with her Saturday date, as she had assured me she would. I felt sorry for him when he presented himself at the back door, a slightly older man, all spruced-up for his evening out and thinking he was about to outwit the lines of disappointment that were already gathering around the eyes.

Really I should have escorted Anna further down the aisle at the Odeon. We should never have sat in the back row. But then I would not have come into such sudden knowledge. And I would not be wrapped in this strange harmony.

One moment I thought I was with Anna, the next with Koki. Anna passed me upstairs with the laundry basket and the smell of freshly washed towels, so redolent of her skin under the sweater, triggered a clammy embrace between the airing cupboard doors. I went down to the yard and there was Koki, slim and poised in her fitted hacking jacket, asking me if I would like to ride with her over to Bushey Park. That morning the back roads of Esher and Thames Ditton were uncannily empty. As the horses carried us past a backdrop of suburban trees, cherries and copper beeches, finials of porch roofs and sweeping ends of gables, we were the romantic leads in a black-and-white film, the only silhouette in each other's sky.

The revived romance lasted for my first term at Oxford. Koki came to visit me and we hired two horses from Stella Aldwinkle, an eccentric lady who ran her stables when she was not working on a philosophical proof of the existence of God. I even took Koki to the Merton Christmas Ball, where she wriggled and glowered in a gown stiff with brocade. But when I came home for the Christmas vacation, we fell back into the old pattern: the eager suitor and the froward belle.

One day at lunch she cut me dead. There was a party coming up, a New Year's party. That evening I told her I would be going to the party with Anna.

I expected Anna to be triumphant. I expected us to be necking as passionately as the impromptu couples all around us. I remember one of the stable girls murmuring to herself as she broke off between kisses, 'Oh feel, feel!' But Anna had brought a half-bottle of gin: I sat bored while she leant against me and sucked at the bottle.

Was she feeling rotten now she had pushed Koki out? Afraid now she had what she wanted? Or was it simply the extra burden of guilt that girls had to carry in those days? The first time in the van she had said to me, 'In Denmark we have a phrase, sympathy prostitute. She doesn't do it for money, just out of sympathy. I think that's what I must be, a sympathy prostitute.'

'Well,' she said that night in her attic room, 'now there are two red stains on that beautiful white dress my mother gave me when I left home.' Colourless, I thought. The second stain would be colourless. Just the smell of gin.

Then I heard a tread on the twisting stair, the heavy breath of someone climbing the narrow turn. My father was coming to check that everyone was back from the party.

I huddled down between Anna's legs. Her room-mates froze under their blankets. On the edge of anger my father would snuff the air like a bull, drawing a breath so deep that it shook him. We felt the first weight of that as he entered the room and stopped, each breath drawn slowly and deliberately, as if in suspicion. This was back before words, which my father hardly used at such moments: it was animal presence, the breathing of the dominant male.

He turned and we heard every creak of the stair as he went down, every step of the search below, the house so stilled by fear that the scuff of his slippers on the kitchen tiles seemed just outside on the landing.

He came back up, straight to Anna's bed and pulled back the blankets, exposing me in my huddle.

'What on earth do you think you're doing?'

Immediately he seemed comical in his anger. Was this what I had been crouching from under each slow, searching breath? This man who stood on the landing and stared at me, his eyes straining out of their pouches, his chest heaving so that all the loose skin on his face shuddered?

In the morning I went downstairs braced for a confrontation. My mother was weeping at the ironing board, the tears in a helpless flow as she worked her way through a stack of shirts and blouses.

Sometimes, when I talked to my mother, I would glimpse the face she must have had when she left school on completing her matriculation. For her, as for my father, university had been out of the question. She became a lab technician at Bemax, a firm that made nutritional supplements. She always insisted that we pronounce 'vitamins' with a long 'i' because it came from 'vital amins'. Once I came across a book she must have bought as a young woman, a tattered wartime Penguin edition of Freud's *Psychopathology of Sex in Everyday Life*, half hidden on a high shelf in the house in Surbiton, alongside *The Intelligent Woman's Guide to Socialism*. But I found it impossible to locate the young scientist who might have read that book. The face I glimpsed was younger, the face of an aspiring schoolgirl, turned to me with an eagerness I found painful.

'No one', she once said to me, 'can know what a mother feels for her son.' But beneath that feeling lay an unrealised life, the sixth-former's dream I had come to embody as I grew up. Which was why successive daughters of old school friends were presented to me as they came of age. And why the tears fell so helplessly that morning.

She sacked Anna, saying she could not bear to look at her.

# PART THREE

## Oxford   Barcarès   Amsterdam
## London   Surrey

## 1963–1968

. . . but why did you leave your father's house?
  To seek misfortune.

James Joyce, Ulysses

*No hay mensaje, hay mensajeros, y eso es el mensaje.*
There is no message, there are only messengers, and
that's the message.

Julio Cortázar, Rayuela (Hopscotch)

The college clock struck every quarter of an hour. It sounded companionable enough at a quarter past, the fall of the chime almost casual. It was a confidential briefing, a word in your ear.

Deferential, too, was the double chime at the half-hour, struck lightly, as between scholars and gentlemen. *The Odyssey* open in front of me, Autenreith's *Homeric Dictionary* to my left hand and E. V. Rieu's Penguin translation to my right, I bent my head to the oar and cut, phrase by phrase, through the wine-dark sea. I had taken up my place on the benches, taken up a stroke unbroken for seven hundred years, and this was the beat of the timekeeper.

But who could work to the three-quarter chime? Or quell the doubt it left in the air? The double chime completed, the notes began to descend again, and descend differently. You followed them down, you could not help but follow them down, until there was a pause in the cadence, a fractional pause. They dropped to a note struck harder with the hammer, a note ominous with mortality. You were left with the gap, the gap between the interval you had been expecting and the darker note that came.

*Redeem the time!* the gap said. But what could redeem it? Not my notes, which were so complete as to be a form of superstition: every grammatical oddity was logged, and then logged time and again through the three books of Homer I had to read every week, because I dared not leave any instances out. The cross-references ran down the pages, *fingers crossed! fingers crossed! fingers crossed!*

The first *tings* came from the University College clock, which did not so much strike the hour as dispense it. They marked the last quiet, a walled garden of quiet, so intimately was that last minute paced and known before the hammers began to move through their relay to the full chime. The final notes climbed to another pause, a pause in which doubt became a mathematical impossibility, so inevitable was their progression. It was a showman's pause, the college summoning up its seven hundred years before the tenor bell struck and sent the hours out across the city in their academic dress.

Impossible not to feel dwarfed as that great procession swept overhead. Sometimes I wanted to become part of it, to work in romantic obscurity as I elaborated some new insight, like Milman Parry, whose papers, published as a young man in Paris and not understood until years after his early death, had transformed our reading of Homer. And sometimes I heard it as an assertion, Merton making its voice heard before Great Tom began to toll from Christ Church, and felt an odd kind of loneliness beneath it, as if I were just grist to the mill.

The hours were silently marked in the fall of sunlight on the other side of the quad. In early afternoon, when my daily stint was still ahead of me, some three hundred lines of unfamiliar usages and steady, hexametric swell, the sun was still high enough to slant over the corner of Fellows' Quad and through the wrought-iron gates of the Fellows' Garden. The far side of the quad glistened white, as if it had been built of York rather than Cotswold stone. The lead lights flashed on the study windows and in each one there was a long blind drawn against the sun.

By mid-afternoon, the blinds were beginning to rise as the shadow in which I sat, chill but undazzled, tilted across the quad. I would glance up to see it sniffing at the staircase opposite, nosing from step to step until its angle fell across the sharply pointed Gothic Revival arch. Become absorbed once more and find it in possession of the first floor, a line of shadow ruled across the flat stone between the bay windows. Derek's blind was up and I could see the anvil gleam of his forehead, bent over the same books of Homer.

By late afternoon all the blinds were up. The sun had sunk to an upward slant on the topmost courses of stone, a last reach of sunlight in which I could see that even Stubbins, as we called St Alban's Quad, stiff and starchy Stubbins was built of the same stone as Mob Quad, Oxford's oldest quadrangle, which had weathered to the colour of groundsel, the long seed heads my Uncle Fred used to give to his canaries. All it needed was another six centuries' exposure to the air.

The November dusk was already over the roof, a martial blue. But there was a resonance now in the sandstone, a steadiness of colour that seemed to hold back the chimes, inserting a moment of eternity before the hammers struck. The afternoon passed as if somehow it had been redeemed in its passing.

Behind me the electric fire, a barony of embossed tin, burned on one of its three bars. There was security in study, in switching on a second bar to make toast when I had reached the last fifty lines. And a comradeship in seeing Derek's small figure rise from his desk on the other side of the quad, unplug the kettle on its side table and fill it out of sight in the bedroom. 'Is that a judo move you practise every afternoon?' someone from the floor above me once asked him. It was the little twist he did at the back of the room, two hands swilling a shadow as he warmed the pot.

But there was a contrary impulse, an instinct that took me out, the moment my work was done, into the early dark. I headed up

151

Magpie Lane, the passageway to the High, as most people were heading down it, denser darks that glanced up as I jinked past and seemed to be glancing out of themselves, all the lines of preoccupation caught in the light from the street lamp. Behind them, pitched against the blue-black of the sky, were the libraries they were leaving, the floodlit dome of the Radcliffe Camera and the long cornice of the Bodleian, so serene in its umber that a Tuscan afternoon might have descended on it rather than a North Atlantic night. But the night was there, a mass you sensed rather than saw, blacking the blue of the upglare. One evening I stood under Hertford's Bridge of Sighs, staring up because I was sure I had seen some dark current pass beyond its lit lantern, some movement out in that unglimpsable gulf.

Buildings were floodlit because they had just been restored, the scab of coal smoke lifted off the stone in a six-month soak. Some we still had to skirt on our way to lectures, stepping out into the road past screens of three-ply that gave off a distinct chill. There was the drizzle of hosepipes and skeins of water ran into the gutter.

There were almost no faculty buildings then. Going to lectures gave us something like a taxi driver's knowledge, forcing us to seek out rooms in obscure college extensions we would never have found otherwise. On the way I made discoveries, places I would return to in my own time. Some were obvious enough: New College cloisters, Lincoln's innermost quad. Others were incidental, such as Brasenose Lane, which I invariably took, relishing its cobbled width after the Turl's narrow, crowded pavement. But I walked them all in an exaltation that never quite faded, never became indifference or hurry. It was a kind of betrothal. I knew how ephemeral I was in the history of these streets. Fresh faces arrived in their thousands each autumn and took that corner from the Turl. But I took it as if sheer concentration could leave me incised on the air.

Sometimes, as I worked on a passage from Homer, an image would come back to me of a stone wall or a handsomely framed doorway or a hollowed flagstone, some detail I might have seen on my way to lectures. It would shade itself in beneath the phrase I was poring over, as if there were something to be teased out by walking there again. Sometimes I felt that the city itself was the concentration and I was the thought it was trying to form.

But then parts of it were built for thought. To turn from the High into Oriel Square and then into the cobbled preserve of Merton Street was to feel the business of the city ebb away as the noise of the traffic died. Merton was built on the old city wall and beyond lay the wide silence of Christ Church Meadows. To reach the focus of this quiet you had to cross Merton's Front Quad, which was possessed of a strange emptiness, like a parade ground after the battalion had marched away. But turn right under the arch and you came out into Mob Quad, whose plain walls, low doorways and small windows seemed to preserve the university in its first impulse. All but monastic in their enclosure, they contained a library that would have been acceptable to Abelard and rooms that might have housed Chaucer's Clerke of Oxenford, who

> Was levere have at his beddes heed
> Twenty bookes, clad in blak or reed,
> Of Aristotle and his philosophie,
> Than robes riche, or fithele, or gay sautrie.

Sometimes I would try to dispel this impression, reminding myself that proportions that looked humble now may not have looked so humble in 1264. And wasn't the mystique simply the effect of the Cotswold stone, of the extraordinary depths of its patina, where gold was slowly turning brown? But the sense of crossing some subtle threshold persisted. Entering Mob felt quite different from entering Fellows', which was as handsome a quadrangle as you could wish to see. Fellows' took a quiet pride in itself and expected you to do the same. None of that was in the air when they built Mob. Mob looked through itself. Its focus was elsewhere.

Derek was from Merseyside, a wing of Brylcreemed black hair over his broad white forehead, and street wary in a way the rest of us found amusing. Once, when we were caught up in an argument outside a pub, he lit two cigarettes and handed one to me. 'If it comes to a fight,' he exhaled in my ear, 'jab it in the bugger's eye!'

He was intellectually wary too. Most of us talked in a fluster of abstractions, a kind of polysyllabic stammer. Derek often stopped short of words, delivering himself of an 'aah', a note of such vehement caution, in the dark, lower register of his Scouse vibrato, that we would all pause, feeling suddenly specious. Or a snort would herald some scabrous aside, some skirl of black humour.

Peter, the other classicist with whom I struck up an immediate friendship, could hardly have been more different. Peter was Hungarian, the stepson of a leading Hungarian playwright, Julius Hay, who had been imprisoned after the 1956 Uprising. Peter was smuggled out to his grandmother in Hampstead. He had won a scholarship to Haileybury and his English was faultless, with just the merest trace of an accent. But you had only to look at the poise of the carefully barbered head on the slight body, at the angle of black moustache and the trimmed line of chinstrap beard, to know that you were meeting a member of a distinctively Central European caste, the intelligentsia.

Each of us was making an attempt at sophistication. Derek had a smoking jacket, made by his mother from a black and brown plaid so that it looked like a cut-off dressing gown. I had a set of coffee cups from Prinknash Abbey, small black cups of an angular elegance that might have materialised from a print by Aubrey

Beardsley. Into these I poured Viennese coffee with fig seasoning, pounded in the percolator until it was like drinking burnt toffee. But Peter had the manner, a way of leaning back in his chair, or against the chaise longue he inherited in his second year when we had the choice of rooms, cedilla of beard flourished against the light as he read out a phrase from one of Mozart's letters or let his fingers fall with a cadence from Schubert's *Trout Quintet*.

What redeemed the manner was its playfulness, the hint of self-parody. As someone who had grown up in the business, Peter was alert to its snares and delusions, to just how easy it was to go off-track. I would float a name, airing my knowledge of the latest talent to be reviewed in the *Observer*, and Peter would confide his misgivings, his concern at the course that career was taking. As we sauntered down the steps after Hall, our scholar's gowns shrugged back and our hands in our pockets, we knew that we were canny enough to avoid any such mistake. Like two Homeric gods watching the battle below, we seemed infinitely far-sighted.

If I had the coffee cups, John had a proper China teapot, its handle woven from split bamboo, and small, handleless, saucerless cups that looked, to our untravelled eyes, more like egg cups. The only China tea I knew was jasmine, ordering which was part of the courtship ritual of taking a girl to a Chinese restaurant, the final grace note after the lychees, whereas John had little screws of grey leaf that were called Gunpowder and dark, kippery twists of Lapsang Souchong, teas he bought, as if from the local agent of the Silk Road, from an austere Pole in Oxford market.

He had also built his own hi-fi, housing the components in a long pine case into which he had cut a discreet hole for a small metal switch. The speakers faced the half-circle of chairs, their oblongs of black mesh as impassive as cult stones. As the tea steeped in its china basket, we would listen to John Williams on the Spanish guitar, the notes falling, at the low volume the speakers made possible, like a skitter of rain across the windows. Or relish the sudden deepening of Georges Brassens's voice, the roll on the 'r' like a recovery of appetite as, shrugging off his landlord, his boss and everyone else who had been giving him grief, he thought of his date: *j'ai rendez-vous avec vous*.

John was reading Philosophy, Politics and Economics but his rooms were on the same staircase as mine. When first invited to tea, I had squatted, as we all did, to look at the books on the bookshelf, running my eye over the thick spines of the set books and focusing on the brief spectrum of paperbacks at the end, the area of free choice where I had *Dr Zhivago* and *The Alexandria Quartet*. There was a thin black book with the title reversed in white on the spine: *HOWL*. The first trump, the revolutionary long poem that had been a legend until then, not to be found within the modest confines of the Penguin *Corso Ferlinghetti Ginsberg*. John had the original, the City Lights edition, brought back that summer from West Berlin. It only took the admission that he wrote himself for us to be committed to the scrutiny of each other's handwritten manuscripts, one of us in a high-revving suspense, the whole engine block rocking, the self shaken down to the last rivet, while the other puzzled over the phrases, weighed the rhythms and sought for the lenient word to convey the exact shade of disappointment.

John became part of the group, his tall figure our marker for which of the long tables to colonise in Hall. He lived in Oxford and insisted we should hurry from Hall to the Scala, the old cinema halfway down Walton Street that showed concentrated seasons of foreign films, changing them every couple of days. One week we would be watching the knight in *The Seventh Seal*, cropped white hair and lit cheekbones bowed against a dark sky as he prayed to the god he feared did not exist outside his hunger for him. The next we would be listening as the gentle, doomed poet of *La Strada* picked up a stone off the beach and explained that everything depended on whether it was part of some greater pattern, whether it was held, as it were, in God's eye, or was simply a stone, simply the debris of a geological event.

At such moments we would be reading the subtitles and you could sense the cerebration of row upon row of seats, the focus of our educated suspicion. But mostly we were all eyes, the images replaying in our heads as we walked back up Walton Street: the charge of the Teutonic knights across the frozen lake in *Alexander Nevsky*, the ice breaking under them and one long cloak dragged across it, wrapping itself round a floe and gripping before it was pulled under; or the moment in *Ashes and Diamonds* when the girl came to Cybulski's room and we saw the blossoming of desire, the lit cloud of her skin moulded across the screen.

Any student of Animal Behaviour would have been able to read our stance, the submissive, forward lean with which we asked our questions, and the distance we kept, holding to our little round tables while Ted Hughes leaned against the bar. He had just read to the University Poetry Society, his broad shoulders hunched over the book, his introductions terse to the point of impatience: 'The next poem is called "Otter". It's about . . . an otter.' The poems seemed to build like floodwater and break over the room, so that it came as something of a surprise when Craig Raine ventured, 'You don't actually read them that well, do you?' Ted Hughes must have been surprised too but he didn't show it: 'Well, you get fed up with them towards the end.' We asked him whether he had published anything at Cambridge and he said, 'No, it's difficult to write anything that's any good before the age of about twenty-four or twenty-five. There are so many abstractions whirling around in your head at university. You have to wait for all that to die down.' Robert Graves was the Professor of Poetry at that time, renowned for taking his poems

157

through thirty drafts. We asked Ted Hughes whether he redrafted: 'When I have to. But the best ones are the ones that come straight out. Don't you find that?' None of us answered – we were stunned to be asked, as if there might be some sense to us after all, some relationship between the elemental music we had just heard and our rushes of words to the head.

Mine seemed to be born of the body's rush, of the impulse that took me out into the early dark. Northern Europeans quicken at the onset of winter, as if the blood needed the cold to race against, and I would walk across the city just to see it embattled, its floodlit roofs ranged against the night sky and the dusk suddenly thickening in the streets, a palpable dark through which I flitted like a disembodied spirit, or not even that: just a perception, a race of perception on the race of the blood. Mostly it was wordless. And I kept it wordless if I could. But every so often a phrase would shape itself, Mephistophelean in its promise, and whisper that its syllables held the key to all things visible and invisible.

It was Ted Hughes's name on the cover that prompted me to buy his selection from Keith Douglas, the finest poet of the Second World War, who had gone into the army from his second year at Merton. His was one of the names chiselled into the wall of the arch that led from Front Quad into Fellows' Quad. It was strange to see the chill strokes of those letters, 'K. C. Douglas Foresters', while I carried his voice in my head, so alive in its control, pacing his anger down to the last line and a bit of 'Egypt', '*My God, / the king of this country must be proud*', or keeping his compassion, not for the dead gunner who had hit his tank, but for the girl whose '*dishonoured picture*' he finds '*in the gunpit spoil*', the girl '*who has put:* **Steffi. Vergissmeinicht** / *in a copybook gothic script.*' His voice was personal in a way that Ted Hughes's wasn't and I wanted to write with that degree of tension, with a strength won from difficulty.

Just how shaky my control was became apparent as soon as I started to read at the small, informal workshops John Wain, Peter Levi and C. A. Trypanis hosted at the end of each term. I launched into my new poem, emboldened by the fact that it had an echo of Keith Douglas's *'Remember me when I am dead / and simplify me when I'm dead'*:

> Do not ask me in
> under a hall lantern.
> Go out into the cold.
> Watch from over the road
> the way I walk,
> and for whom I step aside.

But then came the point where I had to look at the second person with the same detachment:

> As I shall not be held by your eyes' long looks,
> nor trace the flicks of your pixie lips.

The room resonated as John Wain threw back his head and laughed, the only person I have actually heard go Ho! Ho! Ho! like a fairy-tale giant.

'Oh dear,' he said, wiping the tears from his eyes, 'and this one was going so well! There was something really strong and individual coming through. And then – what was it? – your pixie lips?' and the ceiling shook once more.

Impossible to resent that laughter: not just because I had, as we say, asked for it, but because it was so characteristic of John Wain, whose responses were wonderfully unguarded. One evening there was an open invitation to his cottage at Wolvercote to meet David Wright and John Heath-Stubbs. Derek and I went and perched on two upright

chairs, feeling ourselves on the edge of bohemia because John's wife
Eirian was sitting there in a low-cut black sweater, smoking a cigar.
Larkin's *Whitsun Weddings* had just come out and John was musing
on the little poem 'Days', wondering how it was that it could move
from lines of simple enquiry, lines he might have written himself,
*'Where can we live but days?'* to an ending that was pure Larkin:

> Ah, solving that question
> Brings the priest and the doctor
> In their long coats
> Running over the fields.

C. A. Trypanis, Professor of Byzantine Greek and the kindliest
of the workshop leaders, was also there but had to leave early. No
sooner had he made his excuses and bade us goodnight than John
exclaimed, 'The man who has just gone out of that door has written
the greatest lyric sequence since the *Duino Elegies*. It's all about his
childhood in Greece and it has lines like *where time flows like the
shadow of a fish*', and he gave a little groan of involuntary admiration. 'People laugh at him now: but in a few years' time they'll all
be saying that they knew him.'

We duly listened when *The Elegies of a Glass Adonis* were broadcast on the Third Programme and begged a typescript from
Professor Trypanis. Some years later I came across the Faber edition,
*The Glass Adonis*, which I still have, and it *is* a fine sequence, its
restrained passion driven by the early death of Trypanis's wife,
Rania: but is it the greatest since the *Duino Elegies*? Even at the
time we sensed that this was an animating hyperbole, a rallying cry
in what was virtually a group manifesto. This was the moment
when John broke away from the short, neatly constructed poems
of his first style and brought out his freewheeling sequence,
*Wildtrack*. And when Peter Levi, who had returned from Greece

fed up, as he put it, with the way that he was writing and everyone else in England was writing, embarked on his surreal sequence, *Pancakes for the Queen of Babylon*, which he read to us several years before it was published. One image from it lodged in my memory:

> And one hoof of a star printing the dark
> is ringing like a nail of a new metal.

That became another model of how to write, so surprising in its movement and yet so exact.

The angel of chance had laid another trail, a review in the *Sunday Times*, the paper my parents took, that led me to the ICA, the Institute of Contemporary Arts, membership of which, cheap enough for a student, brought me a cyclostyled bulletin every month. Invariably, on the last half-page, there was a note of who was playing at Ronnie Scott's.

In my first Easter vacation it was Stan Getz, one of whose LPs, selected from his first sessions as a leader, I had bought, in the unlikeliest turn of this trail, as a Special Offer from my parents' other point of vantage on the world, the *Reader's Digest*. It was not, as it happened, my favourite record, the blend of his tenor saxophone with Jimmy Raney's guitar sounding filter-tipped after the fierce little roll-ups of Charlie Parker I had found on that 45. But the name was enough to impel me over the fields one evening to catch the train to Waterloo.

I had known Soho since I was fourteen, my first licensed adventure being a trip with two school friends to the 2 Is, the coffee bar where Tommy Steele was discovered, and to the split-level bar, the Heaven and Hell, where we drank our coffee in Heaven and packed into the cellar of Hell to watch a singer with a rich, bluesy voice and an unassuming body shape, Cuddly Dudley. So I walked fast, eyes down, past the touts on the pavement outside the strip clubs, past the doorways with their hand-printed cards below each bell, and down steep steps to the cellar in Gerrard Street, where I bent to the doorkeeper in his cubicle, a thin young man with black hair and black-rimmed glasses who looked as serious as one of the clerks of Death in Cocteau's *Orphée*.

LP covers glimmered on the wall beside the bar. Blow-ups of reviews lifted their frayed typefaces into the half-light, speaking of *Jazz Samba*, which sounded odd to me, and of a revolutionary album with strings, which sounded even odder. Led to a table a good way round the half-circle, I ordered a whisky mac, which I drank at Christmas and was the only drink I knew.

When Ronnie Scott came to the microphone to announce the Stan Tracey Trio, I thought Stan Getz must have brought them over to play with him and focused my attention on the pianist, whom I was now seeing as a New Yorker, hair swept back like one of the Jets in *West Side Story* and sharp face set like a street fighter. He kept a knife on the piano, though it was a kitchen knife he used for running repairs, slipping the blade down the front of a loose key and jerking it back into place. The offending key was just to his left, in some home register he must have needed, but his hands were continually picking notes from the far ends of the keyboard, releasing unexpected resonances and setting up descants the ear had not imagined until then. Sparse as the notes were, they made the piano seem limitless.

Ronnie Scott returned to the microphone to introduce 'someone we've always wanted to have at the club . . . the best tenor saxophonist in the world', applause rose to the occasion, and a suit ran under the spotlight as if it had silver in its weave. He stood well out from the rhythm section, fingers poised over the tenor's levers and discs as the applause turned to appraisal. What sound would the best tenor saxophonist in the world make? A sound so pure the metal seemed to forget itself, to dissolve into the voice of the reed. We listened breathless, as if between us we had to sustain that perfect control. And then the phrase he had been shaping lifted away, ancient and elusive as a piper's lament.

The control, I saw, was in the stance, in the working of the shoulders as much as the pressure of the fingertips or the closing of the mouth round the reed. The saxophone itself was almost incidental: the real instrument was Getz's body moving round it, the shoulders closing as they shaped a note, the small of the back flexing to keep the column of breath constant. I noticed the angling of the breath, the way he brought a ballad down into the depths of the horn but kept it clear of vibrato until the final note, which he would push, shoulders squared and neck muscles braced, so that it touched off the brass of the bell. It came back as a chrysanthemum of sound, streaks of resonance that seemed to grow in perfect symmetry. In the semi-darkness of the club they were almost visible.

I returned to Ronnie Scott's whenever I could, and quickly realised that Stan Tracey, far from being a visiting New Yorker, was the house pianist. I found myself as intent on his playing as I was on the roll-call of stars he accompanied, leaning forward over my little table in the silence he left at the start of his solo, the rhythm falling in soundless beats out of which his right hand would find some quite unexpected path. The left hand would follow like an earth tremor, its geological events hardly sketched in before the right had leapt to another brink. Even when the pulse felt rock solid, the cadence so inevitable that I was held to its descent, silence would complete it, firm as a cut step. The right hand was away, on another goat's path.

My skin kept the memory of its initiation, the astonishment of it so complete that it instilled a kind of patience. Which was just as well: there were only five women's colleges at Oxford then and as freshmen we could hardly compete. But we did pick up a tip for our second year: to try the Oxfam lunch on the first Friday of term, when the freshers had just arrived.

One o'clock had barely struck before I was poised with my plate of bread and cheese, talking to a girl whose long dark hair broke becomingly over black-rimmed glasses. That was what had drawn me across the room: long, straight hair, the Jean Shrimpton look. That and the glimpse of a green miniskirt and black lacy stockings.

She was a first-year chemist, which meant she was spared my literary allusions, multiplying like the eyes of a peacock's tail. We talked of home and family, and found we had something in common, one of those casual links attraction seizes on as a secret sign. She came from Wiltshire, where my father happened to be stationed during the war, and where I was born. Not that I remember anything of it. But my parents took us once to the village where they had been billeted, the houses spaced as in a dream, on wide skirts of grass without a pavement between them. I must have been about twelve at the time, surprised when their old landlady suddenly pulled me to her, in a way that would never have happened in Surbiton: 'Come here, my little bit of Wiltshire! Oh, aren't you going to break some hearts!'

That lunch was held in a room lit by the October sun but I emerged from it as from a darkroom, with exposures of the sheen on a curtain of black hair, the rim of light on a dark eye. I kept glancing at them, checking that they were to my satisfaction. The next night I was taking her to the Scala.

The Scala, the Moulin Rouge, the Playhouse: we were out almost every night, Su's hair brilliantly black against the magenta of the soft leather coat she had found in a sale in Bristol – a little ahead of its time, like the spelling of her name. She had dropped the 'e', convinced it made her look buxom and apple-cheeked, a proper Wiltshire maid, whereas she was slim and pale, the nose fine-boned and a little tentative, cheeks sloping back from the lips I was soon to immortalise as pixie lips. By which I meant, I think, their puckish corners. It was her lips I would reach out to during our long goodnights at the college gate, running the tip of a finger along them – just as the tip of her finger would move across the arch of my eyebrow and down over my cheekbone.

The images of her I carried in my head had changed. The sheen had gone, the fencing lights in the dark eyes. What I saw was her inward look, the lips just parted in an uncertainty that drew me more powerfully than any provocation. What I carried with me were sensations, the successive textures of her skin under the thick mesh of the navy-blue sweater she wore on Sundays, when the cinemas were closed and we lay on the floor of my attic room in Mob, listening to records. We would start, inevitably, with *Kind of Blue*, intimacies I knew so well that the first notes of each solo would form in my head before they rose from the needle. We would build up to *Blues with Bechet*, which stretched across two LPs: eighty minutes of roughhouse gave us the cover for each stealthy transition, from the first cool my fingers met as they slipped under the sweater, the inlaid cream of the small of the back, to the india paper over the ribs as they climbed with a sense of peril; from the firm cotton band of the bra, so steadfast in its modesty, to the fine line I ran as two sensations passed across the fingers at once, the film of the cotton and the skin of the breast.

By the time Bechet was launching into 'Revolutionary Blues', the bra was unhooked, its shucked pod on the back of the fingers as they took the speedway curve to the dell of the nipple. It was addictive, that curve, the skin sliding under the palm as if glossed by the touch, and my hand would circle lighter and lighter, faster and faster until the breast seemed to glisten and the palm was in orbit. Our eyes were closed unless I glimpsed her in a kiss, her pupils flooding through narrowed lids and the light flashing off their dark. Sight was in the fingers and direction in the skin, its surface so intent we were held to it whatever the tempo overhead, whether Pleasant Joe was demanding 'hot biscuits with my pork chops' or Hot Lips Page threatening 'blood on the moon'.

We were clenched together from the waist down, my black cords against Su's blue jeans, but that was blind, that was the id. If my fingers dropped to the ridged denim and started to smooth it over the hips, a hand would descend like the claw over the prizes at the funfair and lift them, with a precision never seen on any fairground, back above the waist. For some eight months, until the evening halfway through the summer term when I finally wrestled the jeans off her and Su conceded, 'I always knew that I would go to bed with you one day – but each time I thought it would be another day,' the fingers became the adepts of the skin, its adepts or its acolytes, so devout was my desire.

There is a Latin poem, '*Pervigilium Veneris*', the 'Vigil of Venus', which describes how the whole earth is quickened by desire. That may have been in my mind because I remember Peter Jay reading his translation of it and the repeated music of the refrain, for which he had found a lovely natural flow in English:

Tomorrow let there be love for him who has never loved and love for the lover tomorrow.

What I remember quite clearly is suddenly glimpsing the presence of Venus in the Latin verb *venerari*, to worship, to revere, and realising that reverence and desire must spring from the same root: we revere what we desire, and desire teaches us reverence. I rushed to the Bodleian and checked in the biggest dictionaries I could find. My instinct was right: reverence and desire did go back to the same root in Sanskrit.

For days this discovery coursed through me like a physical energy. And in a sense it was physical: I was breaking the mind-forg'd manacles, unbinding the briars from my joys and desires. There were moments of dizzying ambition when I thought that if I could only uncover Venus in a poem, two thousand years of Christianity might be reversed. And moments when I seemed to be standing just inside a temple in a diffused, reddish-brown light, an earthly light rather than a heavenly light, but one of great depth and calm.

My fingers adored her skin. I could have thought of it in English if I hadn't been so used to thinking in Latin. But the word 'adored' never came into my head, perhaps because it was not helpless desire. I was always aware of my own calculation. That was why conscience assailed me when we said goodnight at the college gate, why my eyes were 'tactful in their redoubt'. And why I had needed that glimpse of Venus, that licensing of desire.

Though desire was already there, in the skin, the notions in my head not quite up to date with what I could feel under my fingers. I once apologised to Su for the fact that there was nowhere I could take her on a Sunday, as if the Lord's Day Observance Society were ultimately responsible for her seduction. 'I like Sundays,' she said quietly.

At the branch of Moss Bros on the High where we were discreetly guided through the male mysteries of hiring a dinner jacket – Single-breasted or double-breasted, Sir? And will you be requiring a dress shirt? Cufflinks? A cummerbund? – the different types of detachable collar were displayed on a board leaning against the wall. It was there I saw a wing collar – rarely worn these days, Sir, except by lawyers of the old school – and liked the flare of it, the hint of flamboyance. There was something submissive in the wearing of a tie that the wing collar seemed to subvert, turning it into a rhetorical flourish. I bought one and took to wearing it with a dark-blue corduroy jacket, tightly fitting grey trousers and the only tie I actually liked, a charcoal-grey slim jim.

The ensemble was completed when I saw a silver-topped cane in the window of an antique shop, the silver intricately embossed so that the rounded top seemed to emerge from the petals of a rose. It was rounded to fit into the palm of the hand but I did not grasp it like a walking stick, I walked the cane, taking long strides and letting it swing between forefinger and thumb, carrying the rose head into the world as if it might recompose it.

To step out of the college gate, in the daytime at least, was to step into self-consciousness. We had to wear gowns to lectures and even the look we adopted for the street, gown flung over one shoulder, was self-consciously casual. At five minutes to the hour when lectures ended and dons emerged on to the narrow pavements, strips of paper fluttering conclusively from the books clutched to their chests, we would flood in their wake, talking to each other over the heads of the tourists as if we had to stay in role. But I had just made matters much worse for myself. Hair swept back so that it flared off the forehead, I had become a procession, conscious of my every step from the moment someone's curiosity locked on to me at the end of the street to the unspoken challenge of our passing, my carefully enacted nonchalance under their close scrutiny. And yet I persisted, determined there should be a flourish of some sort, even if I were the only one making it.

Inwardly, I was much less assured. My own poems sounded hit-and-miss beside those of John Birtwhistle, who came up in my third year and stunned everyone at the very first workshop he attended by reading 'Village Carpentry', a poem so well made that it went beyond craftsmanship and achieved eloquence:

> . . . these go under the grass:
> heavy oak for the parish wealth

(polished furniture-grain and rays),
elm and linseed for the poor.

Elm forgets faster than oak,
painted names before gold-leaf,
calico is a harsher bed
than swansdown. The scent of Death
fate orders in advance.

And then there was Michael Hewlings, whose lines were so relaxed they could be mistaken for conversation and yet so artful they stayed in the mind, the ear replaying their ebb and flow like music, especially the ironic sound pattern at the end of 'Lord', his imagining of old age:

The walls you walk around
with half an eye upon the goings on inside
are thinner than they were.

From the tower you have looked
on the receding lands.

He stood tall to read, lifting his voice and phrasing each line carefully, and that last line was spoken with particular care, 'the' given the first of three long 'e's that stretched in sound even as they diminished in meaning. It was the first time I had heard someone of my own age use his voice like a violin bow, drawing out from the words exactly the sound he wanted.

By my third year I had exchanged the three-quarter chime for a back lane behind Walton Street, its stillness broken twice a day by the girls issuing from the gates of a small factory at the far end, their shrieks and shrills suddenly in full voice under my windows and as suddenly gone. The middle window was a cottage window but the outer windows were porthole windows, which gave this large room over a garage the look of a houseboat moored in mid-air. Behind it was a small kitchen that doubled as bathroom, a long shelf covered in oilcloth lifting to reveal the bath. There was just room for a toilet before you came to the flat's Yale-locked door, its gloss white opening on to whitewashed stairs.

The kitchen window looked down on to the brief back garden of my landlord's house, part of a four-storey Georgian terrace that was all front, a chequered path between rose bushes and a flight of steps up to the front door. For me it was a front of another kind. Undergraduates had to live in registered lodgings, with a resident landlord or landlady, and my registered address was 10 Walton Street. But I had my own entrance from Walton Lane and a degree of freedom that was quite unusual for those days. As I sat over my books in the mild melancholy that comes of prolonged study, I would listen for the ring of Su's stilettos on the alley's stone setts, such impetus in her stride that for a moment I would be lifted above her life and mine, and hear only an energy finding its place, incisive as the notes of a blackbird.

My own energies seemed to be in abeyance. I had switched to English after Classical Mods, the exams we sat at Easter in the second year. My scholarship was for four years, which gave me seven terms to read for English Finals, just as if I had taken English Prelims. At long last I was free to lose myself in *The Prelude*. I was even being taught by John Jones, who had written on Wordsworth and was writing on Keats. And yet I felt a sense of displacement, of having to mark time. I did not realise how deep this feeling went until I was introduced to Edmund Blunden, the newly elected Professor of Poetry, and took the chance to ask him what he remembered of Keith Douglas, whose tutor he had been. His impression was that Douglas himself, had he survived the war, would have made a good college tutor. I simply could not marry that to the voice I knew from the poems, to what Ted Hughes called 'his impatient, razor energy'. I imagined a Graham Greene figure, restlessly travelling the world but without the recourse to mystery, the escape clause of Catholicism. I was much more impressed when Robert Graves, Blunden's predecessor as Professor of Poetry, told us that Cecil Taylor, an astonishing jazz pianist, the most advanced of the avant-garde, had come to play for him one evening in New York. He had played non-stop for an hour and a half until his voluminous black sweater was drenched in sweat – only to be mugged on the way home and have his arm broken.

The sounds of New York floated out over the back lane at night: Coltrane's 'India' with Eric Dolphy's mesmeric entry on bass clarinet; Archie Shepp's rampage through 'Prelude to a Kiss', its tenderness won from excess. Possibilities were accumulating on the long planks I had set up on bricks as bookshelves: slim Faber volumes of George Barker I had bought for a knock-down price when a bookshop on the High closed down; back numbers of *The Review* that had hung on a wire rack in the doorway, the Black Mountain issue, the Sylvia Plath issue. I found another model in the opening of 'Mary's Song' where sound pattern and visual image fused as perfectly as anything in Hopkins and lifted the poem, in just four short lines, on to another level:

> The Sunday lamb cracks in its fat.
> The fat
> Sacrifices its opacity . . .
>
> A window, holy gold.

But glimpses such as this came fitfully, in a truant ten minutes when I would take the latest *Agenda* off the pile by the bed or reach down the far end of a shelf for one of the Penguin Modern European Poets, anything to lift me out of *Daniel Deronda*.

Much of the time, too much of the time, I was still the grammar school boy, anxious to satisfy the examiners. I would get up from my work table under the cottage window and stare down at the green gates of the yard opposite, which seemed to be a storage depot for the factory. Every week a lorry would back up to the gates, delivering carboys wrapped in straw, and I would hear the storeman's slow Oxfordshire voice curl under the quick London speech of the lorry driver. One week, it must have been just after Remembrance Day, they were talking about the poppy sellers and the storeman sounded doubtful: 'Well, I reckon half the money you put in the tin goes to the bloke holding the tin.' 'No, it don't, mate, I'm the Pearly King of Tottenham and I can tell you it don't. I've got seven thousand buttons on my coat and my wife, she's got eleven thousand buttons on her coat, and I can tell you, every penny that goes in that tin goes to charity!' The Pearly King was stamping the length of the lorry, wrenching each carboy on to its rim and growling it across the boards as he reeled off all the money they had collected that summer, so much on Derby Day, so much on August Bank Holiday, 'and every penny of that went to charity, mate, every penny!'

Or I would allow myself to slip up to the grocer's in Little Clarendon Street for a pint of milk or a quarter of bacon, coming briefly to life in the sun silvering the brickwork and flashing off the stone setts. The alley would be deserted but for an old man I occasionally passed, availing himself of the same bright interval:

> Down an alley fresh from the rain
> an old man
> on his gingerly walk;
> his body leaning to the stick,

his weight withheld from footstep,
the persistent flair for balance,
showed how dear was the custom:
that, in the waning of strength,
he sought the tread of familiar ground,
as a woman newly in labour
might reach for her man's
press of the hand.

The long dark hair on the pillow was not Su's. It belonged to Leluka, an American postgraduate who wrote under that name in *Isis*, the glossier of Oxford's two student weeklies, which had just done a feature on me. As Leluka had explained in her opening column, her pen name was Ancient Greek for 'I have loosed you', 'I have let you go'. She seemed to have blown in from bohemia but there was the glint of ambition too. 'Roger,' she said, 'do you realise that one day we're both going to be in a book of modern English and American verse?' 'Well, at the moment,' I replied, getting out of bed, 'it would be a book of muddled English and American verse.'

Poetry, I was beginning to realise, was a matter of listening rather than speaking. Of listening for a rhythm that would draw into itself the words it needed. There was a soft-spoken Irishman a few years older than us, Michael O'Higgins, who had come up to Ruskin, the trade union college, and gone on to read English at Magdalen. When Michael read at a workshop, you could hear him listening. He leaned forward and placed his words on the air like a chess player keeping one finger on the piece, the poem sensed as the shape they were moving to complete.

'I think there's something wrong with my poems,' I confided to the other Michael, Michael Hewlings, as we walked back from the Poetry Society one evening. 'What one feels about your poems', he risked in the third person, 'is that you don't work on them enough.' 'What do you mean, work on them?' My poems just occurred to me. They formed in the back of my head as I walked across the city. 'Well, you know that poem of mine you like?' He meant 'Lord', his imagining of old age. 'It took me three months to write that poem. And when it was finished, I looked back over my drafts. To get those sixteen lines I had covered seventy sheets of paper.'

That set a benchmark, though it would be almost obliterated before I was ready to measure up to it.

The best register of how little progress I was making was the reticence of Nevill Coghill, the Merton Professor of English, whose door I would knock on every few months with a fresh sheaf of poems, the latest in the procession of aspirants he had been doomed to receive ever since he became Auden's tutor and heard him declare that he was going to be 'a great poet'. All of us were seeking confirmation from Coghill, the nod that would send out streams of Pentecostal fire.

By the time I presented myself, he looked like one of the Irish squires he had sprung from, tall and white-haired and a little battered about the cheekbones, and his kindness was almost palpable, furnishing the room as securely as the large sofa he settled me on with a glass of sherry. In my first year I took him a poem about a statue that had found refuge in New College cloisters, an aged king whose figure was almost weathered away. He read it in silence, his finger travelling down the page and pausing just once:

> In the head of the king
> the cargo has shifted.

'That's a good line.'

In my second year I took him a long poem, 'Fear', the subject set for that year's Newdigate Prize, which I had failed to win. The finger travelled silently through my dramatisation of boyish fears and adolescent self-consciousness, pausing on

> The girl kept within the rim of her eyes.

and again on

> He is dumb, and the girl is light on his arm.

'That's a beautiful line.'

In my third year I managed to elicit a chuckle, 'Poor old boy!' I had taken him 'An Old Don', for which I had used the physical characteristics of Robert Levens, my Classics tutor, who was actually the most liberal of men:

> This old dog
> will not unclamp
> till the bone shows a crack
>
> jaw sprung like a mantrap
> and the wide head
> domed
>
> but eyes thin
> bark weak
> neither bell nor bay
>
> as a whelp
> keener to snap
> than to sound
>
> Well, the odd bone . . .

'Well, Roger,' he conceded, 'I think you have an angular muse but she has her points.'

I was happy with that. The muse might flesh out in time. And quite unprepared for what Peter told me when he rushed round to the flat one afternoon in a state of barely concealed elation. Peter was writing himself and had shown some of his poems to Stephen Spender, whom he knew socially. But he had just come from a consultation with Coghill, who had given him his opinion of me: that I was the most narcissistic person he had ever met and that my poetry – and here Peter gave me a straight look, as if this information might be of some use to me – was all tied up with my narcissism. 'He's hoping that, if you carry on, you'll break out of it and one day you'll just burst into song.'

There was something else, apparently, the other reason Peter was so elated and, to be fair, the primary reason: 'Anyway, you have a wonderful invitation coming to you. I won't spoil it by telling you what it is.' And off he went, exit stage back.

The most narcissistic person he had ever met! Looking back, I can see that it was not just the wing collar and the silver-topped cane. The Fellows' Garden sloped up to a promenade along the old city wall, overlooking Christ Church Meadows, and a curved bench in the round of a turret. One afternoon the previous summer I had settled there to read, endragoned in the green silk of a Chinese smoking jacket a young don had passed on to me as being too dramatic for him to wear, when Coghill strolled up with Peter Jay. 'Just like Rupert Brooke!' they had exclaimed and Peter posed me for a photo, pulling open the wide black collar and tucking my shirt under it to create a V of bare Georgian chest. 'Look down at the book!' they said but the camera did not show another Brooke, let alone another Hopkins in the fine delight that fathers thought. I looked turbid with self-consciousness. But when Peter sent me the photo, I had sent it on to Coghill, thinking it was the thing to do.

Perhaps that had surprised him. Worried him even. But was it enough to make me the most narcissistic person he had ever met? I was shocked back to where I had been that morning in Athens when Frances tried to explain to me how friends usually behaved. All the conviviality of Oxford, the wit and the films and the music, even the wordless intimacy as lovers, fell away. I saw in myself the psyche of the firstborn who has only to live as the apple of his mother's eye.

That night, as Su slept trustingly at my side, I lay awake, trying to earth the shock:

> To build an edifice
>      and the base is rotten
> To build it again, honestly, gingerly
>      it gives way again
> To rebuild now, the third time, slowly,
> to place each brick in the fear
> that somehow it cannot stand
>
>      is work for the damned.

The invitation was to a lunch Coghill was giving for Auden, who was in the country to launch his latest collection, *About the House*. I had my copy already and had come to value the final modest affirmation of 'Whitsunday in Kirchstetten' –

> if there when Grace dances, I should dance.

177

– a modesty mirrored in the glimpse Coghill once gave me into his own religious belief: 'It's just that sometimes you can be walking across a field and you have the feeling that there is someone walking with you.'

But this was not to be a quiet conversation, this was to be a formal lunch, the chosen few bidden to appear for sherry in one of those upper rooms in Fellows' Quad known only to the dons. I was relieved to see Hugo Dyson, an Emeritus Fellow whose tutorials extended to a grandfatherly chat. He had already told me the familiar story of Auden as an undergraduate going into people's rooms to read their letters. 'Wystan, you just don't do that!' 'Nonsense, I'm a poet, I need material.' 'And yet, you know, I always felt a sense of peace in his company. Strange, like a personal charisma . . .'

Not that we felt that, all keyed up as we were. And all dandied up as I was. I was displayed rather than introduced, Coghill directing Auden's gaze across the room as if this should be a particular pleasure. A dandy should be self-sufficient, caring for no one's approval but his own. I bowed and then looked up, as if seeking a response. And saw myself through his eyes, the little deference of the cane held out to one side, the ungainly half-crouch in the tight trousers.

I strode out of it and for a moment we had the conversation I was expecting: 'Who do you take after?' 'Hopkins.' 'A great master but a dangerous model.' 'It's the rhythm I go for.' 'Oh, the rhythm's all right.' And then he glanced up: 'How much a year do you spend on your hair?'

No sooner were the introductions over than Auden reached into his jacket pocket and took out a cutting from *The Times*. He had a look of peculiar satisfaction, as if his quest for material had been vindicated once more. 'Here,' he said to me, 'you read it out!' It was a report of widows solacing themselves by fondling men's genitals as they were strap-hanging on the Tokyo Underground. 'Of course,' the article concluded, after interviews with widows who were poignant in their own defence and strap-hangers who seemed stoical about being taken unawares, 'such behaviour is entirely natural. Whether or not it is intellectually justifiable is another question.'

'I knew I'd never be able to hold you,' Su said, 'but I thought it would be fun trying.'

Did I know how much I owed her? Not as clearly as I do now. I had written, in rather a quaint phrase that must have gone back to bible class, of her *'loving-kindness'*, of *'green wood / slowly bent / through years / to hold the light'*. But did I realise it was her very quietness that had allowed me to grow? That only a sensuality as shy as hers could have meshed with mine?

Bereft of it, I walked the streets at night, becoming so used to St Giles as a long gallery of lit paving stones between columns of tree shadow that it came as a shock when office doors opened by day and people stepped out of them, as if the street's character were being dissipated for no good reason. One night, lifting ahead of me as if he had finally become a thought form, I saw Charles Cameron, who had just organised the first international exhibition of Concrete Poetry, the visual form pioneered by Apollinaire, whose poem 'Rain' drifted across the page in long, thin columns of print. At that time there was a revival of interest because poets like Dom Sylvester Houédard had taken it away from the pictorial towards a purer form in which typography and graphic design were used to bring out the possibilities inherent in just one or two words. Charles had staged the exhibition at St Catherine's, the new college designed by Arne Jacobsen, and to encounter that spare lettering on those austere walls was to feel the kind of excitement students must have felt at the Bauhaus.

Charles's ideas came so fast that he always did seem to move in their slipstream, the round forehead surging ahead of the broken tooth that gave him the look of a Bisto Kid, the thin wrists sticking out of the sleeves of his jacket and the trousers almost swept off his slim hips. But that night was the last night of the exhibition and he was walking the streets in a state of helpless elevation. 'I need someone to play me some slow blues,' he said.

I had just the thing, Red Garland's 'Soul Junction', but it was the early hours before we stopped talking and I let him stretch out on the spare mattress to the long opening piano solo. As if some limiter had been lifted from my brain, circuits that had been dead for weeks suddenly fired. By the time he asked plaintively, 'Where's my slow blues?' I was scribbling down the first words of a poem.

Another night I stumbled out into the empty streets, having written myself into a state of exhaustion. All I had to show for it were four lines of self-reproach, which I mumbled to Charles when I met him:

> For the shy doe
> Fool the hunter's bow.
> Into mound pain
> Quiver arrows of spat strain.

'The only thing wrong with that is that you're saying it wrong. You just need to break it up a bit, give it some air.' And he went into a dance on the pavement, placing the words with his hands:

> for the
> > shy
> > > doe
> fool
> > the hunter's bow

into
mound pain
quiver
arrows of
spat
strain

'From the central seat in heaven which I am currently occupying, that sounds fine to me. Mind you, it's a well-known fact that the central seat in heaven has a habit of suddenly tipping up and dumping you on your back in the gutter, blinking up at the stars.'

Hugo Dyson had a letter from an old pupil who was recruiting for a Canadian university. Would I like him to put my name forward? 'No,' I said, possessed of a very strong intuition that, if I were to do anything but write, I would be conscientious about it and all my energies would be diverted, 'I'm going to be a poet.' Hugo was surprised, even a little intrigued. 'Who knows, Roger, perhaps you'll have a lyric outburst in your late twenties. People can sometimes, you know.' 'No,' I said, 'I'll probably be in my forties before I know what I'm doing.'

But what to do in the meantime? John was going to be a banker, Derek a don. The only one of my close friends I could imagine, not in a garret, perhaps, but in a setting out of John Cowper Powys, an abandoned cottage in the shadow of an Iron Age hill fort, was Redmond O'Hanlon. Coghill had alerted us to his arrival – 'a young friend of mine is coming up' – and at our first gathering at the flat in Walton Lane he had stood, a freshman among third years, to read a very short poem, an image of rooks flying against a winter sky that ended with the simple command, '*Remember!*' Sensing we were not quite convinced by that, he had commandeered a large room in Fellows' and given a performance of *The Waste Land*, his voice going into drag for the bar

room scene with just the right shade of scarlet and hard edge of
lip pencil,

> And if you don't give it him, there's others will,

and pacing 'What the Thunder said' so that the final '*Shantih shantih
shantih*' fell as it should, as a benediction.

Most freshmen were schoolboys in sports jackets. I had been like
that myself, no more than a hint of the aspiring teddy boy in the
way my hair was brushed back for the college photograph. But
Redmond had arrived with a distinct physical presence, more than
a hint of the motorbike boy in the tall figure in the leather flying
jacket, his hair blown back and an aerodynamic wave in his sideburns, as if he had only just got off the bike. There was an untidy
honesty to those long sideburns, thin over the cheekbones and then
tufting out on the cheek. They sharpened the broad face, sharpened it and yet somehow disarmed it, making Red's expression one
of intense friendliness.

He had taken the bike with him to Marlborough and kept it
hidden in the school grounds, prompting his housemaster to the dire
prediction that he would be dead before he was twenty. And he did
tell of coming off on a bend and looking up to see his friend Martin,
who had been riding pillion, passing overhead in a perfect parabola.
Even in his home village, where he was the vicar's son and obliged
to sing in the church choir, he had joined the local bikers and been
accepted as one of the gang. One Sunday morning, as he processed
up the aisle, he saw all their leather jackets bunched on one side
and all the village girls he had been screwing decking out the pews
on the other. He fixed his eyes on his hymn book, forgetting that
the choir divided either side of the font. One of its stone bosses was
at just the wrong height and the processional hymn ended in a gasp
of pain. He stumbled into the choir stalls, groping under his surplice.

That story was typical of Red, his wild streak undercut by comedy. But the story that really fired my imagination was of his riding around Ireland and coming across a girl who lived in a cabin with her grandfather. They were only twelve miles from the sea but she had never seen the sea and, needless to say, she had never been on the back of a motorbike. He carried her down to the shore and watched as she came face to face with the element. She took off her black dress, she took off no fewer than eight starched white petticoats, and ran naked into the sea.

Red had already written a road novel and sent it to Corgi Books. They hadn't taken it but they had offered him £250 for two chapters of a second novel, which suggested that they sensed some potential. Red never showed me the novel – the more closely we touched on his underlying ambition, the more diffident he became – but I began to imagine the episodes. The night in Paris, for example, when the hero and his girl smoked hashish and discovery became as relentless as desire.

'I'm stuck in a rational cul-de-sac,' I decided, and asked Red to initiate me. This was in the early summer of 1966 when hashish still belonged in the pages of Baudelaire or the alleys of Tangier. That evening I might almost have been in Morocco, so completely had Red transformed his college room, the curtains drawn, one lamp lit and a thickness of rugs and cushions undulating over the floor. There was not a hard surface anywhere, only this cushioning, several layers deep, and it struck me that this was both incredibly thoughtful and oddly like a seduction scene.

'There's a whole ritual to this,' Red said, 'it's all part of it,' and sat bent over the LP cover in his lap. I watched the cigarette papers being assembled with distinct misgivings. Was this going to be another version of Airfix, something else for a boy to make and do? But then came the moment when he put the little nub of resin in a screw of tinfoil and held it in the flame of a match. It was not so much the smell in itself, warm and dark, as the way it lifted and thinned, its edge of nothingness.

Not that much seemed to happen at first. I lay on the sea of cushions, feeling stark sober. 'Perhaps it has no effect on you,' Red said, 'perhaps it's like putting lawnmower fuel into a jet engine.' And then came the first effect he had warned me about, the nausea for which he had provided a tin waste-paper basket. I had just finished vomiting into it when I heard him talking to someone at the window, which opened on to Merton Street. 'No,' he was saying, 'nothing's happening here.'

It was another head, checking out the scene, and Red was keeping him away. But that's not how I heard it as I clung to the waste-paper basket. Red was pronouncing his verdict on the evening and it was the most damning of all judgements: 'Nothing's happening here.' Was it my embarrassment that triggered the memory of an episode from Dylan Thomas's travels round America? He was being driven to his night's lodging and his hostess, who had been making every effort to impress, had just committed some irretrievable error, such as congratulating him on someone else's poem. At which point her husband, cigar in mouth and thick rolls of fat round the back of his neck, spoke his only words of the evening, 'Wrong again, Emily!' By the time Red turned round from the window, I was up on my feet, an American matron in some distress. I straightened my stockings, I shook out my dress and I trudged up and down the unsteady surface of his Eastern divan, crying out, 'Oh, take me home, Henry dear, take me home!'

Red's room was already in shadow the next time I called, the curtains drawn against the afternoon light. Which should have prepared me for the Zapata moustache, cross-legged on the floor and leaning forward, travelling on even as he sat.

'This is Bryn,' said Red, 'just up from London.'

Denim jacket over a blue and white striped shirt. Sharper look than a student, the black hair trimmed, the oblique angle of the moustache razored against pale, urban skin.

Bryn must have been reading my own appearance – twist of neckerchief in an open shirt, hair almost shoulder-length – because he glanced over at Red, as if to say, 'Are we all right, then?' Red nodded. 'Thought so' and Bryn's grin as he reached into his pack had an unmediated animal zest, the Zapata black as a dog's lip against the white of the teeth.

None of us spoke as the joint went round. I was focusing on my newly acquired technique, taking extra little sniffs to suck in the last of the smoke and sounding like a bicycle pump in reverse, when I heard clasps being clicked back, *one, two, three*. Where Bryn had been was an open guitar case and he was positioning himself on the front of the sofa, finding slow chords and spacing them out until our enclosed afternoon opened into a summer's evening.

'Oh, I see,' said Red, 'we're at transference of mood.'

'Here comes a little girl skipping,' confided Bryn, skittering up the top string in a series of little trills. 'And here's her old granny, keeping an eye on her,' moving up the string a little stiffly and halting with a tremor where there had been a trill. 'Here comes the girl from Ipanema,' and her hips swung on the strings, so seductive in their delay that for a moment you thought she might actually give you a glance. The samba rhythm held the world in its summer. 'And here's an old man with a wooden leg,' an abrupt slide up the bottom string and a slap on the body of the guitar, *jerk, slap, jerk, slap*. That animal glint of black hair on white teeth as Bryn chuckled, the world's summer flew apart and we were back in an English music hall, in one of its merciless routines.

The atmosphere changed again when Bryn took out his harmonica. He covered it with his hands and blew softly, two or three notes whose ghosts seemed to gather as his hands opened and closed. He was playing for himself now, going on down the highway I had glimpsed when I first smelled the resin heating in its screw of tinfoil, the highway I felt we were moving along that evening as we walked up the High, our feet strangely in step, Bryn's black boot in its tube of denim coming down on to the pavement in the same moment as my old-fashioned sandal, and the long black neck of the guitar case lifting ahead of us. He needed somewhere to crash and I had offered him the flat.

'I like the way you do that,' said Bryn as I drew on the last of the joint and threw my head back, sucking in the smoke. 'You really want to get everything out of it.'

A few nights later he might not have been quite so sure. An American girl had turned up, someone I had met at Koki's party when I was home for Easter. A strong, open face gave her the look of a farm girl on her way to becoming a flower child and there was a rush of attraction neither of us quite knew how to focus. We had slipped out of the party to go to the Crawdaddy Club, only to drive fruitlessly along by the Thames, unable to find the bridge over to Eel Pie Island. I thought of leading her up the long ladder to the hayloft and turned the van for home. We coasted into the yard with the lights off, high on stealth. And crept up the ladder to find the loft crammed with bales. They had bought a lorryload in. Where I had promised her an ascent in an Elizabethan airship with starlight winking between the tiles, we had to clamber to find a ledge we were soon to abandon as too awkward, too hot and too prickly.

That night in the flat, though, everything seemed to be conducive. She had arrived in the afternoon and left her rucksack. She had other friends to see and I was out that evening. I came back to find her basking in her sleeping bag in front of the electric fire, in a musk of animal warmth she found words for as I bent over to ask if she was OK on the floor: 'Yeah,' she said with a slow smile, 'I'm in a pretty good state.'

Bryn's bed and mine, two singles I had pushed into a double when I was with Su, were in an L-shape round the fire. Bryn sat up on one elbow and rolled a joint we passed across the glow of the one lit bar. Then I unplugged it and moved down into the animal warmth.

All I remember of that act of love is the *thump thump thump* against the floorboards. The more energy I threw into it, the more blatant we became and the more inhibited she must have felt. Better next time, I thought, as we moved over to the bed.

But next time she said no. The blood had risen, the muscle stretched to its shimmering edge and she said no. The blood went to my fingertips where it pulsed like the blows of a cold chisel. The nerve endings rang until I thought my fingers would burst and I would start to spray blood like some parody of Padre Pio.

I lay back and closed my eyes. But the familiar refuge, the warm dark I had been able to seal myself into ever since I was a child, the inviolable dark that was, lucky child that I was, the childhood I still carried inside me, that had become a bloodstream, red corpuscles hurtling down the screen of the lids. There was a moment's fear, the feeling of being on a brink. And then the realisation that I must be watching the film of my own heart attack.

'Bryn,' I called out, 'get me a doctor!'

'Can't do that, man.'

'Then get me to the Radcliffe!'

It was only just up the road.

No reply.

'No, seriously, get me to the Radcliffe! I'm having a heart attack!'

'Can't do that, man.'

No longer a free-floating consciousness, able to slip in and out of the body at will, self-aware one moment and abstracted the next, I had a vivid sense of myself on a narrow bed in a room over a garage in a back alley, the law like a Berlin Wall between me and any possibility of help. Beside me was a warmth I dared not touch or the pulse would return to the muscle, the small of the back arch off the mattress and she would shrink away once more. I was alone with the apocalypse behind my eyelids, the blood in spate and the heart driving, driving.

*Ayeeyah!* Too embarrassed to scream openly, I ritualised it, releasing a wordless wail I imagined as Arabic, the muezzin's cry I knew only as a phrase in one of Harry Fainlight's poems from Tangier. *Ayeeyah! Ayeeyeeyah!* It was that or the heart would blow a valve. On the other bed Bryn kept his head down. While the American girl must have huddled into herself as into a storm cellar, waiting for me to blow over.

There were moments when I thought I had wailed all the wild energy out of myself. I would lie back on the pillow and look up into the dark, the indifferent dark. 'Hi!' I would say and back would come her voice, 'Hi!' Warm and companionable, as if all along she had been waiting for me on the threshold of the normal. Then I would close my eyes and there was the blood colour, relentless at its high pitch. 'Hi!' I would shout as the shock of it swept me away again, 'Hi! Hi!' but there was no answering voice, no way back down to the spaciousness of that minute when I had looked up into an ordinary night, its unhurried pace the simplest state of being but guarded, it seemed, by the most exacting of gatekeepers. The least tremor in the voice and she would not answer. That was just some anxious impression of myself, trying to slip across the threshold. Only once I was back, and the voice had reaffirmed itself as I stared into the dark, would I hear a response, 'Hi!'

By the morning it had become a source of pride. I had had the horrors. But it was too much for the American girl, who found herself another floor to sleep on. 'I don't usually do that,' she explained of her initial surrender to the animal warmth, 'but I thought, oh well, why not?'

'Chick like that shouldn't be on the road,' said Bryn and proceeded with my education. That evening I came back to a flat that looked twice the size. He had taken the beds out of their L-shape and turned them into four, the mattresses set against the end walls and the bases under the round windows. My work table was still under the cottage window but everything else, the chairs formally poised for conversation and the one free-standing book-shelf, had been pulled back against the walls. All the assumptions had been taken out of the room, all the small talk. The floorboards gleamed in the light from the windows as if we had recovered an earlier human space, an arena or a dance floor.

Bryn completed the rearrangement by moving in the Rolls-Royce of radiograms, a varnished wooden cabinet on whose record changer you could stack no fewer than ten LPs. He had borrowed it from Bernard, the son of a Belgian diplomat, on the grounds that Bernard could only play it at low volume in his college room whereas in our back alley he could hear the high notes flare like shooting stars and the low notes resonate in the stone setts. Bryn was not quick-fingered on the guitar, not like Humphrey, who would bend over the strings, looking very Left Bank in his dark-rimmed glasses, and play the most intricate of jazz solos, but he had a very good sense of time – during his months in New York he had sat in on drums for Charles Mingus – and he made me listen to moments in the music I might have overlooked, like three notes on the bass, perfectly spaced but held just long enough for you to feel the beat gathering in them. 'That's really hard to do.'

Time slowed once you were stoned and the brain seemed to be tuned differently. Words felt far off. If they came at all, they came as a reflex, supplied from some distant memory bank. Look at them closely and they would turn nonsensical. But sounds were immediate, close and spacious. The moment the needle dropped on to an LP you seemed to be synchronous with it, not listening to something that had been recorded but inside it as it was being played. Almost stunned by the sound at first, a shaft of sunlight in which the dust had begun to move, I would start to sway, dancing in my own space until the detail of the music moved me out into the room, my hands picking up one line, my feet another. Then I had to dare the space, arcing across it and half-spinning back, trying to paint the music into it until my foot went to the floor in a last step and a last note completed it.

Bryn had been up to Brixton and come back with enough hashish to sole a boot. 'Look at that!' he said as he pulled it from his shirt. Grey-green leather, the resin so compressed that it had a faint shine. Slightly thicker, in fact, than a boot sole. Most of it he cut into tiny squares that he weighed carefully on a pair of kitchen scales, hashish being sold by the ounce or the half-ounce. The rest he hid behind the board of the electricity meter on the stairs, that not being, technically, on our premises.

The melancholy of the back lane had gone. To walk up it was like that moment in *Steppenwolf* when ethereal neon outlined a hitherto unnoticed door and Harry Haller is given admission to the magic theatre. Sometimes the repeated riffs of 'Wednesday Night Prayer Meeting', the opening track of Mingus's *Blues and Roots*, would tell me that someone had already stacked up the LPs, selecting them to take us deeper with each click and shift of the changer so that in a couple of hours' time, crashed out on the mattresses, we could lose ourselves in the intricacies of *Money Jungle*, Ellington's avant-garde piano trio with Mingus and Max Roach. Sometimes I would hear rapid finger stops on the guitar's upper strings, a run brought off with a clipped, almost Chandleresque wit, and know that Humphrey had come down from his room over the Poodle

Parlour on Walton Street. And sometimes the lane was silent, the flat in almost complete darkness, lit only by the pilot light on the radio Bryn had placed on the floor, just behind the rolled-up jacket that served as his pillow, the sound turned down so low that it can only have functioned at the level of instinct, keeping him company through the night.

Another effect of the slowing of time was that everyday encounters seemed to take place in slow motion. Going into the off-licence to buy some straights, as we called ordinary cigarettes, I would watch the successive changes in the owner's face, the lips gathering themselves to open in a smile, the corners of the eyes crinkling as he went into his act and became the obliging shopkeeper, 'Good evening, Sir!' He was a youngish man with a look of my Uncle Peter and for a moment I was a small boy playing shop, finding the right words to advance across the counter. What came was a voice that discounted the 'Sir' and used the undertone of one working man to another, a voice I must have learned from my father on our trips to the builders' merchant. Then some small joke as the money changed hands so that, as I went out of the door, I left the sound of myself on the air, breath with a fuel injection of laughter that was really just the impetus of my twenty-two years, carrying me out into the summer night.

Air that had its own texture, air that might have come from a bakery were it not for the dry smell of dust cut with the scent of Mivvi wrappers and lolly sticks. City-deep air through which I could hear the traffic moving on St Giles, the blur of engines waiting at the lights, the revs of expectation as they sprinted away. And then a lull in which I imagined the door of another off-licence closing somewhere across the city, the eagerness ebbing from the face of another shopkeeper as he went offstage, and someone else out on the pavement, the night charged as if there were thunder in the air but with a subtler electricity, a breathing presence that, all this way inland, felt oceanic.

'Tune in,' said Timothy Leary, as if the pulse were always there and only our attention intermittent. Ron used to dance as if he were listening for it. The most philosophical of us, his expression deepening from thoughtful to doubtful under a ginger moustache and beard, he would stand poised as the first notes came from the speaker, his head bent and one hand in the air, and only gradually start to move. And yet he was possibly the youngest of us, not a student but an emissary from the anarchists in London who had become concerned that the Oxford anarchists seemed to be dropping out of politics. He had been working as a messenger boy on the Stock Exchange and arrived in a jacket and tie and pressed trousers, with a suitcase of neatly ironed shirts. Now his hair had bushed out and his face mossed over. There was a scarf loosely tied in the neck of his open shirt, the look we all had of an Edwardian navvy. And he was as likely to talk of *samsara*, the Vedantic notion of the veil of appearances, as he was of Bakunin.

When time slowed and you saw faces in transition, in the moment before the mask formed, the veil was almost visible as a veil. But speed was built into me too, and sometimes I could not see for speed. In the absence of Su I was back to scanning the horizon, turning every distant figure into the longed-for shape, the elusive ideal. Sometimes I could only laugh at the tricks my eyes played on me, the continual flicker of illusion and disillusion:

> In the distance
> I saw two girls gaily
> swinging a bag.
>
> I hurried closer, and found
> they were two mothers
> rocking a baby.

I rejoiced
in girl-gay mothers.

A woman sitting on a bench,
legs up under, mermaid-fashion.
Closer, a middle-aged woman.

I rejoiced
in a middle-aged mermaid.

And a girl alone
on the grass.

Now to cross the path
would be stark.

I shall wait
for a cocktail party.

Sometimes I did not wait. I would walk up to a girl in the street
and start talking to her. It was like another dare. As I nerved myself
to approach, the adrenalin would pulse through me and I would
see her in sharp relief, every detail of her face etched against passing
time, against the certainty of disappearance. Then it seemed impossible to let her go.

That was how I met Anke. It was early June, the last week of
the Trinity term. I was walking down to college for Early Dinner,
a quiet meal that I preferred to formal Hall. She was standing with
another girl at Carfax, the main crossroads in Oxford, staring up
at the city map, trying to work out the way to the youth hostel. I
glimpsed long blond hair, a slim figure in jeans, and responded as
any twenty-two-year-old would have responded: I stopped and
asked if I could be of assistance.

She was standing in front of me, no more than child-high, the round head between the straight curtains of hair tilted as she looked up at the map. I saw the curve of the cheekbone, the fineness of the cheek moulding round to the chin, and felt the horizon contract to a small vertical, perhaps five-foot-two.

I remember the quietness of the streets at that moment. The traffic of the day had died down and it would be another hour before the pavements filled with couples out for the evening, knots of students on their way to the Scala, bevies of drinkers crowding into pub passageways. The day was in suspense – and the suspense held for a moment as the surprise filtered through. She was bone-perfect, just enough of an oval in the line of the jaw to balance the round head and the broad cheekbones.

That was important to me then. Later it ceased to matter, and I lived in the changing expressions of her face, in her different ages: the clouded forehead of a serious child, the woman's humour that stirred in the long line of the lips. Most of all, perhaps, in her eyes' river light and shadow. But what I saw at first glance was a sculpted Saxon head, a bone helmet I could set beside Modigliani's Jeanne or Picasso's Sylvette, posters that hung on student walls all over Oxford.

I looked into myself and thought: *Don't lose her*. It was as if I were back in Beech Wood before dawn. Everything in me concentrated and became still.

What went through Anke's mind, I don't know. Apparently, as I led the girls towards the flat – I had managed to persuade them that the youth hostel was a long way from the city centre – Hannah had hissed in her ear, 'You can't just go off with everyone you meet!' But when I opened the door at the top of the stairs and she stepped out into the room's buoyant width, she recognised it: somewhere she knew from a dream, a room moored like a raft at the edge of the sky.

Just as a third person can become crucial to a relationship, providing some balance the lovers lack in themselves, so that summer would have been unimaginable without the flat. Though what it provided was not stability but continual change: crowded nights where we danced in a room full of surging shadows and fell asleep in each other's arms, naked to the waist on one of the mattresses ranged around the walls, as the record deck changed down into a slow blues and sent Major Holley's bass humming out into the dawn; sunlit estuaries of the late afternoon when we found ourselves alone, the light brimming at the round windows, and coupled as fiercely as if we had just bitten the apple. Without that element of surprise, the days might not have seemed so paradisal. Nor ended in such tragic confusion.

Nights were communal. We lay on our mattresses, listening to music, moving into sleep as our ancestors must have moved on migration, picking our own paths, foraging along a gully or staring from a small height, but never losing the sense, even as we moulded ourselves into a hollow, of others moving on the same tide, across the same landscape. We were more intimate for that restraint, Anke whispering on my shoulder in the small hours. 'Anke is only my nickname,' she confided on the second night. 'I was christened Marie Bernadette. My father was a Belgian jazz guitarist.'

She said it so quietly she might have been thinking aloud, telling herself the story: almost happy with it now, much less puzzled than she had been, but still needing to say it over.

Little by little, over the next few days, she told me the rest. There were moments when her voice quickened and I could hear the shock. Moments when she was still witness to the accident of her own life.

She had grown up with her mother and her stepfather, a Dutch painter. Then her mother went into a deep depression and her stepfather blamed himself.

'He felt that he was destroying her. He almost went mad himself. I've seen some of the drawings he did then and they're terrifying. At first you just think it's a self-portrait. Then you look again and you see that he's turned himself into a monster. He's a metallic little demon, a scissorman.'

They were the last drawings he ever did. Painting seemed a selfish passion. He gave it up and became a social worker.

When she spoke of her mother, it was with an affectionate calm: 'Sometimes she's fine. She's happy and she comes out of hospital and lives in her flat for a few months. Then she begins to do strange things, the neighbours call the doctor and she has to go back in again. It doesn't upset me now, I know it'll happen.'

Anke had been in an orphanage since she was twelve. Her step-father had remarried and had a daughter of his own. Anke stayed with them at weekends and thought of the little girl as her sister. She talked about her eagerly and each time, for a moment, she would become abstracted. Odd term for so vivid a state, and indicating movement in the wrong direction: it was the child who came into the room. Anke would look down and smile, as if she were playing at her feet.

That was my clue. I should have caught that look. It is only now that it registers, too late.

I had listened to the wrong half of the story. My imagination seized on the Belgian jazz guitarist and the Dutch painter. Even the orphanage seemed romantic. What I had missed was Anke's wistfulness about home and family, her longing for all the securities I had grown up with, and needed to strip away.

And yet I came so close. In that first glance in the street, seeing her intent on the map, tired, a little white in the face, it was a child's intentness I saw. She looked as if she had been carved out of holly, that bright, virginal wood. Finely cut. Uncompromised. Reading that map as if it charted the course of her future life.

So serious about herself. And innocently so, quite unaware of it. Concentrated in herself, a bud forging its spear point. I kept my distance as I shepherded her along the Cornmarket, I chose my words. None of the rhapsodic chat with which I usually accosted girls.

In those first few steps I had fallen into place, walking slightly behind her, attendant, guide and protector. Looking over her head, seven inches taller than she was, and four years older. But walking watchfully, I remember, eyes flicking left and right.

Languid and alert, I stalked in her shadow, a gunfighter in a Western escorting the beautiful young heiress from the East through a wild frontier town.

Which suggests that I was not quite old enough.

I took up my place each morning, slipping out of bed while Anke slept and making her china tea. It was mid-morning and the sun had already moved from the kitchen window, leaving it in a warm shade. I remember each detail of that ritual: the electric kettle's first, fugitive stir of sound, like a bush roused by the wind; the teapot warming between my palms as I swilled water round it; kneeling by the bed, waiting for the tea to steep; pouring it, a little at a time, first into one cup, then into the other. It seemed transparent and I would be afraid I had made it too weak. Then the colour would begin to rise, a lemon yellow darkening to gold. It held like a well-struck note and I felt that the ritual had worked: our luck was secured for another day.

It was then, as Anke sat up on one elbow, heavy-headed and full of sleep, and I handed her the tea, watching the fine lines come into her forehead as she bent to sip it and softening my voice, spacing out my remarks, that I realised there was something fatherly in this care. I felt the responsibility you feel talking a child to sleep, when it takes you over the border with it. It murmurs half a sentence and hangs on your reply. For a moment you sense a country where you are blind and it can see. You listen, trying to read the lie of the land and mould your voice to its contours. You are looking for the word that will hold this world in place. Then it slips away from you. You are back where you were, sitting on the edge of the bed.

Anke was surfacing from sleep but there was the same sense of a trust that was almost a trespass, of waiting for her at the border. She would tell me her dreams, just as she had told me her real name, in a voice that was more reflection than speech. I could hear every surge of amusement, every muddying of doubt.

Then she would reach for the navy-blue shine of her tobacco pouch, Samson's halfzware shag, and roll the first cigarette of the day, so strong, she said, it made her dizzy. I rarely smoked before the afternoon and I watched as her fingers lifted and teased out the tobacco, straightening the dark strands along the white paper. She leaned on one elbow, the sheet drawn across her breasts, her shoulders soft and heavy with sleep. She inhaled and her body shuddered slightly as it took in the smoke, a tremor that ran down through the skin from the collarbone. Her breasts quivered under the sheet. It was like watching her move under the hands of another lover.

She leaned back, eyes half closed, and her features seemed to blur for a moment. Then her forehead cleared, the same bright forehead I had seen in the street, and we began to make plans, talking in hushed voices on our side of the room while the others slept, or pretended to.

It was then, as I watched her move into the day, that I noticed the difference. That taut girl-child had blossomed. Her travelling clothes, the wine-dark shirt and the grey jeans, had gone into the rucksack. Now she wore a green miniskirt, no more than a wraparound of cloth, like a short, unpleated kilt. Bare-legged and bronzed, she looked like a young Amazon.

Or she astonished me by appearing in a pierrot costume, a

skin-tight mottling of purple and white, with frills at ankle and wrist. Hannah had seen it in a shop window and dared her to wear it. It was part of the play between them, a way of burlesquing the difference between Anke's unequivocal beauty and Hannah's comical looks. It was Hannah's nose that made a clown of her, pushed up at an oblique angle to the long, white, oval face framed by ringlets of ginger hair. Almost, you could say, they wore the pierrot suit together: Anke provided the sensation and Hannah the wit.

Between them, they drew me into the game, laughing at my innocence. I had no idea, for instance, that eyeshadow could be green. I had only ever seen mascara and mascara was black. But I was happiest when my presence was taken for granted and I could savour the late-morning stillness, the sense of being backstage as Anke leant to the mirror, brushing on the eyeshadow, or bent over the rucksack, pondering a belt or a silk scarf, some small final touch. Our plans were laid. The day brimmed with promise. But the day could wait. In their intimacy, in my closeness to this woman as she shaped an eyelid or tied a long scarf round her neck, these moments seemed the last of the night.

Out in the street, when I sensed the eyes of passers-by brush over her, I felt an odd satisfaction in the line of her collar, the fall of the hair against her cheek, as if they were preparations I had made myself. In my memories of our journeys together – to the Cotswolds to show her Lower Slaughter, to London for the second Poetry Incarnation at the Albert Hall – Anke herself hardly ever appears, except in these side glimpses. What I have is a sense of accompaniment, of other eyes directing me, or following mine like a second glance.

Occasionally something separates us – a knot of people on the pavement, a speeding car as we cross the road – and she appears a few steps away. I am struck through with surprise, like any stranger glancing after her in the street.

There is a moment somewhere in London, crossing the road

towards an Underground station. Anke is ahead of me, bare-legged in her green miniskirt. Outside the Tube, a young man my own age turns to watch her as she comes up to the safety barrier on the kerb. No apparent pause, not so much as a waver as she ducks and steps between the bars. A hurdler's rock of the hips and she is through, pulling up out of the lift and swing of her skirt into the stride that straightens her back and carries her down into the station, the long blond hair breaking over her shoulders, burnished by the dirt of London and almost green-gold.

I was like someone walking on water. This miracle would last as long as I did not doubt.

I made love to her as if my life depended on it, which in a sense it did. I knew nothing then of delaying tactics, of slowing my rhythm or varying my movements. I came and carried on, remembering a friend's advice: 'If you keep going, it stiffens up again. Hurts a bit at first.' I bowed my head and sprinted through the pain barrier, hammering against the thought of losing her. And was rewarded by hearing her say, slowly and quaintly, struggling to express something sacred and profane in the English she had learned at school, 'You are the first person . . . with whom I have . . . reached the highest point . . . twice.'

There was an admission in that sentence that did not escape me. 'The first' implies a series. In this case, two series. Before me. And after me.

Oddly enough, I was not disturbed by it. We were at the age for experiment. The same curiosities moved in us both. I put my lips to her sea cave, exploring the soft, saline cleft. Suddenly the roof arched under my tongue. It hardened into ribs of muscle, like ridges of sand at low tide, and shot salt into my mouth.

I reported on this discovery to Redmond, who sounded dubious: 'What was it like?'

'I got rocks of the sea and a gush of salt.'

'Christ!' he said, and went off to find a sea cave of his own.

Sometimes her curiosity ran ahead of mine. She had grown up in a city and wanted to make love in the grass. One morning we left the flat at dawn and walked down through the empty streets to Port Meadow. On the railway bridge we met Michael Hewlings, sitting on his bicycle, contemplating the sunrise. I introduced him to Anke.

'He's a very good poet,' I said, 'but he likes to keep that a secret.'

Michael smiled. 'Of course, or I'd have to be Manager.'

We walked down to the car park and out across the meadow, glancing back at the railway bridge to make sure we were out of sight. I began to realise how cold it was. The sun had only just risen. The night's chill was still in the ground, which was wet with dew.

'Here!' said Anke and began to take her clothes off. We were not even in a hollow. I scanned the horizon. All I needed was one intrusive silhouette and we could call the whole thing off.

'Come on!' Anke insisted. She was lying naked on the wet grass, that compact, perfectly muscled body looking as if she had stripped to wrestle in the act of love. I braced myself for the cold and the bout.

There was a purple clover in the grass. I fixed on it in my mind, trying to give her that colour, trying to make it stand for all the flowers that should have embowered us on that flat ground at the city's edge.

Afterwards, I picked it and put it in the top buttonhole of her shirt.


'I think you are the most beautiful person I have ever met,' Anke said. Girls of eighteen are prone to say these things. But at the time it was like a touch of a sword on each shoulder, dubbing me into manhood.

201

We were lying on my bed at the farm, in an early evening hush that seemed to mirror our first meeting in the city. I thought back to what I had felt then: the alertness, as if I were back in Beech Wood before dawn; the recognition that, if I lost her, something in me would be diminished for ever. Beech Wood, I realised, was just the shape the intuition had taken. What I had glimpsed was the wide wood of the world. I had come into a mythical clearing where a horn hung from the branch of an oak and the adversary waited in the shadows. It was my untried self, the knight with the mirror shield.

I told her a story Hugo Dyson had told me, Malory's tale of Sir Galahad drawing the sword out of the stone. Only one person could draw the sword, the most perfect knight in Christendom. When it yielded to his grasp, Galahad wept, out of despair that there should be no one better.

I thought of myself shivering in the dew on Port Meadow, wanting to be quit of this adventure. Of the nervous boy in the body of the young lover, head down and sprinting for the finishing line. Of all my improvisations, my careful choice of words, the fragile balance I had kept. At that moment, briefly ensconced, as Charles would have said, in the central seat of heaven, I had some inkling how Galahad must have felt.

But we had been lucky. No sooner had we met than the flat had drawn us into its magic theatre. There had only been one moment when the enchantment trembled on the point of dissolution. Early on that first night, when we were dancing, someone had passed me a joint. I had slowed to give it the attention it deserved, drawing on it deeply and holding my head back to suck in all the smoke. Anke looked at me suspiciously. 'You don't want me,' she said, 'you want that.' I looked down at her, outlined in the half-dark, and my voice seemed to rise from the soles of my feet and go through me like a shock: 'I want *you*.'

Later that night, watching attraction flicker around us like summer lightning, Humphrey laid down his guitar and told us a story. On a beach at night somewhere on his travels – Greece, the South of France, I can't remember where – he had joined a group of young people sitting around a fire. As he stared into the flames, they parted for a moment and he caught sight of a girl's face, framed in the fire. Every so often, as he played and people talked and sang, he would look up and their eyes would meet through the flames. When the fire died down and everyone else drifted away, the two of them were left, face to face. They stayed and made love beside the embers.

This was just the story we wanted to hear. It seemed to consecrate our chance meeting, giving it a fabulous authenticity. By implication, Humphrey took our story and wove it with his own into a chronicle of fortuitous lovers that stretched back to the troubadours, in whose songs the European ideal of romantic love was born. As Graves wrote, *'there is one story and one story only'* and ours was another telling of it.

Love, like poetry, is a return to magic. All lovers have a sense of ceremony, trying to shape the small events of each day into significance. My kneeling at the bedside with a cup of china tea was a part of that. So too were the ceremonies bestowed on us: the immense flourish with which Redmond emerged from his room on to the college lawn, bringing us each a glass of port; the tray laid with a white cloth on which Michael Horovitz served us breakfast in his flat, the morning after the poetry reading at the Albert Hall. It consisted of one boiled egg – all there was in the house – served with great state in a black pottery egg cup from Prinknash Abbey.

To be in love is to be briefly the hero and heroine of your own story. Almost, for a moment, of the world's story. It is that moment that is so magical and so elusive. We were at the axle point on which so much of literature turns. Love can be cast into forms more lasting than bronze. But being in love cannot: it belongs to the present tense.

Trying now to cast this story into a lasting form, I realise that what I want to do is impossible, even in a medium like prose that thrives on detail. I want to preserve that summer's ephemera, its shimmer of circumstance: the final whisper, for instance, at the end of Them's version of 'Baby, Please Don't Go!', a last, humorous, heartfelt plea that we always sang to each other as we danced; or the plangent undertones of 'Guantanamera', the song that had become the anthem of the Cuban revolution. We saw Vanessa Redgrave sing it at the end of the Albert Hall reading, in khaki fatigues and a Fidel cap. Che Guevara was still alive. A generation's hopes were still voiced in the song's hesitant fall, its recurrent rise and reassertion. But for us they were the very cadence of that summer, our held breath as one incredulous day opened into the next.

'Nine perfect days' I wrote in my notebook and had no idea how to continue. I felt like a blank page between chapters.

Anke and Hannah had hitchhiked up to Newcastle, promising to return. They had remembered that they were on holiday. They wanted to see Hadrian's Wall.

Bryn did not believe in falling in love. It prejudiced his cool. 'One of these days,' he warned me, 'a chick is really going to screw you up. You put too much into it.' But he had permitted himself a light-hearted romance with Hannah, whose irony won his respect.

With the girls gone, the magic theatre went dark. Or rather, in the mirror world we lived in, it went light. The flat filled with the western sky. It went back to its first solitude.

Bryn went out of business. He had come to the end of his Brixton boot sole. He got himself a job in a café, working lunchtimes and evenings.

One hot afternoon when he was trying to sleep between shifts, I put on a new Duke Ellington record I had just bought. A Latin American album, full of strange rhythms, difficult to sleep to. Bryn got up and turned it off. Bored in the heat, and impatient to hear the record, I put it back on. 'After all,' I said, 'it's my flat.'

Fatal words. I apologised, but it was too late. Bryn had packed his rucksack and was out of the door.

He went up to James Street, where a colony of heads had taken over the hulks of two old houses. Which has made me wonder if the row wasn't a pretext, if he wasn't hankering after Maggie, who lived just over the road from the battered bedsits.

Maggie was a wandering bluesman's dream of home: a warm smile in a head of dark curls, a slim figure in a check shirt and jeans. She was living with Mike but married to an older man, an anarchist, who was the father of her young child. She also had an eleven-year-old daughter, a girl of deer-like grace, whose father had been an African student. Maggie had said she wanted to live with Mike and, true to his principles, the anarchist let her go. Later, I believe, he asked her to come back and she went.

Mike was out at work and rather resented the amount of coffee we all drank, the loaves of bread and jars of honey we consumed during the day. But how could we help being drawn to Maggie's kitchen? It had spice jars on shelves and jugs hanging from hooks along the mantelpiece, a warm smell of baking and a fresh smell of drying clothes, the alluvial sounds of the washing machine trickling in more water and pummelling a new load in the background: a rich domestic harmony that none of us quite allowed ourselves to recognise as home. If asked, we would have said we came to talk to Maggie. Her humorous perspective lightened our troubles, just as, I suspect, our company lightened her child-rearing.

I wandered up there one afternoon, looking for Bryn, and found a girl in the kitchen with Maggie. They were just putting two trays of flapjacks into the oven. She turned and I came face to face with someone I had first seen on a cold night in March, sweeping the floor in a coffee bar on Little Clarendon Street. Tiny, pale and stick-thin, a waif, a gamine, she had been wearing a black battledress jacket and a short black skirt that emphasised her bare legs. It made you shiver just to look at her.

I was with Peter and John, on our way back from the Scala. As she swept around us, I wanted to acknowledge her in some way. I wanted to buy her a coffee – as if you could buy coffee for someone who worked in a coffee bar. The next day I went back on my own to ask her out – only to see her leaving the coffee bar and walking down the road in front of me. I hurried after her but she crossed and turned into Wellington Square. I wanted to shout after her but I did not even know her name.

Now she was standing in front of me, in the same short black skirt, and I had time to consider my fascination. Straight brown hair, cut in a helmet round her head. Snub nose. Delicately curved lips that ended in sharp points. Eyebrows that were hardly there, two charcoal strokes, slightly arched over eyes so narrow they seemed Chinese. It was her eyes that made her elusive, puckish, fey.

In that first glimpse I had felt like Orpheus in Cocteau's film, the conventional poet suddenly getting intimations of another reality. I was a cloistered student and she seemed to belong to a demi-monde whose life I could only guess at. Now I had stepped through the mirror to find myself in a world that was strange, yes, and yet strangely down to earth.

Maggie seemed delighted by my arrival. 'Ah, here's Roger. He might know Cosmo.'

Expressions of disappointment when I confessed that I did not. I felt disappointed too. How could I not know someone with a name like that?

'He's just gone into the Littlemore. Lesley here's trying to get up a party to go and visit him but no one seems to be around.'

The Littlemore: another potent name. One of Oxford's mental hospitals, set up on the city's southern hills. I imagined a spaced-out philosopher, so far out he could feel time bend and see the smear of the galaxy beneath him like the gloss of oil on a puddle.

I felt some misgivings. I had never been to a mental hospital. But I was anxious to advance in the degrees of knowledge. And determined not to let this strange guide slip again.

'Hey, look!' I said, 'why don't I come with you anyway?'

I went off to buy Cosmo some tobacco, wondering what brand could possibly be adequate. Newton's Counterpoise? Einstein's Special Flake?

'There he is!' said Lesley and pointed to the third bed in a double row that ran alongside the living area. The Littlemore was surprisingly modern: pine furniture, lemon-coloured walls. A television enthused in the corner. Drinks were being served from a trolley. It was like a youth club whose members had aged prematurely. They moved heavily between the bright surfaces.

Cosmo was wandering up and down beside his bed. Below a bent, bony face, a greying moustache ran down into a little beard. He looked like a billygoat moving at the end of his tether.

On the way Lesley had told me his story. He was an Oxfordshire village lad who had taken to the road years before. Now he was back living with his elderly mother, a situation that threw him into periodic depressions. Depression started him drinking and drink brought him here.

He was almost embarrassed to see us. We gave him the tobacco and some books Lesley had collected together. I found his conversation a complete puzzle, which I was never to solve. It was as if he had mapped the world for himself, without reference to the existing charts. But over the next four years I came to value his friendship. Cosmo had a shy nobility. If I found him sitting on one of the benches in the Cornmarket, or on the steps of the late-night shop in Walton Street, I would stop and sit with him. We said little: but I felt as if I had dipped my hand in holy water.

He was arranging the books in his bedside locker as we left. We saw that it was empty and knew that we had been right to come.

Outside, it was evening. The blanched light of midsummer. The tarmac of a suburban path, the light grey stone of the kerb. A place of such resolute ordinariness that it was odd to be so aware of each other, so alert to the inches of air between us. The visit was over. We no longer had a pretext. Only the tremor of possibility that made us linger on this spot where there was nothing to detain us.

'Let me take you out to dinner,' I said, giving myself away completely. I might as well have asked her to a Commemoration Ball. We stood there, Lesley in her T-shirt and old black skirt, me in my shirt and black jeans, and smiled at the ludicrousness of the suggestion. But I had given her a glimpse of myself, just the kind of glimpse that filled Bryn with foreboding: a small boy coming across the school field to garland her with daisy chains.

I took her back to the flat and made her an omelette. I played her Debussy's *L'Après-midi d'un Faune*, not telling her I imagined her in that forest at the edge of time. She asked me if I knew *La Mer* and tried to describe to me how the music stilled into calm and swirled back into storm. As she paused, lost for words, Cocteau's enigmatic messenger disappeared. She slipped off the mask I had given her and looked me in the face. She was as young in the world as I was.

'Why don't you stay?' I asked. And then, as if it was the most natural thing in the world, she explained to me the curious obligation she was under.

At an impasse with her boyfriend in London, she had run off

to Oxford, homing in on Lizzie, who was like an older sister to her. She did a drawing once of herself as a little creature with shredded wings, an impish sort of fairy, clinging to Lizzie's ankle. Lizzie's legs rose above her, shaped and sassy, a force of nature in flared jeans. But Lizzie had her complexities too, which at one point took her off to a nunnery. Her consort was a junkie, whom I shall call Phil. Junkies were suicides, which gave them a certain glamour. Death fascinates the young. You have to live longer to see through it, to get the full force of D. M. Thomas's lines:

> death must be a poor thing
> a poor thing

It was his death pallor that had won Phil his place on Lizzie's arm.

But even junkies have a survival instinct, in the early stages at least. Phil had gone into the Warneford, Oxford's other mental hospital, for a cure. In his absence, Lizzie had taken up with Kevin, a Glaswegian who had drifted down to Oxford. People were wary of Kevin. Tall, thin and jagged, he looked like lightning about to strike, though a glance at his startled eyes would have told you it was the other way round: it was Kevin who had been struck.

Which was why Lizzie was worried when she learned that Phil was coming out of the Warneford. There was no knowing what Kevin would do. Lesley's arrival must have seemed a godsend. Lizzie went off to look after Phil and asked Lesley to look after Kevin.

I did not like to think what that might entail. But I understood what Lesley was telling me: her relationship was not with Kevin, it was with Lizzie. She was acting out of sisterhood.

At least I knew now why she had been asking me the time all evening. 'I must get back,' she said, 'or Kevin will think I've gone and left him.'

I walked her across Oxford and up the Cowley Road. It was eleven o'clock by the time we got to James Street. Early evening in our world but already too late: Kevin had taken an overdose of sleeping pills and been rushed to the Radcliffe in an ambulance.

Everyone in James Street was markedly unsympathetic. 'Kevin'll be all right. He's all bluff.' But I walked Lesley down the Cowley Road and all the way back across Oxford just to make sure. We walked in silence, both a little shocked. Then Lesley seemed to brighten.

'Roger, would you do something for me? Something very special? A great favour?'

'Yes,' I said eagerly.

'The hospital's near the flat, isn't it? I mean, we'll be going right past it?'

'Yes,' I said breathlessly.

'And you have all those shelves of books in the flat, don't you? All those books of poetry?'

'Yes,' I said guardedly.

'Would you let me choose one to leave by Kevin's bed. Something he can read as he's coming round? Something that will fill his mind with the right images? Whatever it is, I'll get you another copy.'

I was awed by the idea. To think of a poet forming his thoughts as he came round from death, of a particular phrase being the gate through which he re-entered the world. The rest of his life might go back to that moment of choice on the bookshelves, to the phrase that had shaped him.

Part of me wanted Lesley's glance to fall on a poet that I valued. Part of me was afraid that it might. Some books, like the George Barkers I had bought when the shop in the High closed down, were irreplaceable. Others, like my Keith Douglas, I wouldn't part with. There were phrases in there that had shaped me.

210

'How about this?' I asked, lifting down the Penguin Robert Graves and opening it at 'Love Without Hope':

> Love without hope, as when the young bird-catcher
> Swept off his tall hat to the Squire's own daughter,
> So let the imprisoned larks escape and fly
> Singing about her head, as she rode by.

It seemed to fit the case. And it just so happened that I had two copies. 'Perfect!' Lesley declared and we carried on to the Radcliffe.

Casualty was almost deserted. Lesley negotiated with the nurse, explaining that she was Kevin's girlfriend. He would be fine, the nurse said, he had had his stomach pumped and he was asleep in a side room. Lesley slipped in to leave the book while I waited on the other side of the green canvas screen.

Once more we traversed the empty streets. By now they had ceased to be streets. They had become blank urban material, outlines of the nullity our lives had to pass through, the rooftops and shopfronts of Babylon. We felt eerily light, detached, like two spirits moving across the face of the earth.

It was the early hours of the morning by the time we reached James Street. Kevin's suicide attempt must have cast a shadow over the house, which was dark and silent. I saw Lesley to the door. There seemed no need to say anything. A glance was enough as she stepped inside.

I turned to walk home and she called me back. Held her body against mine for a moment. And vanished into the house. This was the only time in the entire twelve hours that we had touched.

My skin retained the sensation. It was like walking into a light wind.

I turned into the Cowley Road and yellow blossomed strangely under the street lights. Roses were growing along a low wall, in a little shoebox of earth between the house and the street. The city became human once more. Restored to me in all its detail, its accommodations and improvisations.

The thought of the roses stayed with me as I walked. But I felt obscurely rebuked by their colour. The night demanded a red rose. I remembered where some grew, against the front of one of the houses further along Walton Street. In the twilight I crept through the white gate and picked one to carry back to the flat.

Putting it into water, I noticed that one petal was touched with a darker colour. At that moment the poem which had been swirling in my head all the way down from James Street, huge, cloudy and ambitious, became precise.

The night had one more trick up its sleeve. I was just settling into bed when it occurred to me that the Graves might have my name in it. I did sometimes write in the front of my books, a spindly *Roger Garfitt, Merton* that had none of the confidence of the double-barrelled names I used to find in the front of my Latin set texts but that would be quite enough to send Kevin's thoughts off in another direction from the one Lesley intended. I hauled myself out of bed and looked for the other copy. It was unsigned. I put my clothes back on and walked down to the Radcliffe, where an amused nurse effected the swap.

By the time I returned to the flat, it was light and I had abandoned any thought of sleep. I sat up in bed and worked on the poem. It may be thanks to that final mischance that it came out as clearly as it did:

### For Lesley
The last thing touched me

the way you said

Oh, and Roger . . .

212

and for a moment
                    laid yourself against me

                Before I thought to kiss your cheek
you were gone

                    In the street next to yours
a flood of yellow rose

In the Georgian street
                    the next one to mine
I found a whole cluster
                        small roses
of a deep red
                    This house will never miss one

I searched the full flowers
                            for one
still tense
                    Ah, there!
I reached
            snicked it carefully
at the base of the stem

                    I found my smallest glass
                    washed off every stain
                    dried it with a hand of cloth

Now the bud is alive
                        in clear glass
                one petal
                    seems to burn


Anke is walking with my arm round her shoulder, not so much
telling me about her travels as telling me by her quietness she is back.

213

The city frames us like two figures in a manuscript illumination, heading down Walton Street into the aureole of late afternoon, the white haze of sunlight over the bus station.

'We got to London last night,' she explains, 'but it was too late to hitch any further. We were wandering through the streets, feeling really tired, and then, it was so lucky, we found a café that was like a Café des Beaux Arts. Bands play there and they sell records and posters. It was about to close but there was a black boy running it and he was so kind, he let us in, he gave us ice-cold Cokes, he made us some food. And he said we could sleep in the room at the back.'

The luck of the road. Why do I suddenly grudge it to her?

'You know, he was so nice. When I lay on the floor to sleep, he lay down beside me and just put his arm over my shoulder.'

She pauses for me to admire his restraint.

'And then in the middle of the night we just turned to each other. It was so beautiful.'

I had dropped my guard. I was wide open. The blow took me right over the heart.

Ride it! A split-second of self-knowledge, like that first moment when I thought, *Don't lose her!*

This is what comes of being a thread in the troubadours' chronicle. The weavers weave on and there is no telling them when to stop.

Chivalry and romance. His arm over her shoulder. Their bodies turning like tides under the moon. Almost as poetic as glimpsing each other through the flames of a fire on the beach.

Suddenly I am very grateful that Lesley had called me back, that I had felt the wind on my skin.

I kiss Anke on the top of the head. I tell her about Lesley, all the alarms and excursions of that night. I can feel us holding ourselves intact, can feel the concentration in our steps, light,

214

suspended steps, like a firewalker moving across his bed of coals. There is pain down there but we can choose not to feel it.

Then the pain is behind us and our feet are falling casually on to a pavement in June. Anke is under my arm, talking on my shoulder just as she does in the night. I can hear all her voice's inner fluctuations: the hesitations and ponderings, the sudden confidences, the way she breaks into laughter on a particular word.

As long as I can hear those, I believe, I have nothing to fear, whatever she tells me.

Charles comes round to borrow my suit for his degree ceremony. Anke has just left and I am in full flight.

'Pure Anglo-Saxon features,' I exclaim, 'but from another world. She makes you think of the Vikings in Byzantium or the Rus in Nijny-Novgorod. She's like a memory of Nordic beauty, carved out of ivory in Cathay.'

An appraising light comes into his eye.

'Which way is she heading? I'll be travelling all summer. Our paths might cross.'

I hesitate, looking a little unhappy, and Charles gives me one of his disarming smiles.

'Oh, come on, Roger! It's going to happen anyway. I'm sure you would rather it was with a friend.'

'The South of France,' I murmur, as if this will enable him to pinpoint her exactly.

Tilbury Docks is at the end of the line. One by one, the towns of the Thames Estuary fall behind us. The train begins to move through an anonymous zone. Service roads run between blank-faced warehouses. Chain-link fences divide empty lots. If it were not for the other passenger in the carriage, a Thames pilot going on duty, I would be convinced we were being shunted down a siding. We will clink gently

215

off the buffers and come to a halt among cinders and rose bay willowherb.

This morning a letter came from Barcarès, a fishing village in the Pyrenees. 'We're going to be here for a fortnight,' Anke had written on the back of the envelope. 'Why don't you come down and join us?'

By midday I was at the Headington roundabout, making for Dover.

'Dover?' said the driver who was giving me a lift to London. 'Why go all the way down there? Take a train to Tilbury and catch the Townsend-Thorensen. It's much quicker.'

The station was only waiting for our arrival to close. Townsend-Thorensen sailed just once a day. I would have to wait till morning. I walked down to the terminal, past three buses parked on a piece of waste ground. It was dusk and the only light came from a café, a grim little buffet, set in a line of closed offices.

Beyond it was the walkway to the ships. Opposite, the swing bridge to the lower docks, for which you seemed to need a pass. An inspector in a long blue coat was chatting with a port official in a gaberdine and brown trilby. They shifted their feet, they took a turn across the worn grey boards, and I could see all the late rosters they had whiled away together, I could hear the familiar phrases, the creaking of the boards. There was an odd kind of comfort in watching them.

It was a mild night and the café door stood open. I might have gone in had it not been for the noise, the stoked roar that comes from men who have been drinking all evening. For hitching I was wearing my old school boater, a rather superior white straw speckled with black. Cut a dash on the kerb! But I knew just what the reaction would be if I appeared in the doorway with a boater and shoulder-length hair. I sat outside and leaned against the wall.

It felt as if I were leaning against the men's voices. They were

216

ferrying me into sleep, steady as a ship's engine, when there was a whoomph, like the gas igniting in a gas heater. A whoomph of catcalls and wolf whistles.

I looked up, just in time to see an elated smile, a blond head tipped back and a short white raincoat, of the kind that was fashionable then, swirling around white flares and white plimsolls as they moved in a high-stepping, hip-rolling stride. He paraded out of that café as if he were leading the Mardi Gras.

Beside him trotted a small man, dressed in black. An older man, his trim figure just beginning to run to flab. The contrasting clothes suggested they were a regular couple but the little man's were drawn tight as if he shrank from the uproar, just as the other revelled in it.

That blond head was tipped back like an athlete's breasting the tape. I had never seen such exultation. I tried to imagine what it must be like to be the crowd's flashpoint, to live in that dangerous moment. If all else failed, I could always come down to that. A dandy's last resort, scraping for match flares of sensation in a dockland bar.

I was still indulging this fantasy when the blond sailor came back. The raincoat had been discarded. His shoulders were hunched in a white T-shirt, a massed, brooding hunch reminiscent of James Dean in *East of Eden*. The room fell silent as he walked up to the bar. He bought a stack of beer cans and I heard the woman talking gently to him as she handed him the change. He had caught them up in his arms, he was carrying them out, his bowed shoulders filling the walkway, when he turned and began to hurl them at the wall, one after the other, as if he had a particular quarrel with each one. They rolled all over the corridor and he snatched them up and threw them again.

One rolled down past me and I thought, *Don't notice it! Keep looking the other way!*

217

He stood for a moment, swaying slightly. I thought he was going to lurch off, leaving the cans scattered. But he bent over them, almost tenderly, gathering them up. Cradling them in his arms, he carried them up the long walkway back to the ship.

I reached out for the one he had missed and slipped it into my pack.

That night I shared the can with two unemployed men who were waiting for a ship. The top was stove in and the ring pull jammed. We had to knock it in with a stone.

Getting a ship was no longer easy, they explained. The union had organised that once casual profession. You were supposed to enter as a boy, on an apprenticeship. There were qualifications and grades, a whole career structure. The only way in for an outsider was to wait around on the docks on the off chance. If a ship was short-handed at the moment of sailing, it was allowed to take you on. One trip and you had your union papers.

So much for running away to sea, I thought. Next thing the French Foreign Legion will be asking for references.

My new friends had been waiting around for nearly a week. They had just spent the last of their money on the halves of beer they had nursed all evening in the café. Now we sat on the top deck of one of the parked buses, eking out the beer in the can.

They were both from the East End. One was dark and silent, the other a typical Cockney, small and indomitable. He had had a greengrocer's shop until his partner had run off with the money. He grinned and began to tell stories of life's little surprises.

One night he had been sitting on a park bench with a mate, both of them penniless with nowhere to go, when two women pulled up in a smart car. 'How about a little fun, boys?' they said and took them off to their flat. At dawn he had found himself back on the park bench, well-fed, well-liquored and well-pleasured, with a couple of quid in his top pocket.

At that point something clicked. A memory of Bill's loft at the farm, of sleepless nights with bottles of brown ale. It was his story of the officers' wives and the men with commando training. We had entered the region of consoling myth. These were the tales of Rock Candy Mountain, the legends of Cockaigne.

I spent the next night in a barn in the Pas de Calais with a girl in a black dress. I had spotted her as soon as we got off the boat, hitching along the road in front of me. More chance of a lift with a girl and I caught her up.

A strange hitchhiker. No luggage. Walking along the verge in a simple black dress, looking for all the world like a French village girl. I spoke to her in French, only to discover that she was a student at the American College in Paris, on her way back from visiting friends in London.

We got a lift almost at once, two French boys in an old American car. They were very proud of the car, which was on its last legs.

'We need some petrol,' they explained and turned off the main road. They coasted down to a garage, where a friend seemed to be in charge of the pump.

'This is our village,' they said. 'While you're here, you must see the church. It's very modern.'

We drove thirty yards to the church: one of the stained-glass tents the Roman Catholics threw up everywhere in the 1960s. Audacious, if you had not seen twenty others like it.

We made approving noises and were invited for a beer in the village's little bar. At which point we realised we had been kidnapped.

Blame it on rock'n'roll. They had only seen hair like mine on record covers. To them I had stepped out of another world, out of the mythical streets where the Rolling Stones lounged on the corner. I might have taken the Ferry 'Cross the Mersey, I might have danced at the Cavern. I confessed that I had not. But I had once seen the Beatles land at London airport, their blow-dried mopheads shining in the floodlights like little silver busbies.

These French boys lived within sight of the car ferry. In a few hours they could have been in Swinging London. But they were tied to their homes and families, to the peasant traditions of the Pas de Calais, which stretched around them like an endless Middle Ages. All they wanted was to touch the hem of the modern world. All they wanted, in the end, was for me to send them a postcard.

Religiously I wrote down their address and they released us on to the main road. But it was too late. All the ferry traffic had gone. We walked until the road glimmered like a comet's tail in the dusk, like the promise of a millennium that would come to lift us out of these interminable fields. Like two vagrants from any century, we slept in a barn, innocently locked together in the narrow, old-fashioned sleeping bag I had inherited from my father.

The twentieth century picked us up early next morning, in the form of a freaked-out policeman. He was storming back from his mother-in-law's in Calais, where he had left his wife after a row that had lasted all night. At eight he had to be at his desk in Paris.

'Don't worry!' he said as he hurtled into a bend, pumping on the brakes. 'I've done the police driver's course.'

The car swooped on its springs. The body tried to fly off the chassis and was brought back with a crunch.

'Lie across the back seat!' he shouted to the American girl and we realised we had been picked up as ballast.

On the policeman's instructions I took the Metro out to the Porte d'Italie. It felt odd, midway through the intensity of longing that had carried me from Oxford, to come across so many like me and take my place in a line of hitchhikers at the head of the N7; as if there were some midpoint in dreams where spirits had to queue in their crumpled clothing.

Then a car stopped, a black Citroën DS, and I was caught up into the delusion of a lawyer in his early forties, a slightly podgy man with black hair brushed back and gold-rimmed spectacles.

I was surprised that he had given me a lift at all and started to thank him in my most formal French.

'I am giving you a lift', he explained, 'because I have to give you a warning. I have been entrusted with a great secret, with a revelation: the world is going to end in 1970.

'All the evidence is in the Bible. I'm writing a book to prove it but it will take me five years. Three to track down all the quotations. Then a year to write and a year to publish and distribute. It can take a book six months to go through the printers, particularly a book like that. All the cross-references. All the numerological charts.'

'But by then there won't be any printers!' I pointed out. 'We're already in 1966. Your book will be coming out a year after the world has ended.'

He waved this aside as mere arithmetic.

'I was given a sign. One day when I was praying in Notre-Dame. I was given the revelation and then I was given a sign. I saw a great light and felt a great heat around me. I was touched with fire and ever since there has been a flame burning in my forehead.'

He touched the spot, just above the bridge of his spectacles.

'A little flame that burns day and night. You can't see it but I can feel it.'

A warmth came into his voice as he said that. He seemed to draw reassurance from the syllables, '*mais je peux la sentir*', as if he were naming his wife or his child, and I guessed that the flame had to burn in their place.

He drove on round the ring road and turned off, appropriately enough, for Chartres. So much for my swift progress down the N7.

The next night I was in Orléans, in one of the outposts of the Cold War. Taken in by an American airman and his girlfriend, who had looked up and grinned when they saw the boater. The first and only time. The French seemed to resent it. Someone had spat on me from a passing car.

Louie was stationed in Orléans with an air force band. There were worse places. He could have been on ceremonial duties in Saigon. Or in a little mobile jazz combo, being flown around to perform on rafts in the Mekong Delta. But in a sense he was already a casualty of Vietnam. Louie was a song-and-dance man. He had just broken into musical comedy in Hollywood when his draft papers came. His agent had investigated all the loopholes. There were only two. He could convince the Medical Board he was a drug addict, which was almost impossible: even real addicts were being passed. Or he could declare that he was homosexual. Louie had thought it over and refused: 'It would have finished my father.'

He was turning the boater in his hands, looking at it with a wistful half-smile. Short of a top hat and cane, I could hardly have produced anything more reminiscent of vaudeville. 'Try it on!' I suggested. But he shook his head. 'It makes me think of a curtain number. You know, you take it off and give three little waves as you dance into the wings.' He jumped up and set it at a fetching slant on Kathy's head: 'Let's hit the town!'

There was not much of a town to hit. We sat in a little bar, its door open on to the street. Three teenage girls paraded slowly past on their bicycles. An elderly couple, arm in arm, were taking the air. 'Hey, look at those two!' said Louie. 'They're a complete production.' The panama hat, the white linen jacket, the cane coming down slowly and precisely, like a waterbird planting its foot. All the fine details were there: the tiepin in the tie, the watch chain looped across the waistcoat. The old lady's little hand, tucked into the crook of his arm, was enclosed in a white lace glove. On the brim of her dark-blue hat was the shadow of a veil. 'I can't bear it,' murmured Louie. 'I can smell the eau-de-cologne on her handkerchief.'

We did not like to laugh out loud with the old couple so near. The laughter rose inside us as a distillation, a pure spirit. For once, three was company. Louie and Kathy leaned back on their chairs, looking at the town they had come to know so well. I had given them my traveller's immunity, my glimpse of it as an overnight fair – illuminated windows, the music from a café, strollers and a solitary drunk – and they had remembered that they too were travellers. That little bar was like the inn in a folk tale where we met to exchange our stories.

Mine was all intuitive leaps and immediate decisions: the chance meeting in the street, the sudden departure for the postmark on a letter. Theirs, a slowly dawning, incredulous sense of luck: they had found each other where they least expected, on an overseas posting to a provincial town. Kathy was the daughter of the base commander. Their only fear was that they might have grown almost too close, that isolation had given their relationship an intensity it could never achieve again. They were like Donne and his young wife during their long banishment from court:

> She is all States, and all Princes, I,
> Nothing else is.

How would they feel when they were back in the States, when Kathy had to go to college and Louie tried to relaunch his career?

'It might even be the end of us.' Louie was becoming sombre. 'Who knows? Lovers are gamblers. You risk everything on a hunch.'

'But it's always been like that,' I protested. 'The world is not as

223

logical as it appears. We are like ships in the days of sail, subject to immense and unpredictable forces, trusting to the winds to see us round Cape Horn. What do you think people said fifty years ago when that old lady first appeared on the old gentleman's arm? Was it a good match, approved by both families? Or did everyone shake their heads and say it was *un coup de foudre, un amour de folie*? Look at all the houses in these quiet streets!' I was warming to my theme. 'They look so orderly, don't they, as if they were governed entirely by thrift and good housekeeping. Don't you believe it! They're all founded on dreams and illusions. Every one of these marriages was a leap in the dark.'

I was falling under my own spell. The more I talked, the more intolerable it became that I was still so far from Anke. Three days on the road and still only in Orléans! Destiny should not be subject to such delays.

'It'll take you two more days at least,' Louie pointed out. 'Two more days on the roadside, smiling hopefully into slipstream and spit. Who needs it? The Southern Express goes through here at midnight. Why don't you catch that?'

The prospect was irresistible. We raised our glasses and drank to my departure. We began to imagine the girls' surprise. They would be sitting at one of the tables outside the little café, lingering over their coffee, when the waiter presented them with two enormous ice creams, 'with the compliments of the Englishman in the corner'. They would be standing on the quay, watching the fishing boats unload, when I walked up behind Anke and placed my hands over her eyes: 'Guess who?'

Louie and Kathy were still inventing scenarios as they waved me off at the station. I felt as if I were making this journey for them too, as if I were rolling a double six in the face of boredom and frustration and doubt.

\* \* \*

I could only see into the middle distance. Beyond that the sand shimmered and went out of focus. Spots slid across my eyes. No doubt they were sunbathers too.

It was like trying to find two dots in the Milky Way.

I stepped out on to the sand and a wolf whistle went up. A thousand pairs of sunglasses swivelled in my direction. *Wretched boater!* I thought. But it wasn't the boater. On the beach, in the midday sun, that looked almost sensible. It was the hair, the blond pelt curling to my shoulders. The angel's mane, as Anke once called it, in one of her inspired bendings of English.

They had never seen anything like it. Or only in photos of the one French rock singer to cash in on the beatnik vogue. His name began to rise all around me, in long, derisive jets of sound: *Antoine! Antoine!*

Children pointed and shrieked, dancing on the edge of their family circles. Deckchairs leaned back to consider me over their aperitifs. Sunglasses dandled their smiles, curious, amused, mocking. Oiled backs sat up like seals, stretching their necks to look at me. I dodged between them, scanning the horizon for that one proud head with its straight fall of hair.

I remember that beach now as if I had been flying over it, skimming the white sand and the upturned faces, the cries of *Antoine! Antoine!* flaring around me like tracer shells.

There were some young people sitting in the shade of a bamboo screen, beside a couple of beached dinghies. I homed in on them as if they were a friendly airstrip.

Yes, they had seen two girls with rucksacks. But not recently. Last week. Or the week before.

I walked on into the salt-bright haze, confirmed and dispirited. They must have gone off somewhere else for a couple of days. The little groups thinned out, the last beachcomber bent over the tideline, and I went on treading the sand's starched sheet until it melted into the glinting grain of a small river running into the sea.

Hope postponed is an acceptable state. You can live in it. It becomes a temporary home. I went back to the group under the bamboo screen and asked them where the post office was. Anke might have left me a note at the Poste Restante. 'Leave your rucksack here, we'll look after it,' they said, with an adoptive eagerness that I recognised from Calais. The blond pelt had its uses.

I should have said, Don't be fooled, I may look like something out of *Desolation Angels* but I don't really know what I'm doing, I've only just turned on. My psyche ought to be wearing L-plates.

If you were facing the beach, Barcarès seemed infinite. If you faced the village, it was almost as I had imagined: buses came in on the dusty white road from Perpignan and pulled up in front of the Café Loup de Mer. The road opened out to form a little marketplace and drew itself in again before the brown-stained bulk of the church. Between the café and the church there were two rows of little shops, separated by a street that ran down into the marketplace. The first row contained all the essentials – *boulangerie*, *épicerie*, *droguerie* – and ended in a big bar on the corner. The second row was more nondescript and ended in ordinary houses. You walked along this row and turned the corner, as if you were going round to one of the back doors, and there was a half-door in the end wall. This was *La Poste*.

Part of the charm of summer places is that a lightness attends all the usual offices. You go into the chemist's and there, beside the pharmacist's sober brown bottles, are racks of beach shoes and bright revolving stands of towelling wraps. You go through the half-door into the post office and there, in place of the mausoleum chill, the mahogany partitions and the marble counter, is a whitewashed room that smells of sand and salt. There was no letter waiting for me but I sat and wrote a note to Anke, letting her know I had arrived. In that family atmosphere, with the summer colony greeting each other as they despatched their postcards and opened their parcels from home, it seemed impossible that she should not be in the next morning to collect it.

The beach cleared as if someone had just blown a whistle. Five o'clock: time for the colony to go back to their summer homes and shower and change. They had to prepare for the round of evening visits, the drinks on the crumbling terraces, the elaborate improvisations in the old farmhouse kitchens.

My friends padlocked the dinghies to their chains – they were for hire, it appeared, though there had not been so much as an enquiry all afternoon – and came to wish me goodnight. '*Tu as l'air content*,' one of them said. 'You look happy enough' and it was true. I was leaning against my rucksack, writing to Redmond. When it was too dark to write, I could roll out my bag and sleep in the shelter of the screen. For once, I felt snug in the universe.

A wind sprang up. The screen wheezed and the dinghies lifted on their chains. The halyards rattled against the masts. Long strips of tinfoil, pinned to the mastheads, flittered and tinkled. The wind stiffened and they began to whine like musical saws. A memory stirred of one of the shamanic peoples – the Inuit? the Tibetans? – setting up wind drones to keep away evil spirits and the shrilling took on another significance. I felt as if I were camped between worlds.

When the first twang came, I thought it was just a note the wind had struck from a wire. When it came again, insistent, imperious, I listened and caught the rest of the riff. Someone was starting to play 'Satisfaction' on an electric guitar. Red's letter was never finished. I tucked my notebook into my pack and went to find the

227

music. It was coming from a concrete hut at the back of the beach, next to the toilets. I opened the door and there were a drummer and two guitarists building up to the tune's final frenzy. They must have been playing for themselves because there was no room for anyone else. A few kids had collected inside the door, leaving just a narrow space in front of the band.

Time for Antoine to show his paces, I thought, and launched myself into it. I had never danced in public before and there was an elation in having this small space to command, this little audience to stun. The drummer was good and I danced as if I were part of the rhythm section, kicking out as the hi-hat skished, boogying down as the pedal thumped on the bass drum. By the time the number finished I knew that I had danced clear of all my shadows: Rimbaud; Kerouac; the sailor in white. Between us, the drummer and I had made something real. Momentary but real.

But I was too young to leave it at that. Too young and too full of illusions. If I could dance, perhaps I could sing. Perhaps I could break the lock on my voice. I thought back to my first slow swayings in Walton Lane, to that shaft of sunlight in which the dust had begun to move. I went outside and walked up and down the beach, singing the opening words of 'Satisfaction' over to myself. I could hear the effect I wanted to get, a slow, breathless chant that would end in a holler.

I went back in and negotiated with the band.

'I want to try something,' I said. 'I'll start and you pick up from me. Don't worry if it sounds strange, just improvise.'

I put my lips to the microphone and began to intone: 'I can't get no . . .' But it didn't sound strange. Just horribly familiar. Horribly flat. The drummer gave a peremptory tish on the hi-hat and sent me back into the dance.

\* \* \*

228

The hut was locked, the musicians were back in the bosom of their families and I was still thirsty.

To everyone's amusement, I had drunk a pint of milk while I was dancing, gulping it down like liquid energy. After that, I had only to pause and the kids would say, 'Tired, Antoine? Drink some milk!'

I looked round the edge of the screen. The *épicerie*, where I had bought the milk, was dark. All the shops were dark. The Loup de Mer glowed over them as the orange juice dispenser glows over a café counter, a rectangle of soft light. Both floors were lit and people were out having drinks on the balcony. The wind carried their laughter and I felt like Grendel in his dark fen, gazing up at the lighted hall where Beowulf and his companions were feasting.

There was a tap, I remembered, set into the little area of crazy paving at the back of the beach, next to the miniature golf course. I crossed the prickling, wind-blown sand and came to the rim of light from the street lamps. There was the tap, in the centre of a broad basin, as if it had been built as a fountain. Brightly lit and in full view of the crowd on the balcony.

Now I felt even more like some poor, bare, forked thing, crawling out of the night. Or an animal coming down to the waterhole under the massed infrared cameras of the safari lodge.

There is only one way to do this: with dignity. I crossed the paving and stepped down into the basin as if it were the most natural thing in the world. Composing myself, as if this were another dance, I knelt in front of the tap and drank from my cupped hands.

The crowd noticed at once and began to discuss me in the philosophical manner of the French. Phrases like '*l'extrême de l'existentialisme*' floated over my head. Which made a change from being told I was a long-haired scruff who needed two years in the army. As I gave my face a final rinse, someone was even entering in my defence: '*Je l'admire plutôt* . . .' I was almost tempted to stay and hear what he said.

Back in the lee of the screen, I composed myself for sleep. This was not so easy. The streamers' wavering cries might have been my own unquiet music. Little jigs of elation when I remembered the dance. A long, sawing anxiety when I wondered where Anke was. I tried to rest on the uncertainty as Jacob had pillowed his head on a stone in the wilderness. This is the nature of quest, I told myself. Between revelations, the desert. But no visitations came, no angels ascending and descending. Only the bedlam in the air above me, which seemed more and more like the howlback of my own thoughts.

What I needed was a drink. *Un petit cognac*. It was much later now. The family parties would have left the Loup de Mer. I looked round the edge of the screen and, sure enough, the top floor was in darkness. Just a low light burning downstairs. I spruced myself up, put on my jacket and made my way across the beach.

The Loup de Mer was closed. The low light was a security light. There was nothing for it but to risk the bar on the corner. I had walked past it that afternoon and sensed trouble. Boys sitting on the steps outside had eyed me as I approached, their silence more threatening than all the whistles on the beach. But there was no one on the steps now. It looked friendly enough.

I entered and a large group of young people, sitting at several tables, immediately called me over. They sat me down and poured me a glass of wine. Word of the dance had obviously spread. I took off my jacket and made myself comfortable. We were just beginning to talk when I became aware of someone close behind me. I looked round and he was crouched, dark eyes in a big, cropped skull, staring at my hair with an avid gleam. '*Je veux des ciseaux*,' he said and made cutting movements with his fingers.

This was too close. I stood up and two or three of the boys at my table jumped up too. '*Amis!*' they said anxiously. '*Nous sommes des amis!*' I put my hands on his shoulders, which were as broad as roof beams, and steered him on to a chair at the next table. '*Tu t'asseois là,*' I said, '*et je m'asseois ici.*' 'You sit there and I'll sit here.' I turned back to the conversation, thinking I had established a distance between us, when I sensed him behind me again. One glance was enough. He had a cigarette lighter. He was holding the flame in front of him with a smile of revelation, of incredulous mischief, swinging it from side to side and bringing it closer and closer to my hair.

I leapt up and threw my wine in his eyes. It worked just as it does in the films. He groped blindly, his arms outstretched. At that moment, if I had remembered my boxing from school, I could have finished him off: a blow to the stomach to wind him and an uppercut as he folded up. But I had seen too many films. In an absurd imitation of God knows whom – Honor Blackman in *The Avengers?* – I tried to land a karate chop on the thick muscle at the base of his neck. This must have looked more dangerous than it was because the others pinioned me. They swarmed over him too and subdued him. But not before he had come swinging at me and landed two ringing blows, one on either side of my head.

'*Va-t-en,*' they said, '*vite! Avant que viennent les flics.*' 'Vanish! Quick! Before the cops get here.'

I ran down the steps, reached the shadow of the beach and realised I had left my jacket behind. Everything was in the pockets: my wallet, my passport. I ran back but it was too late. As I came down the steps the second time, the police came round the corner. They marched me off to the station, which was just up the street, and sat me down in front of the inspector.

'*Passeport!*'

He looked through it carefully but there was nothing incriminating: no stamps saying *Deported* or *Entry Refused*.

231

'*Vous parlez Français?*'

'*Oui.*'

'*Vous le parlez bien?*'

'*Oui.*'

This was a great relief to him. Now he could be as rude as he liked.

'Then what *connerie* is this? Starting a fight in a bar! Where the hell do you think you are? Marseilles? This is a quiet place. A family resort. A little village that depends on the holiday trade. It has to be protected from *salauds* like you.'

He spoke rapidly, as if he had a backlog of bad temper to work off on *salauds* like me.

'*Mais, Monsieur!*'

It seemed to me that we had skipped a stage in the legal process: namely, the trial.

'I didn't start it. I was only acting in self-defence. He came at me with a cigarette lighter. What was I supposed to do? Sit there and wait for my head to go up in flames?'

He caught the note of playground innocence, the cry of 'But, Sir, he hit me first!' and relaxed a little. Perhaps I was not quite the international drifter he had taken me for. But in his book I was still guilty. I was trouble. Respectable tourists did not get their ears singed.

'That's as may be. But I want you off my patch. I want you gone first thing in the morning.'

'*Mais, Monsieur!*' – the note of shrill protest again – 'I can't go tomorrow. I have to wait for my girlfriend. She wrote to me asking me to meet her here. I can't go until she arrives.'

Perhaps only a French policeman would have unbent at the mention of *la belle amie*.

'I see. And when is she likely to get here?'

'I don't know. Some time in the next few days. I've left her a note at the Poste Restante. I'll know the moment she arrives.'

'All right.' He handed over the passport. 'But if you take my advice, you won't hang around. You'll leave the area as soon as possible.'

There was a warning there I did not register at the time. All I cared about was that I had his permission to stay in Barcarès.

'*Merci, Monsieur, merci beaucoup. Vous êtes très gentil.*'

But he was not going to leave me under that illusion. As I reached the door, he reminded me just where I stood in the eyes of the law.

'*Je n'aime pas les emmerdeurs.*' 'I don't like troublemakers.'

The world spun as I came out into the street. I felt bruised and breathless, as if I had been trading punches. For me the real fight had taken place in the police station. I stood there, white in the face, and a policeman coming back off his beat asked me if I was feeling all right.

Suddenly I was glad of the wind. I wanted to lose myself in its primal force, to howl against the element. Slipping past the bar into the darkness, I made for the shoreline. The wind hit me full strength and I could feel my shock like a tide running the other way, carrying me into it. The dunes were breaking up. Coils of marram grass bowled across the sand, which was lifting like spindrift and returning to the surface in a long hiss. A branch of driftwood reared up, two white horns giving me their empty stare. 'Anke, Anke!' I shouted, hurling her name into all that welter as if somewhere along the coast it might slip between the air currents and find her, ducked under the hood of the sleeping bag like a child under the blankets.

The cry had gone out of me. Drawn by their strange half-light, I drifted into the dunes; clambered through the wind's breakers over two or three crests and dropped down into a stillness, broken, somewhere at my feet, by the welt of water on sand. I had come out on to another shore. I looked inland and saw lights rising and falling in the shelter of the ridge I had just crossed. I had found the fishing fleet, moored in the little bay that must have brought

Barcarès into being, centuries back, when the beach only served as a breakwater.

Following the rise of the dunes until they became a deep stone wall, I stood looking down on to the boats. The waves were driving in hard and they jinked on their chains, every rope and wire thrumming. I watched them for a long time. There was something calming in the movement of their tethered weights on water, something domestic in the slap of keels and the jingle of anchor chains. They were like cattle shifting in their stall.

I tried to hold those sounds in my head as I settled to sleep under the demented streamers. I tried to imagine Anke sheltering from the same wind a few miles up the coast, sleeping, as I knew she slept, with her thumb in her mouth:

'Lovers who have learned this last refinement –'

I told myself, repeating lines I had heard Graves read in Oxford,

'To lie apart, yet sleep and dream together
Motionless under their starred coverlet –
Crown love with wreaths of myrtle.'

But it was not easy to dream when you felt like an old rope fender the waves had washed up, wind-frayed and white with salt. One side of my jaw was stiff. There was a bruise behind the other ear. I was beginning to feel the blows I had taken in the bar.

There were shouts. Running footsteps. I sat up and saw a torch flash over by the band's hut. It might be my anxious *amis* from the bar. Or my avid shadow, come to avenge the wine in his eyes. Hard to tell until I was on the brink of discovery and then it would be too late.

I flattened myself against the sand, anxious not to show a

234

silhouette behind the screen, or the white of a face the torch might catch. And was unnerved to hear, so close they seemed imminent, every run the searchers made across the back of the beach. I was hearing them as a rabbit might hear them underground, as vibrations rather than sounds.

The searchers themselves never came close. They dashed this way and that, in a frenzy of disbelief. '*Mais il doit y être,*' one of them shouted, '*parce qu'il existe!*' 'But he must be somewhere . . . because he exists!' and for one dangerous moment I felt as if I had the option, as if there were a border I could slip across, a death I might return from.

Though fear would have followed me even there. Two or three times that night my sleep was broken by the sound of running feet, a *thump, thump, thud* that seemed to end with someone standing right over me. I awoke crying out and jerking to one side, already shuddering from a blow.

And then the sun rose. I felt it as a change in my sleep, a warmth entering and easing the night fears out of me. I drowsed in its gold and woke as our ancestors must have woken for centuries, with a sense of mercy.

By the time the first holidaymaker came down on to the beach, I had made an awning of my anorak, tucking one edge between the slats of the screen and stretching it over my pack. This simple arrangement made me feel like a king of the road. I lay under the slant of shade and my confidence surged back in rough little blasts, like the first notes of a blues on the mouth harp. 'On the road again,' I sang to myself tunelessly, looking up at the sky and feeling the planet move under me like the back of a lorry. I had already forgotten how much of this well-being was physiological. I thought I was a Dharma Bum, riding the turn of the earth. Whereas I had simply reanimated in the sun like a lizard.

A shadow fell across me in mid-chorus. I would like to be able to say that I looked round. Actually, I twitched like a probed nerve. But it was only the little Belgian who owned the dinghies. He sat down beside me and began to tell me his troubles. The onshore wind I had felt last night had been blowing all summer and the seas were running high, too high for the casual sailors his trade depended on. No one was going to take their children out into the backwash of a gale. He had driven down from the north with the dinghies on a trailer, expecting to make his fortune. Now he was reduced to selling Cokes from his icebox.

'Why don't you just go home?'

'I can't afford to. I paid the council in advance, I had to take the pitch for the whole summer. I don't even have the money for the petrol home. I've just got to stay here and hope the weather changes.'

He sounded philosophical. And looked almost meditative, hands clasped between his knees as he squatted in the sun. But he was like me, I noticed, an involuntary glancer, a continual checker of the horizon. One glimpse of a customer and he was up like a sprinter off the blocks.

Gradually the screen's little club gathered around us, the girls arriving in their beach wraps, a shoulder basket swaying over one hip, the boys nonchalantly stripped down to their trunks, a packet of Gauloises and a disposable lighter in one hand. Gravely the girls unveiled their bikinis. They chatted as they oiled one another's backs, but there was a weightlessness about these exchanges, an absent-mindedness. They were like the remarks that go back and forth between lovers as they lock the door, draw the curtains and throw a dark sweater over the bedside lamp: next-to-nothings that will not deflect the body from its purpose. Stretched out on their towels, they gave themselves into the hands of the sun.

The boys had a darker design. Face down alongside their chosen

236

girl, the tip of their elbows almost touching hers, they began a side-long, murmuring courtship, so stealthy it was almost subliminal. I might have thought I was imagining things if I had not seen one of the girls give an answering moue, shrugging her shoulders flatter as she resettled her cheek against the back of her hand. They must have been deep in erotic thought transferences, pheromones swirling over their bodies in chemical storms, the sand between them throbbing like the Atlantic cable.

Time to try the Poste Restante.

Still nothing. Which was like a blow to the stomach. A little gulp of cold in the sunlit room. Swallow and straighten your shoulders. Out into the street.

Only one thing to do. Search the beach. The sunglasses swivelled, the wolf whistles went up. But the space I had danced in the night before was still with me. Move in your own time and you project the space. Eyes slide off you like the eyes you flash past in a dance.

No sign of Anke and Hannah. Just a large group of children, playing on their own. Lighten up. Children are like animals, they pick up the least flicker of disturbance. I imagined James Moody's flute over Milt Jackson's vibes, I said the last stanza of Roethke's 'A Field of Light' over to myself like a charm:

My heart lifted up with the great grasses;
The weeds believed me, and the nesting birds.
There were clouds making a rout of shapes crossing a wind-
    break of cedars,
And a bee shaking drops from a rain-soaked honeysuckle.
The worms were delighted as wrens.
And I walked, I walked through the light air;
I moved with the morning.

The children looked up from their game and smiled: *Bonjour, Antoine!* No mockery in their voices now. Just a child's eagerness to name, to be on speaking terms with all the world's phenomena.

*I am controlling this*, I thought.

A young couple with two toddlers had marked out their patch with two piles of clothing, safety markers, presumably, beyond which the toddlers were forbidden to toddle. Their family dog, a black cairn terrier, was monitoring my approach.

I can control you, too. I have the Horseman's Word. I speak your gruff dialect. If I keep my eyes down and keep to the tideline, staying outside the markers, you won't bark. I'll slip past like a gypsy in the night.

I kept my eyes down. But skirted just inside the first marker, just for devilment.

He bristled and began to bark furiously. He was offended in every hair. The young couple looked up, astonished. Here was someone walking innocently along the tideline and their dog vibrant with rage. They grabbed him by the collar and apologised profusely. But he knew. And I knew. Long after I had gone, his protests shook the air.

Still no sign.

I came to the dunes I had clambered through the night before and threw myself down, leaning back against their warm swell and sinking one hand into the cool sand under the surface. '*Soothe me, great groans of underneath*.' Roethke again. I had thrown his *Words for the Wind* into my rucksack in Oxford, thinking they would be good company on the journey. Now they had become part of it. They had ceased to be lines of poetry. They were logbook entries, sketch maps of where I was.

I wanted to reach right down, to grope for ribs of rock, but the lower sand was damp and impenetrable. I scrabbled at it with my fingers, gouging out a ridge that I gripped like the pommel of a saddle, and it gave a kick like the shock from an electric fence. I was already writing the poem,

> My arm shook and the pulse
> of the earth went through me,

when I realised that it was my own pulse, earthed by the sand.

Last night the howlback of my thoughts on the wind. Now my heartbeat in the ground. This place was too much.

Low dunes ran back into low pines. They crinkled round a salt-water lake and formed an island that was almost silted to the shore. A low wooden building had overrun it like thorn scrub. Salt-whitened planks smoked in the clear evening light, a bluishness of old paint in their grain. The shutters were down on one side and a man's head moved in the darkness behind the counter. A foot-bridge ran out to it across the end of the lake.

I had walked up the beach the other way, towards the distant smudge of the Pyrenees. And here I felt a surge of hope. It was just the kind of dereliction that Anke would find magical.

The man had not seen her but he seemed to approve of my enquiry.

'*La vie de bohème,*' he said, polishing another glass for the non-existent customers, '*c'est la meilleure.*'

'*Oui,*' I said as I turned back across the footbridge, '*mais quand ça ne marche pas . . .*' 'But when it doesn't work . . .'

There was nothing left but the horizon. '*J'allais sous le ciel, Muse! et j'étais ton féal.*' 'I walked under the open sky, Muse! and I was your bondsman.' Rimbaud's '*Bohème*'. The litany of consolations had started up in my head.

I came to the river where I had turned back the day before and waded straight across. The water was running fast and for two or three steps it tore at my thighs. Then I was over. There were no footprints on the other side, no scraps of litter in the dunes, which the wind had scoured almost flat. Just the rounded edge of the fore-shore, white as a cuttlefish bone.

It was broken by a silhouette. The gable of a roof, that seemed to sink back into the sand. A rock, I thought, that had pitched against the skyline. Except that there were no rocks on this beach.

It grew steadily more rock-like as I approached. The outline, that sharp, man-made angle, became irregular. The surface rough-ened. Blotches of lichen appeared, or veins of milky quartz, running its length. And then I saw daylight through them.

It was a shelter, skilfully constructed out of driftwood. Two great curves leaned together to form an inverted 'v', like the arch of a horse collar. Long, sloping sides tapered back to the junction of three branches, the bole of a small tree. This was the point of genius in the construction: the bole balanced the arch. One branch sprang up to form the roof-tree. The other two curved out to set the line of the walls.

Smaller branches were wedged in between. Not enough to keep out the rain but enough to provide shelter from sun and wind. Not a twist of rope was to be seen, not a single clove-hitch. Everything was held by the balance of stresses. The walls were strung like a harp.

I was not sure which drew me more. The untrodden sand beyond the river, far from the lights of the Loup de Mer, the streamers' spirit cries, the shouts and the sound of running feet. Or the shelter itself, the strange, stripped beauty of its bleached wood, grained and gleaming like stone. Though it was above ground and filled with light, the shelter had the secrecy of a cave.

All I had to do was keep them both secret. I moved off at a stealthy shamble. Trudged back across the river, looking bored, as if I had found nothing of interest on the other side. Wandered up to the deserted screen and casually, as if on a whim, picked up my rucksack.

There were lights along the horizon, discreetly spaced as in a hotel lounge: sardine boats, their predatory spotlights softened by distance and transformed into a visual lullaby. They curved up off the black sea in a succession of perfect arcs.

False moons were luring fish to their death: but to me they came across the night as the calls of their kind must come to birds in the evening chorus, lapping them in the comfort of the species. I fell asleep remembering the torches of other climbers on the early morning ascent of Mont Blanc, a chain of lights moving up the great hill of the dark.

I awoke to find myself staring up at a skinned rabbit. It was stretched just over my head, the exposed flesh glistening. I jerked away and it melted back into the roof, a curve of the driftwood, lit by the dawn pallor.

The next time I woke into sunlight. Scrambling out of the shelter was like slipping on a shirt fresh from the ironing board: warmth clothed my neck and shoulders. The heat haze had yet to rise and the beach ran straight into its distant curve under the foothills of Mont Canigou. In all that glitter of sea and sand, I was the only vertical. I breathed the morning in and tasted hunger like the bite of an apple, like a natural good.

I thought of the little bakery next to the Loup de Mer, of the sweet scent of *pain au chocolat* coming through the smell of warm bread, and made for the river.

As I entered the water, my reflection rose like a shine in wood, steadying a moment among the sand flecks and streaming away as I surged forward.

There was a lone sunbather in the dunes, a blond girl in the three scallops of a white bikini.

'*Quelle jolie forme!*' I said and walked on along the shoreline, my jeans already drying in the sun. The cloth lifted from the skin and I felt as if at any moment I might lift off too and take to the air.

But then came the knots of people, the nudges and whispers. I glanced down and began to pick my way through them but it was hard to lose the sense of boundlessness, to pull back from the horizon and shrink down to a self-conscious nub. You'll just have to be impervious, I thought. Spaced-in rather than spaced-out.

There was a market in the marketplace: three or four trestle tables and people stopping to look. I stopped by the first one and found myself looking down on to a jumble of antiques: oil lamps, a leather wallet, an old brooch. Not valuable things but not junk either: what Thomas Hardy called '*relics of householdry*', the sort of things over which he saw the hands of the generations still hovering, '*hands behind hands*'.

I say 'wallet' but it was not stiff and shiny, nor was it meant to hold money. A simple fold of rough leather, it had two ribs of softer leather on the inside, tucked and stitched into a series of loops. A carpenter might have kept the bits of a small drill there, or a saddler his needles and awls. Now you would invent a use for it, just to have an excuse to own it. Even when the wallet was closed, there was something reassuring about those two neat rows of double stitching crossing the brown earth of the leather, something that spoke of the certainties of craftsmanship, of the world brought under man's control. It looked like a book, an old leather almanac, holding the seasons to their cycle, the moon to its waxing and waning, February the twenty-ninth to its punctual reappearance every leap year.

There were darknesses in the leather, liverish swirls in its chestnut. I held them up to the clear meridional light and saw that they were ripples, unevennesses that must have occurred when the skin was first stretched and dried. Over the years they had darkened from the sweat of hands behind hands.

I cleared a space on the table, right in the centre at the front. Put the wallet down and looked for another colour: the deep red of the brooch. Set beside the wallet, the depth and the darknesses seemed to balance. The brass base of one of the oil lamps was a soft yellow, the colour of old gold, and I moved it down so that it stood over the wallet and the brooch.

There were three old wooden spoons bundled together with string. Everything on that table looked as if it had just been unpacked from a tea chest. I took them out of the string and fanned them out so that each one showed against the table, each different hollowing, with the stainings and the little splits of use. I found two glasses, rather elegant tumblers of a thin, clear glass, etched with a scroll round the rim, and set them in the spaces between the spoons.

By now people were watching me. Among them, I was sure, the owners of the stall. Someone had moved to my elbow when I first picked up the wallet. I had the same feeling I had during the first days with Anke, of walking on water. If my nerve held, if I could just finish rearranging this table, they would see the sense of it.

'*Mais, c'est un artiste!*' said the shadow at my elbow. I glanced round: a man in his fifties, hawk-faced with curling white hair, brushed back and receding at the temples, was watching me with a gentle eagerness in his eyes. At his elbow stood a squat, dark-haired woman, her eyes glistening like black olives. Behind her, a tall, broad-shouldered boy of eighteen, his face a blur of puzzlement. Father, mother and son, in echelon. I took it that I had their permission to continue.

It was like tuning an old instrument. For all its jumble, everything on that table had been carefully cleaned and polished. The copper glowed, the wood shone. It was just a matter of finding the right intervals, of clearing a space in which each colour could resonate.

I stepped back, all the spaces finally found, and the hawk-faced man stepped forward: '*Qu'est-ce-que tu fais à Barcarès?*' 'What are you doing in Barcarès?'

I told him of Anke's letter, of the message scribbled on the back. 'Have you seen them? Two Dutch girls, one with long blond hair, the other with ginger ringlets? I've been looking for them for two days now.'

Desperation must have shrilled in my voice because he said, '*Ne t'en fais pas!*' 'Don't worry about it!' and began to tell me a story. He had been in the French Foreign Legion, marching in a column of men through a little town in North Africa, when he saw a girl gazing at him from the pavement. Their eyes met and she threw him a rose. As he marched away, a song came into his head.

By now he was gripping my elbow, his eyes burning into me: 'The girl sees the man, just for an instant. She throws him the rose. But he is a soldier, he can't break step, he has to march away. In that instant, something in her dies.'

He sang me the song as the crowd broke around us. It began gently, sadly, as if it would become a lament, then broke into a note so high it sounded transparent, a note washed clear of longing or loss.

'Listen!' he said. 'That note is not found in Western music but I can teach it to you. It's in the back of the throat.'

He gripped my elbow harder and sang the song again, staring into my face. He might as well have tried to teach the table to sing. But I remember the note. There are moments when I see someone standing clear in his own light and I hear it again.

All the stories he told me are like that. I kept glimpsing him against different backgrounds: in the Legion, in the Resistance, as a singer, or a dancer, or a poet. But his own part was always incidental. The stories were bearings he had taken on experience and he passed them on to me as a master mariner might pass on the finer points of navigation. Every so often the stars fall into a particular pattern and I remember something he said.

All I know of the man himself is his name, François Rovira. He was a Catalan and proud of his race. He taught me a few words of Catalan and I swore that one day I would come back and learn it properly. I saw myself sitting in a monastery library high in the Pyrenees, translating the poetry of corsairs and troubadours. But, forty-five years later, all I have are the phrases I recited one morning for an old scholar as he was crossing the marketplace. François gripped my wrist, I came out with my phrases and the old man tipped me a couple of francs.

Showmanship was one of the tricks of the trade. So, I quickly learned, were little charades put on for the customers. Among the antiques was a single-barrelled shotgun. Whenever a likely customer was within earshot, François's son would pick it up and squint along the barrel. François would turn on him and hiss in an angry whisper, 'How many times must I tell you to leave that gun alone? That's a valuable piece, that is, not a boy's plaything. It must have been made for a crack shot. I've never seen a gun so finely balanced. Take your great hands off it before you do some damage!' The customer would move away, pretending he had not heard a thing. A few minutes later he would be back, taking a closer look at the gun.

Not all our play-acting was calculated. Some of it was just play. I remember a little girl who kept edging up to one of the tables and shying away again, a little girl with a sharp brown face and short dark hair. She was fascinated by a fur collar, a marten's skin that clasped together with the nose and the little black button eyes over the tail. I picked it up and held it round her neck for a moment. She shimmered, as if a wave of light had just passed through her, and her eyes flashed, full and dark.

\* \* \*

The next morning I set out all the tables. I was left with a high-sided cot, beautifully made of black iron with a brass knob at each corner, and a heavy wooden wheel with an iron rim, too small and too ornate for a farm cart; it must have come off a gun carriage. François had taken down one side of the cot so that it could hold other things and form a display in itself. On an impulse, I took the wheel and slanted it between the bars so that it ran at an angle into the cot. The effect was surreal: the wheel looked as if it had broken through from another dimension and was still rolling.

I went to lift it out again, fearing it might be too dramatic, when François said, 'No, that's fine!'

Later that morning he called me over to the Loup de Mer where he was having a celebration drink with a Belgian tourist.

'We've sold the wheel,' he said and slipped a few coins into my hand. 'You've brought us luck.'

Which I was to lose them the very next day. I had decided to make a feature of the two oil lamps. I liked their marriage of the medieval and the industrial, the way the shape of a chalice was topped off with a filler cap and the little wheel that turned up the wick, the way glass rose from a filigree socket and tapered into transparency. I put them in the middle of the centre table and built the rest of the display around them. Everything was in place, the lamps rising like two Gothic windows, when François's wife came to warn me that there was a breeze blowing in from the sea. Perhaps I should take the glasses off the lamps in case the wind caught them and blew them over. I leaned down and held my hand a couple of inches from the glass. The flow of air was almost imperceptible and I decided it was safe to leave the glasses on.

François's wife must have had a word with him, because a few minutes later he came over and repeated the warning. 'The lamps can stay where they are,' he pointed out. 'Just take the glasses off and lay them alongside.' I squinted at the bases, trying to imagine them without their translucent cones: they looked gnarled and awkward, like polled willows. I held my hand in front of the glass again, first at one angle and then at another: just the faintest coolness across my fingers. I looked at the top of each clear column: they were steady, not so much as a tremor in the wind. The light turned in the glass and I knew that I could not bear to take them down.

The fatal gust came half an hour later. I had slipped off to the Poste Restante on the usual hopeless quest. I came back to see one glass lolling beside its lamp. 'We had to take it down,' François explained gently. 'The wind blew the other one over and broke it.' There was no hint of reproach in his voice. Just a general sadness, a sense of the unforgivingness of the material world. Glass was not renewed like sunlight.

'Perhaps you'll find another one,' I suggested, but we both knew it was irreplaceable. Oil lamps without glasses could be found mouldering in the corner of any old barn: but a glass without a lamp?

I saw the accident unfolding just as François and his wife must have known it would: their repeated warnings, the deep courtesy that had prevented them from simply stepping forward and taking the glass off themselves; and I saw myself with my hand out, testing the wind in a gesture I must have learned from some old man somewhere, a bogus gesture, because I knew nothing of this coast or the wind's behaviour. Shamming, there was no other word for it: I was a sham.

'Today felt wrong from the start,' I confessed to François.

He nodded towards his wife. 'She had the same feeling, bad luck in the air.'

What I did not tell him was that my unease was quite specific. I had walked in early. The morning was overcast. There had even been a little rain in the night. As I looked along the deserted beach,

247

I saw Anke on the skyline, on the rise of ground above the harbour, looking out to sea. It was just the way she stood, the weight thrown on to her left hip and the right leg starting forward, as if she had just run up to the horizon and stopped to take a look. Still something of the child in that quick poise, as if she might take off again at any moment.

I shouted out her name and started to run. With the lurch of my first stride, the silhouette corrected itself. It really was a child, a Catalan girl in a long black skirt. The momentary resemblance, that leftward swing of the hip as she came to rest, must have been so strong that I had misread everything else, even dividing the long black skirt into Anke's jeans.

What I felt was more than disappointment. It was anger, a bitterness in the back of the throat. In that moment all the strange wounds of these days, all their curious exposure, had healed. I had seen myself walking the beach with Anke, introducing her to François, to the musicians in the hut, to the sunbathers in front of the screen. She was my explanation, my counterpart. Then she was gone, a corrected error in the visual cortex, and I was returned to my oddity. I felt myself tightening up again, little guards and bracings I had not even been aware of until then.

That night I lay in the shelter and looked up at the great curves of the arch as they twisted over my head. The wood's grain gleamed in the starlight and I felt shielded by its density, as if I were under the earth's wing.

It was Saturday and I had stayed in the village till late, hoping the band might turn up. José appeared and told me they never played on Saturdays: that was the night *la Sardana* was danced in the village square.

'It's a Catalan dance,' he explained, 'and it means a lot to the old people.'

248

For a long time nothing seemed to happen. I sat on the rim of the drinking fountain, listening to the bee swarm of voices from the Loup de Mer. Nine o'clock passed and then ten. I was almost asleep when I heard the swarm divide and people file out on to the square. A moment's self-consciousness, *falsetti* of laughter, and the slow music of the dance came over the loudspeakers.

It did not seem to catch at first. A dark-haired couple in their fifties stepped into each other's arms and began what looked like a slow waltz. Heads held high, they were dancing almost defiantly. Suddenly they turned and held out their hands to the people either side of them, like Greek dancers. There was a wavering movement in the centre of the square, a hesitant sway, that rippled out to the edges. The tide had turned. Everyone was dancing, hands linked in a long undulating chain.

I stood on the edge of the square, watching. The halting rhythm felt strange to me, ground out of a past I did not share. A few years earlier, perhaps, when the long chain still swung thoughtlessly from past to future, I could have stepped into it as a passing stranger, part of the flux of the tides and the seasons. Now it had become a dance of belonging. The village was dancing out its last days before it was developed into a resort, one of the new super-resorts the government was planning to rival the Costa Brava.

I thought of the funeral I had seen earlier in the week, the whole village gathering in the square as the bell tolled, the coffin arriving on a hearse drawn by two black horses with black plumes in their headbands. What would become of that austere ceremony? Would the community still turn out to bury its dead? Or would they go to their graves awkwardly and almost anonymously, the cortège a small embolism in the flow of traffic?

As I moved away, slipping out through the crowd that had gathered behind me, someone tapped me on the shoulder. 'Antoine, there's a gentleman here who's been asking for you.'

A burly man in a blue vest and shorts, the flat blue of French overalls, was looking at me with a prophetic warmth, as if he had just found me a place in the scheme of things.

'He's a lorry driver and he does a run up the coast. He can take you to work on the sardine boats.'

He was so taken with his plan that it felt mean of me to refuse. I thanked him at some length, explaining that in François I already had a *patron*.

Lying in the shelter that night, I wished I were as penniless as I appeared. If I had not had a future to return to, if I really had washed up here like a stranger in a folk tale, these people would have taken me in.

I already had my invitation for Sunday. Before I went off to the Poste Restante, François and his wife had exchanged glances. She came over and asked me, a little anxiously, if I thought I could manage to catch the bus into Perpignan on my own.

So much for the horizon haunter, with his flashing eyes, his floating hair. So much for the Dharma Bum.

I looked into her large, grave eyes and saw myself, distinct and small, some mother's son.

Yes, I reassured her, I could manage, I had come out on the bus from Perpignan in the first place.

The anxiety lifted. She explained that they wanted to invite me to Sunday lunch but had been worried because they could not fetch me in the lorry. They did not come to Barcarès on Sundays, they had a stall in the flea market in Perpignan. But it was right by the bus station, it would be easy for me to find.

Then François came over. 'No point in your getting up early to set the stall out. We have to sell real junk in the flea market. People can't afford anything else. But come in on the bus later and have a look around. It'll be interesting for you.'

In fact, it was depressing. François's stall was much like the others: depleted sets of crockery were stacked up in front of hideous table lamps; bakelite plugs sullenly shone among old spanners and screwdrivers. He was not the showman he was in Barcarès. The customers bent over the tables in anxieties of calculation and he bent towards them, as if under the same compulsion. I felt weightless beside them, weightless and useless. If I attempted to serve, the customers glanced at me nervously and moved on.

I took François at his word and wandered off around the market, looking for anything that was not lacklustre. Anything that was not lack.

Something glimmered behind the stallholders' heads: red and blue paint, dashed on to the whitewash of a wall in two broadening streaks, two horns of a fanfare.

Imagining a poster for a happening or a piece of street theatre, I pushed into the roadway. The paint was fading off the wall. Pasted below it was a handbill, bleached into aphasia by the sun.

As I followed the wall round, looking for the blistered edge of another handbill, the coherent dust of a typeface, I felt as if I were back in the street outside the magic theatre. The door had vanished into the wall. I had come to the right place but in the wrong time.

Only when I was on my way back to François, mooching down the next aisle, did I come on the second-hand clothes stall run by a family of gypsies. A matriarch in a long embroidered dress sat on an upturned wooden box, a little girl at her side, while a boy my own age, slightly shorter than me with a tight mass of curls, stood guard over the clothes rack. All three were studying me with a frank curiosity. They could not place me in their world. Nor in any world they knew.

The boy's eyes widened as he took in the bare feet and the sunbleached mane of hair. He stepped forward, challenging me, half afraid I might not be of this world at all.

'*Qu'est-ce-que tu fais?*'

'*Je danse.*'

The mother smiled and began to clap her hands and the children joined in.

For a moment I stand still and listen: a springy, ankle-flexing sound. Off the ground and turn, the feet finding their own pattern as they come down, one, two and three for balance: four, the last step falling into place and spinning me back the other way, like a ball on a jet of water in a shooting gallery, flicked up into the air and spinning on its own axis.

'Yes,' said the boy, 'he can dance.'

Now he was eager to find out what else I could do. 'Can you drive?' 'Yes.' He crossed the strip of pavement to their lorry and opened the door: 'Get her going!' I started up the lorry, swung the nose out and swung it back into the kerb. This, it seemed, was conclusive. He turned to his mother: 'I want to take him with us on the grape harvest.'

Harder to refuse than the sardine boats. I heard the zinc of fingernails on guitar strings, I saw myself learning to dance flamenco by the light of a campfire. Everything that should have dispelled the myth – the rack of second-hand clothes, the old lorry – only made it more tangible.

But the grape harvest did not begin until the end of September. This was July. I had promised to visit Anke in Amsterdam. Not much chance, it seemed, of her turning up in Barcarès. And then there was the little matter of my final year at Oxford.

I explained that it would have to be next year. I was on my way to Amsterdam to visit *ma belle amie*. This must have been the right excuse because they began to kit me out for the journey. The boy looked along the rack and picked out an old army jacket: not a short battledress jacket, such as I was used to seeing in England, but a long waisted jacket with deep panel pockets that looked as if it should be worn over breeches and boots. It went straight into my mythology, where it became a French cavalry officer's jacket from the First World War.

It fitted me perfectly and the boy began to look for a hat. Not many to choose from. He settled for a straw trilby my grandfather might have worn. I was turning the brim down in front, trying to give it a touch of Bogart, when the little girl darted over to a tin jug that held red paper roses on long wire stems. She picked one out and held it up to me. I bent my head and she reached up and twisted it round the brim.

I should have left then and there. Set out on my journey, wearing the rose in my hat. But I hesitated, wondering if there was something I could give in return. I thought of the boater, how well it would sit on the boy's dark curls, how delighted he would be with the black speckle in the straw. And how curious it would look, a migrant from the green light under willows, from the river world of regattas and picnics, as exotic among the grapevines as a hoopoe in the hop fields of Kent.

'I have a surprise for you,' I said, 'a wonderful hat.' (I did not know the French for boater.) 'I'll bring it to the market tomorrow.'

He looked puzzled. Like the lorry driver, he had taken me at face value. How was he to know I was only playing at vagrancy? He had just given me a hat for my journey. Now I was proposing to give him one. Where was I going to get it from?

'*Danse!*' he said, as if he wanted me to spin like a wind-blown seed all the way to Amsterdam. But he did not clap and I felt heavy under the jacket and hat. Feeling goaded to dance, like a dancing bear, I snarled, hooped my arms and lumbered at him.

He was delighted and led me shambling and swaying to his mother and sister. It was a clumsy imitation but the snarl was real enough. 'He frightens me when he does that,' he said.

253

François must have seen me through the crowd. When I got back to the stall, he was not at all amused.

'And what do you think you were doing?'

'Imitating a bear.'

'That's not the way to do it. That's not the way to do anything. Look, I'll show you how a bear moves. I made a dance step from it, *le pas d'ours*.'

He put his foot down flat, leaned into the step and swayed over a bent knee. No snarl, no clowning. The bear was there, in the flat step and the sinking knee.

'What you were doing was playing the fool and that's dangerous. You can amuse people for a while, you can even frighten them, but in the end they'll turn on you.'

'I was only trying to make friends with the gypsies.'

'But that's not the way to go about it. No one respects a fool. Always be the gentleman, wherever you are. Keep your dignity and you keep control. If you want to go among the gypsies, tell them you're a writer, tell them you're writing a book about them. And at once they'll be filled with pride, they'll throw their heads back and tell you their stories, dance you their dances. That way you'll win their friendship and their respect. Go in as a fool and they'll tear you to pieces. *Les hommes, ce sont des loups,*' he concluded darkly. 'Men are wolves.'

He must have sensed that I was heading for trouble because he gave me another talking-to that afternoon. From the market we had taken an eagle's swoop of a right-hand turn and climbed steeply uphill, the engine racing in low gear. We came out on to a new road on a high ridge where he was building himself a house. The walls were as yet unplastered, the cement pressed between the stones in lines so sharp you could still see the point of the trowel. One long room ran back to the kitchen, which was perched on concrete footings over the slope of the hill. Like a watchtower set over the city, I thought. Or a stockade raised against wolves.

254

Sunday lunch was a stew that had been simmering all morning in the care of his daughter.

'Not long enough,' they pronounced when it was ladled out, thick and fiery. 'It really needed another hour.'

The girl was fifteen and the image of her mother.

No sooner was lunch over than the mother picked up one corner of a large piece of embroidery.

'That's her work,' said the younger son proudly. He was ten and had come with us to the market.

I expressed some surprise that she was starting on it so soon.

'It's a tablecloth,' she explained, 'and I have to finish one every week. I make them for a shop in town.'

'Sometimes she sits up till midnight,' added the little boy, and she smiled down into herself, keeping her eyes on the point of the needle. Tiredness showed white under the brown skin but it was a willing tiredness, composed and almost contemplative, almost amused at itself.

The daughter cleared the dishes and sat across the table from her mother. She took up the other corner, stretching the white linen across her fingers and tipping it towards the light.

François took me for a drive along the coast in the Sunday traffic. We ground under headlands in a haze of exhaust fumes. Windscreens flashed at us across little coves. From one of these the Resistance had smuggled out a captured German general to a waiting British submarine. They had caught him by the oldest of stratagems: a pretty girl met him at a party and lured him into the garden, where François came out from behind a tree with a revolver. It was his most famous exploit. At the end of the war the British had flown him over to London, where he danced with Princess Margaret.

But this afternoon he was not in the mood for reminiscence. He was worried what I might do next. I had told him I was thinking

255

of running away with Anke. The gypsy's invitation had lodged in my mind. The more I thought about it, the more attractive it became. To slip through all the regulations that separated us: the immigration laws, the university statutes, the rules of the orphanage.

'Once we were in the Pyrenees,' I said, 'they would never find us. We could disappear for ever.'

'No,' he said, 'those days are gone. They have Interpol now, they're all in radio contact. There's nowhere in Europe you can hide.'

Ahead of us was the dark line of an old stone jetty. The sea shone beyond it and people were silhouetted against the shine like seabirds, standing out on the end or sitting on the warm stones in the sun. François pulled the lorry off the road and parked under the lee of a wall.

I can still see him as he was that afternoon, lying propped on his elbows with his face into the breeze. Silver hairs gleamed on his cheekbones where the razor had missed them. The wind tugged the white shirt back from the dark throat and hooded it over his shoulders. He looked like an old passage hawk, roosting on migration among its flocks of prey.

'One of these days,' he mused, 'you'll find your wife. You'll sit at home and write your poems. You'll bring her to see me and I'll tell her how lucky she is she didn't know you ten years ago.'

He thought for a moment and glanced up at a young woman who was standing further along the jetty, staring out to sea.

'Look at her!' he said softly.

She was in her Sunday best, a white silk blouse and a dark-blue skirt that ended just above the knee.

'Just look, see how beautiful she is!'

I considered the dark hair, drawn up to the back of the head to reveal the profile of *La Belle France* on the stamps of the time, a long, straight nose and a short, firm curve of jaw; the rounded fullness of the shoulders and the upper arms as they bloomed through the silk of the blouse; the line of the thigh muscle under the short skirt and the swell of the calves over the high heels. She was not striking in that she was not unusual: but, as I saw her moulded against the helter of light off the sea, saw the milky luminescence of flesh the hormones had spun over the bones, yes, she was beautiful.

'*Les femmes*,' said François, '*ce sont des images qui passent. Il faut être l'homme pur*.' 'Women are images that float past you. You have to be a man in yourself.'

From the coast François drove me to the vineyard he was planting for his old age. A shuttered house stood among rows of new vines, like a promise of peace, and I thought of the Roman poet Horace coming into possession of his Sabine farm.

Ironically, François owed it all to the tourists. The stall at Barcarès had lifted him out of the flea market and given him the chance to do a better class of trade.

He did not open up the house but took me into a gallery that ran under one side and formed a storeroom, shaded and dairy-cool. A wooden barrel stood on stocks against the wall.

'It's the strongest part of the wine,' he said, 'made from the skins of the grapes.'

He took the bung out of the top, slid in a plastic tube and stretched it down over the barrel. Bent and sucked on the end, lifting his head to breathe out and bending and sucking again until his cheeks creased in a long swallow. Capped the tube with his thumb and handed it to me.

'Go on, take a pull!'

It was like being handed the pipe of an enormous hookah. I slid my thumb across in place of his, stooped and put my lips to the tube. A fiery sweetness hit the tongue.

'Go on, take some more! It's good against the sun.'

He kept me there, bowed to the god of the wine, until I had taken four or five long pulls. A punch of cold air came up the brainstem. A window opened in the back of my head.

François's eyes rested on me, equable and appeased. If we had been out in the light, I would have seen the hazel of the irises, their fine grain. When the fit was on him, when he had something to teach, the pupils dilated and he would turn on me with a waspish glitter, spots of light over each eye that looked as if they might peel off and attack in their own right.

He took me back to the house and we sat at the long table over a bottle of the wine. The sweetness was still there but in an ethereal form. It was like drinking the ghost of what I had tasted in the barrel.

Farewells were already in the air, the sense of a ritual almost completed, when something in the conversation must have prompted François. His head jerked up and for the last time I saw the glint of exegesis. He reached across the table and grabbed me by the wrist.

'*Non, laisse-le!*' said his wife, laughing and freeing my arm. She had seen me flinch, suddenly frail with fatigue, like a child at the end of the day.

The words, whatever they were, were never spoken. But the glint stayed with me, the way François seemed to rekindle as the energy flared up into his eyes. I thought back to the first morning in the marketplace when he had tried to teach me the song, his grip tightening on my elbow as his eyes burned into me.

The master had been in need of an apprentice almost as much as the apprentice needed a master.

It was early evening by the time he dropped me back in Barcarès. That morning, when I caught the bus, the marketplace had been full of villagers in their Sunday best, waiting to go into eleven o'clock mass. Now a drinking booth had been set up, an open-sided tent with a makeshift bar, and men stood around in shirtsleeves and dark trousers.

One of them called to me as I went past, 'Antoine, will you have a drink with us?'

I ducked in under the awning and the little groups of drinkers half turned, swaying and stepping back on their heels. It was a herd movement, a stir that was almost a bristling – just enough to show what might have happened if feelings had been running the other way and the village had closed against me. It was one of the fishermen who had tried to set my hair on fire, someone with what we would now call 'learning difficulties'.

Just as well I had not landed any of the devastating blows I kept rehearsing in the aftershock of the fight.

I accepted *un petit cognac*, sensing that it meant my own acceptance, and stood there with the drink in my hand, uncertain of my steps in this strange male dance. The man who had bought me the drink was leaning towards me, protective and expectant. I felt like a fighting cock he had just put some money on. The others hovered on the half-turn, waiting to see how I shaped up. I looked to him, as to a natural ally, and the half-turned heads turned away. So much for my command of the ring.

The skin on his face was still taut and he had a full head of dark hair. There were probably no more than fifteen years between us but the difference was complete. He was formed and finished, *un hombre hecho y derecho*, as the Spanish say, at ease with himself and among his people. Only the eyes were restless: they had been ranging the square when he caught sight of me crossing it.

Spits of sound suggested the guitars were tuning up. I could glimpse my kingdom, the strip of concrete in front of the band. But first I had to negotiate this conversation, its odd, short steps.

He asked me which road I had come down on and I gave him an account of my journey, leaving out the kidnap by the rock fans. I wanted to appear competent. I was not going to admit that I had ricocheted the length of France like a ball in a pinball machine. But I did tell him of the wild drive through the dawn with the policeman who had just had a row with his wife and of the prophecy of the lawyer with the invisible flame in his forehead. Then I played my trump card: I told him of my meeting with Louie and of Louie's bitter bad luck in being drafted just when he had the offer of a film. '*La vie est vache*,' my companion said. 'Life's a bitch' and we stood in silence for a moment, two life-hardened men, their heads bowed in mute sympathy.

Perhaps it was the posture that brought the pictures into my mind. They came one after the other. A shot from the film of *Henry V* of a knight in full armour hanging against the sky before he was winched down on to his horse. And then the animals on the game-keeper's gibbet in Ted Hughes's poem, slowly turning on their strings as they swung in the wind, their heads bowed to this worst rain of all.

How armoured men are, I thought. How difficult it is for them to get to know each other. The Catalan was looking down as he talked. The eyes flitted behind their lids and I sensed reservations and manoeuvres. I wanted to ask him, What's it like to be you? To grow up in the village's strict codes and mould yourself to them? To walk into the square on a Sunday and take your place as one of the men? But I was too unsure of the conventions to risk breaking them. And too anxious to join the band.

They were laying down the first chords now, long washes of sound like the first waves coming ashore in a storm. When he offered me another drink, I had the best of excuses. But I made them too hastily and my nervousness must have shown.

'*Oui*,' he said, '*va à tes amis!*'

260

Just a hint in his tone of 'Run along and play!'. Something else in the eyes, a quickly shielded disappointment. He had been as curious about me as I was about him.

I walked away feeling inept. Guilty, even. He had invited me into the circle and I had not earned my place. The man he wanted to talk to was the man I might be one day.

And then, suddenly, between one step and the next, I went from too young to too old. When the energy ran high, I actually felt as if I had winged feet. My heels seemed to rise from the ground as if they were powered by little jets of compressed air. All I could feel in the thirty yards from the bar to the band's hut was a bruised numbness underfoot. The wine and the brandy were taking their toll.

Shouts went up from the kids on the door, '*Il arrive!*' I could see that the drummer had set back his kit to give me a little more room. Expectations rose to meet me like my own shadow. I felt like an old jazzman limping into a cellar club for another night of his Parisian exile.

What I could not manage in surprise I tried to make up in symmetry, spelling out patterns with my feet. As I became intent on my chamber music, and less inclined to flash around the edges of the room, the kids settled along the wall to watch, sitting cross-legged on the floor.

Tall and white-haired, an old man in blue overalls stooped through the door, a blue cap set on the back of his head. Under his arm he carried a little white dog, rough-coated and truculent. With a stealthy insistence, not wishing to intrude and not willing to be challenged, he moved into a space and sat against the wall, drawing his knees up to his chin and setting the dog down between them.

That stooping entrance gave him a strange authority, as though he had stepped down across the generations to see what we were

261

up to. The dog made me think he might be a shepherd. That seems unlikely to me now. What would a shepherd be doing on that sandy coast? But there was something shepherd-like in the containment with which he sat against the wall, the dog alert and composed between his feet.

I felt honoured by his presence. Honoured and put on my mettle. I imagined the dances he must have known, driving rhythms and bare feet stamping on the packed earth, though really I knew nothing of folk music then. What I was remembering was Stravinsky's *Rite of Spring*.

Hazy as my reverence was, it worked. I danced over my bruises as though the steps I was improvising to this rock band had to answer to an old tradition.


Hard to leave the driftwood cave, to turn my back on that braced solitude. One night I had taken Shakespeare's history plays from my pack and lain reading by torchlight with my shoulders against the arch, as if I could learn concentration from the wood. I had wanted to send for my books and stay all summer. The next night, of course, I felt weary of my limits and bought half a bottle of whisky from the bar, as if I could kick-start the visions in the brain. But what came back to me as the whisky cleared was the sensation of lying with my shoulders pressed against the wood, of mentality stilled by matter.

I strapped the boater to my pack, ready to give to the gypsy, and set the straw hat on my head with the rose twisted round the crown. I knew how lucky I had been. The first days in Barcarès, the beach scourings, the blank moments in the Poste Restante, '*Non, Monsieur, il n'y a rien pour vous*,' were all forgotten. I wanted to find Anke and tell her of the extraordinary chances, of discovering the shelter, of the encounter with François. I wanted her to see me while the luck was still flowing through me, like a light between the skin and the bone.

For the last time I waded across the river and splashed through the shawls of surf. 'Where are you off to?' a woman asked as I went on down the beach. 'Amsterdam,' I replied, though I was almost out of money. She glanced up at the straw hat and smiled. 'With that on your head, you should get there!'

I came to the steps that led on to the square and met some of my friends from the screen, among them the only one I might have fallen for, her hair in an urchin cut.

She admired a bracelet I was wearing twisted in a double loop round my wrist, chips of ebony on a strip of elasticated black velvet, African, at a guess. It had washed up on François's stall in the flea market, the only thing there that had any charm.

'Here!' I said, slipping it off my wrist and fastening it round hers. It seemed only right to give away some of the luck.

With that, all my farewells said, I was ready to step on to the bus. I could see it standing on the square, the same bus that had brought me in from Perpignan on the first morning, the same bus that had taken me into the flea market the day before.

'But there is no bus!' my friends exclaimed. 'Not now! Not till the afternoon.'

I checked with the lady in the *boulangerie* and, sure enough, the bus did not run between twelve and three. The driver was having his lunch. I would find him in the Loup de Mer.

I bought a *petit pain*, some slices of *saucisson* and a carton of milk, my usual recourse, and began to wait out the time, squatting on the kerb on the empty side of the square, away from the steps to the beach and the café tables.

As I stared down into the wind-blown sand at my feet, I noticed an edge, a rounded edge. A wind print, I thought, a swirl in the sand, and followed it with my eye: too neat for a swirl, too regular. It sat like a disc in the sand.

I picked it up and it was like picking the cosmos out of the ground.

Soft and black, a black beret a workman must have dropped, so spattered with paint that it was like a night sky by Jackson Pollock. Constellations had dripped from ceilings and wandered the dark cloth, thickening into galaxies and sliding into overlapping star-bursts. Between them, in the vacant, interstellar spaces, pulsed tiny dots of red, gold and blue.

It seemed like some strange return for the boater I was about to give to the gypsy and I slipped it into my pack.

The bus station in Perpignan was next to the flea market and I walked round to complete the exchange.

To my surprise the market was closed. The islands of concrete stood empty with the traders' lorries parked between them.

Monday. It was Monday. I had forgotten that there were Mondays, just as I had forgotten that there were lunch hours.

Disappointment sank in, level below level. I thought of all that would be lost if I did not deliver the boater: not just the gypsy's surprise when he saw it (a promise he had only half understood, and already forgotten, suddenly translated into this elegant black-speckled straw) but the surprise of the boater itself, this musical comedy prop, sitting on his tight black curls and looking so much better there than anywhere else. I felt as if I had been about to achieve a light verse effect, a felicitous rhyme in the fabric of events.

The only thing was to leave it in the back of his lorry. To do that, I had to walk past a small group of men who were sitting in the sun on the end of the first island, drinking red wine out of a bottle.

I had glanced away the moment I saw them but it was too late. Their voices had stopped in mid-yelp. Their silence was focused on me.

Don't give them an opening. Draw right into yourself. Be unquestionable.

264

Slowly past. Treading their silence as if I were treading water. Steering my whole elaborate assembly, the shades, the straw hat, the shoulder-length hair, down the first aisle as if it were the most natural thing in the world, as if I came here every day.

The gypsy's old pick-up was not where I expected. Nothing of the shape I remembered stepping into the day before, low-slung, with wide grey wings. But then there was nothing to tell one stall from the next. Just the spaces where the stalls had been, marked off by rusting iron roof poles.

The watching eyes had seen me hesitate. It seemed simpler to acknowledge them, to turn and ask where the gypsy's lorry had gone. They pointed over to the fourth aisle and there it was, slumped against the kerb.

I clambered into the back, which was empty. No heap of tarpaulin. No upturned box. Nowhere to hide anything. Just the bare boards. I laid the boater down in the corner behind the cab, crossed my fingers and entrusted it to fate.

'*Merci bien*,' I said to the men as I walked back past them, wanting to ensure their goodwill. They must have seen me climb into the back of the lorry. I had to hope that the sun and the wine had sapped their curiosity.

They held the bottle up to me. It seemed churlish to refuse. Besides, it was half empty. I took a swig and handed it back. It went round the circle and rose again.

Clean shaves. Clean shirts. They did not look like winos. They must be men from the market on their day off. I took another swig and saw myself wandering Europe, passed on from little open squares like the one in Barcarès to great glazed market halls with ornate cast-iron roofs, part of a rough brotherhood, living by word of mouth.

The brothers, meanwhile, were eyeing up my rucksack, a German ski-trooper's rucksack Bryn had lent me for the trip. Rucksacks aren't cool but this one was. Just two leather satchels on a piece of deerskin. Bryn had shown me how, when you strapped the satchels up and strapped the two of them together, it was completely weather-proof, deerskin on the outside and leather on the inside. You could travel light, a neat square between the shoulder blades. Or strap on a tent and a bedroll and travel the world.

'What have you got in there?' they wanted to know.

'Bombs against Franco.' I had heard that the Catalans were still fighting the Spanish Civil War and running guns through the Pyrenees.

This delighted them. 'Show us!' they said. '*Faites voir! Faites voir!*'

I took off the pack, knelt down and undid it. By now I was a transcontinental pedlar, the *jongleur* of the lorry parks. And I did have one or two things to show them: the army jacket the gypsies had given me, Su's version of a Russian shirt.

They made a fuss of whatever I pulled out of the pack, applauding as I held up the clothes and reaching out to feel the material. Some they dismissed as ordinary. Others I had to put on. I read their comments as some kind of initiation I was passing, so absorbed in the success of my performance that it was a shock to look up and see one of them waddling around in the army jacket, the tailored waist hugging his bum.

All I wanted then was to retrieve everything, to strap up the materials and be on my way. I was just fastening the buckles when something jigged across my line of sight. It was the waddler. Only now he was drifting up and down with his hands in his pockets, whistling silently into the air. The others were still sitting, gazing up at him, their slowly widening smiles his footlights.

'Hah!' he breathed on his knuckles and brushed them on an imaginary lapel. Threw out his chest and went into a bantam strut. Without the jacket he was Punchinello, a balding, broad-chested little man with black hair springing out of the neck of a white shirt.

He grinned to his back teeth and flexed his legs in their tight black trousers, a clench of the thigh, a brag of the buttock. All that was missing was Punch's song, 'That's the way to do it!'

I shrugged the rucksack on to my back and settled the straw hat on my head. Went to put on my shades and realised they had gone. This was the initiation and I had just failed it.

I should have smiled. Started a round of applause for the bantam cock, who was still stepping the walk in triumph. He could have handed them back as the climax of his show. But I was too green to read the signs. So green that he went on preening himself as if I weren't there.

'My sunglasses have been stolen!'

The others, who had been quick to look away when they saw me watching, fluttered in their concern. Had I put them in my pack? In my jacket? In my trouser pocket? But the brotherhood had dissolved. All I could see were the eager faces who had made me the patsy.

I leaned over them, one long shriek of outraged innocence, and the smiles went out.

'If they are not returned immediately, I shall go straight to the police.'

The strutter came to a halt, looking aggrieved. I had rained on his parade.

He glared at me so long I could see his eyebrows bristling on their arches, each separate hair stirring as if it had an animus of its own.

The others were slurred over the concrete, grey-faced and uneasy. The last thing they wanted was trouble.

He reached inside his shirt, where the glasses were nesting against the chest hair. Glanced into the air, as if asking the gods to agree that such deft work deserved better, and handed them back.

He could not believe the injustice of it. He had been robbed of his triumph. 'Leave us something else,' he suggested, 'in exchange.'

But I had turned away. Shock, the adrenalin rush, whatever it was I had flung into that threat to make it convincing, was already carrying me out of the gate.

Only once I was safely in the street did I realise that I had left him something: the boater. No going back for it now. It was there for the taking.

I found myself walking uphill, fording crossroads after crossroads, sheet after sheet of light, as if I were crossing the sky at low tide. By the time I came out on to the ridge below François's house, I felt like a penitent on the Walsingham Way.

At least he could explain to the gypsy why I had failed in my promise.

'You should have left the thing with me,' he pointed out. 'I would have given it to him.'

He didn't say any more. He didn't need to. I had said it all to myself.

The only hint of his displeasure came later that evening. We were standing on the ridge, watching the light fade over the city, when a man strolled up with the air of someone who regularly came by, a tall, slim, military-looking man with a neat shirt and short greying hair.

'You should tell him what happened,' said François. 'He's a police inspector,' and introduced me with a shrug: '*Il joue le bouffon*.' 'He plays the fool.'

I jumped back as another lorry revved up and pulled away from the kerb. Still no prospect of a lift but every prospect of being run over.

I had to scan the pavements for men who were turning away as they talked. Watch for the moment when they gave a last laugh and jumped up into the cab. Be round there with my plea before the door slammed.

'Get down to the fruit market early,' François had advised, 'and find a lorry that's going to Paris.'

I had slept under a low stone wall, just across the road from the house, and set out at first light.

In the time it took me to walk down the hill, the city awoke. Shutters were thrown back as I passed. The barred gate of a patio opened and an old lady emerged on to the street, a shopping basket in the crook of her elbow. The stalls were already under fierce scrutiny, old ladies picking out the best fruit and greeting each other with quick nods of approval.

No one stared at me. No one had time. The lorry drivers did not even seem to notice when I jumped clear of their wheels.

'Ask around the cafés!' François had said. 'That's where the drivers have breakfast after they've loaded up.'

The waiter stepped past me and shouted his order over the counter. Behind me the door opened to a grunt of '*Bonjour*' and an answering rumble from the little tables as if the men in blue overalls were all clearing their throats.

This is how a ghost must feel, outside the movement of the day.

'*Il y a quelqu'un qui monte à Paris?*'

My question washed up against the tables, where the conversations paused, as if someone had just found a fly in his coffee, and resumed.

'*Tu veux un café?*'

The offer came from a man sitting by himself, tall, dark and well-dressed, at ease and apart in his corner. He was in his late thirties, just enough of a gap between us to justify his use of the *tu* form, which he had voiced with a careful courtesy.

It came like the offer of a truce, a chance to assume the anonymity of a customer, to become part of the day. I took it gratefully but I doubt if my gratitude showed. I sat at the corner table and sipped at the small black coffee like a ghost trying to reconstitute himself.

There were questions I should have asked, simple, practical questions, like how to get out of Perpignan. And questions I should have answered, complex, emotional questions, like what I was doing there in the first place. I suspect that, like the man at the Sunday evening bar in Barcarès, he was prompted by a kind of brotherly curiosity. He was buying me coffee because I was a younger version of himself.

But the mist of invisibility was still over me, a prickling in the air like the beginning of a faint at school. I could hear the voices of my upbringing, warning me not to accept sweets from a stranger. I refused a second cup when it was offered and stood up, ready to leave.

He smiled to himself, as if he had expected no less, and sat back in his corner.

I looked down the curve of the old street that led north out of Perpignan, wondering how far the thin stream of traffic would carry me. Amsterdam seemed impossibly far. And I was honour-bound to turn off into the French Alps and visit the Coutagnes in their chalet at Argentières.

The last thing I did before I left Oxford was to send them a postcard, letting them know that I was going to be in the South of France. Barcarès was not so far from Le Défends, the old family vineyard outside Aix-en-Provence where they would be in September, and I had imagined returning there with Anke and wandering the sandy paths between the evergreens, rather forgetting that it was the domain of a traditional Catholic family. Monsieur Coutagne was one of seven brothers and the other six were all priests. He in his turn had seven sons, thus ensuring a supply of servers when his brothers came home for the summer. Every morning before breakfast the boys would be shuttled around the outlying chapels so that each of the uncles could say his daily mass.

But it was only July. They would still be in the Alps, just the oldest of the brothers, perhaps, L'Oncle Pierre, and the immediate family. The car that lifted me off that street in Perpignan was going all the way to Paris. 'Why go off track?' François had said. 'Stay in the jet stream!' But I remembered my manners and asked to be set down at the Grenoble turn-off. Some rather sophisticated French campers in a big car swept me along to Chamonix, where I took the train down the valley to Argentières.

This was a village the French had managed to keep to themselves, an enclave of the *bonne bourgeoisie*. Three years before, I had arrived just as the results of the Baccalauréat were published. All the talk was of places and percentages: who had come where, who was going where. I had listened, half-comprehending, as the names of the *grandes écoles* took shape on the air: I-Math, I-Chem, magical doors through which the technical élite of France had to pass. But then I had my own sesame. I had only to say 'Oxford' and the dreaming spires shimmered. The incantations were different but the magic was the same. I was like a young Brahmin among mandarins.

Now I arrived with hair down to my shoulders and a paper rose round my hat, babbling of gypsies and flea markets, of a fight in a bar and a driftwood shelter, like someone talking out of a dream from which he had yet to wake. I washed off the salt of the beach in the chalet's pinewood shower and still did not wake. As I sat in the circle of family and friends, enjoying the summer ritual of a long aperitif, all I could hear was the way the voices echoed. They seemed to be going in and out of phase, fractionally delayed, as if I were listening to them across a transatlantic cable.

It began as an inclination of the knees, a sketch of the wrist. It began as a dance under my breath. Left alone at the roadside, I felt the rhythm rise like a recovered memory. I began to dance to myself as I thumbed the occasional car, swinging out with my thumb and swaying back over my rucksack, making a dance out of the mooch on the kerb.

The Coutagnes had run me up on to the back road into Switzerland, where there was more chance of tourist traffic. They had also lent me some money, enough to see me through to Amsterdam. For the first time since I left Barcarès, I really believed that I could get there.

The rhythm quickened, breaking into single-note runs, irrepressible rills of joy, like Charley Christian taking off on 'Swing to Bop'. I began to dance them out, visibly dancing now, stepping out along the line of a phrase and jackknifing back, keeping to the narrow strip of verge.

There were watching eyes in the café across the road. Let them watch. I could feel my journey rise out of Haute Savoie into Switzerland and feed into the flow of the autobahns north. I was half gone already, spinning on the empty air of the roadside as if it were a strong wind or a succession of riffs on a stratocaster, zigzagging across it as if I were dicing with it, stepping into the rush of distance, then pulling my body back to let the distance go.

I had come back down to a dawdle on the kerb when I heard a voice behind me. Someone was calling to me from the other kerb, a round-faced little man with balding black hair. He was leaning towards me and making soothing gestures with his hands, almost doing a dance of his own.

'Come in and have a drink with us! I'll run you down to the main road later. You'll stand more chance there. But I have a little bit of business to finish here first.' He pointed to a Rickard van parked outside the café, one of those *deux chevaux* vans with crinkled sides. 'Come in and have a drink!'

The café had looked nondescript from the road: a glass door between two half-curtained windows. I stepped in and it opened before me like a wood, a deep, wide, pine-boarded room that ended

272

in a horseshoe bar. He led me to a table at the back where a drink was already waiting, a small glass of what must have been eau de vie, with a slice of pineapple in a saucer.

'It's our local drink,' he said, ushering me into a chair. My mouth was dry from dancing and I sucked at the wedges of pineapple, whose honeyed warmth carried the rumour of the same liqueur. He watched to see how I would react and nodded his approval: 'They go together well, don't they?'

'It's his speciality,' said his friend, 'the cafés and the eaux de vie of the French Alps. He drives all over Savoie conducting his research. Rickard think he's working for them but really it's just a form of sponsorship.'

The round face exuded well-being. He was clearly a man who had found his niche. His friend had a thin face and short, dark hair that sprayed out from his forehead. He was giving me that prolonged appraisal that was a speciality of smokers. Studying me as he drew on his cigarette, as if the quickened glow gave him a sharper focus. Exhaling and looking at me over the smoke.

'My friend here is very taken with your hair,' the round face explained. 'He's just itching to get his scissors and style it. He's down here on holiday but back in Paris he has his own salon. A whole chain of them, in fact. Ten salons all across the city.'

The thin face glanced down in self-deprecation. Then looked up at me with what was almost an appeal. 'With hair like yours,' he said, 'I could really do something.'

I had a fleeting vision of the Paris salons, of men in Pierre Cardin suits stepping in off the pavements and moving through white and silver light, their reflections tripling in wall-to-wall mirrors and sliding across polished metal surfaces like well-cut clouds. The mirrors were about to dissolve – how could they hold the old army jacket? Or the gypsy rose twisted round my hat? How long since I had sat in a barber's chair? – when I remembered that I was on my way to see Anke. The gleam deepened and I saw myself arriving on her doorstep transformed: no longer with simple hair but with a *chevelure* like Hermes' winged helmet.

Thin Face borrowed a pair of scissors and a towel from the woman behind the bar. 'Take your time,' he said, 'finish your drink. There's no rush. I want you *bien tranquille*, nice and quiet, nice and still, so that I can concentrate.'

Better have a pee, I thought, and walked round the bar to the Gents. As I came back, the woman called out to me, 'Don't let him cut your hair!'

I let her into the secret: 'He has salons in Paris. He's going to give it some style.'

She turned away. No more to be said.

He posed me carefully in the chair, head bent forward with the bar towel tucked under my collar, and repeated his instruction to sit quite still.

My obedience would have satisfied any Zen master. Head devoutly bowed, I went into a kind of trance. I could feel the comb and scissors on my neck, I was aware of the attention of the room, which had fallen silent as he began to cut, but I was somewhere down below these sensations, in a luminous calm that was my travelling self. This was like drinking from that tap under the eyes of the crowd on the balcony, a curiosity of circumstance I would pass through, curious and unscathed.

Both his hands pressed on my shoulders. '*Bouge pas!*' he whispered. 'Don't move!' Insistently, as if he were about to make some delicate final cut.

I held still. Nothing for a long moment. Then the *ting!* of the café door and the sound of a *deux chevaux* taking off.

I put a hand up to my head. The fingers passed through where my hair used to be. Stretched and probed the rough edges of stubble and what felt like a deep rut.

For a moment I was afraid that I might have been trepanned as well as cropped. I hurried round to the mirror in the Gents and saw the grub of myself looking back at me, two doubtful eyes under their dubious skullcap.

Stubble is too smooth a word. It was the torn earth after autocross. Just under the crown of the head there was a skidmark, a puddle of bare scalp. I had felt the scissors wrench across it and assumed it was some special effect he was improvising in the heat of creation. But it looked as if he had tried to give me a tonsure.

All eyes were on me as I re-emerged from the Gents. 'I shall come back,' I said to the woman behind the bar. 'I shall have my revenge!' in a shaken undertone that rather defused the threat.

Then a glimmer rose out of that luminous calm: I shall just have to be French, I thought, and I took out the beret I had found in the dust of the roadside and moulded it round my hairless head.


'*Vous avez peur de moi!*' the beerbelly laughed as he barged round another bend on another back road. Too right. I was afraid of him. This had ceased to be a journey. It was becoming a drunken eddy between one village bar and the next.

Just a local lift, I had thought, when the old lorry stopped. Never mind. It would get me away from the scene of my discomfiture. An unshaven grin shouted something round a fag end and we set off with a judder like a cross-Channel ferry.

It seemed only polite to shout back but he was as foxed by my accent as I was by his. I leaned across the hump of the gearbox, trying to edge my vowels into his black-haired ear. The eyes stared ahead, unblinking. For a moment I felt helpless. This was the system of sounds that had carried me the length of France. My second language, of which I was unduly proud. Then the lips tightened, giving the fag a downward tweak that might have been a smile.

No sooner had I settled into my seat than he turned off the main road. 'Back roads are always best,' he said, and drove down into a little hill town. 'No rush!' he added, and parked below a terrace of shops and cafés.

Actually, I thought, I am in a hurry, I want to get to Amsterdam, but I followed him up a flight of stone steps and into a long narrow bar where I stood at his shoulder, sipping beer. A holidaymaker in checked shirt and shorts started to advise me on the small towns of Savoie while the driver stood locked with his cronies in a communal gaze at the floor. Every so often one of them would raise his head and bark out half a sentence. The others would grunt and suck steadily on the rims of their long glasses.

Their silence left with us, closing around us in the cab. No more philosophy about short cuts. He seemed to be driving in a dream of his own. Let him be, I was thinking, let him be, when we drew up on a dusty space in front of a *café-tabac*: all that had ever come of a village, one side that had never grown into a square. This was the barest of bars, two or three wooden tables and a hatch where men stood drinking bottled beer. He joined them and passed a bottle back to me.

I sat at one of the tables, wondering how I was ever going to get back on the road. These men were younger and the conversation more animated. I would look up to see the driver in the thick of some friendly dispute, wagging the neck of his bottle to make a point. This was the oasis he had been looking for. How much of the day would pass before he could be persuaded to leave?

I felt angry that I had been trapped. And trapped in my anger. He had been sullen enough on the way here. I could not afford to rile him.

In the end I decided simply to walk, to take my pack from the lorry and walk. I asked one of the men at my table how far it was to the main road. I didn't want to hassle the driver, *je ne voulais pas le déranger*, but I did have to be on my way.

276

He went straight up and tapped the driver on the back. A glance round. A droop of the shoulder and a jiggle of the bottle. Which I took to mean that he'd be along when he'd supped up.

He seemed to bear me no grudge, setting off again in high good humour. So high that I began to wish I *had* walked. As the lorry surged round corners, I felt like someone caught on a fairground ride that was going out of control.

'*Monsieur*,' I began nervously, '*vous êtes très gentil*', 'you're very kind . . .' But I had a long way to go. Could he just drop me on the main road?

'*Vous avez peur de moi!*' 'You're afraid of me!' His astonishment filled the cab, a great, billowing genie of astonishment that nothing I said could dispel.

'*Vous avez peur de moi!*' He was still relishing it as he dropped me off and I was still repeating hopelessly, '*Non, Monsieur, non, vous êtes très gentil, très gentil.*'


No more local lifts, I said to myself and tried to recover my poise at the roadside. I am not sure which I minded more, the loss of time or the loss of face.

Almost at once the jet stream lifted me off, two young French couples who were driving into Switzerland for the day, a little older than me and so sleek that I was surprised to find myself in the back of their car, the knee of my beach-stained matelots nudging the knee of an Italian suit: two engaged couples who must have picked me up on impulse as they might have thrown coins in a fountain or bought a rose from an old gypsy woman at their restaurant table. I was their lucky charm, part of the romance of the day.

The Italian suit bent over his girl in the corner seat, whispering in her ear, and I was left to contemplate the swings of the road as they came at me over the driver's shoulder. Hardly time to be bored before a familiar sensation began to rise out of my childhood, a dull taste like the inside of a torch when you changed the battery, the taste of dead air. I tried to swallow it down but it rose up inside me, a bitter little gulp I must not spill.

Look out of the window, I thought desperately, but the world was tipped at an odd angle and sliding past me in the diminished colours of a bad dream. I focused on the space between me and the back of the seat in front, the square of space in which I held myself upright, carefully swallowing.

Quicker and quicker until I knew there was no time to swallow again . . . I tried to ask the driver to stop but the sentence ended in a splash of vomit. I pulled out a handkerchief and held it over my mouth but the smell of sick was already filling the car.

He stopped on a straight with the traffic swerving past us and I stumbled round to the verge. Up came the eau de vie and the beer, all the morning's shock and all its perplexities. It was a poor thing who shrank back into the car, mumbling his apologies over and over again, '*Je suis désolé, je suis désolé*,' and dabbing at the remains of the sick with his one remaining handkerchief. It had got into the ashtray, under the door handles, into the runners under the driver's seat: all the nooks and crannies of a car that you only discover when you've just thrown up in it.

The girl in the front fixed me with a motherly eye and asked me if I had eaten. 'Only a couple of beers,' I explained, 'with a lorry driver.' 'You can't live on beer,' she declared and instructed her fiancé to stop at the next café. It was some time before one appeared, an elegant establishment with a gravelled courtyard. He pulled in, glanced at her and switched off. Charity was not going to come cheap.

I sat in the gleam of a round polished table, taking in tiny sips of pale French tea and steadying myself for the sandwich the motherly girl had ordered. She had vetoed my choice of ham and substituted chicken. The girls made a show of drinking mineral

278

water but the men had ordered nothing. They simply sat and waited for the embarrassment to be over.

That was all it took to complete the work of the scissors. As the men shuffled in their chairs, easing back a cuff to glance at a watch, I saw myself reflected in their boredom, a roadside oddity, a cropped little creature the girls had decided to adopt.

In Lausanne it rained all night. I slept under a bicycle shelter in a deserted square of offices, just round the corner from the railway station. I had already changed my French francs into Swiss and bought a ticket home.

Why continue? Why struggle all the way to Amsterdam? To give Anke a nasty shock? To appear with my maggot's head and my lost luck?

Writing by torchlight beside the empty bike stands, I told her of my journey and its abandonment, all in one scrawled-out note. 'They cannot destroy us!' it ended, as if I were Che writing from the Bolivian jungle.

The session behind my shades was going well. I had just brought in muted trumpets over the bass, a light, uninsistent swing that was a Dukish translation of the movement of the tram, when a woman said, 'Shut yer row!' and I was shaken out of my black skin.

What had I misheard? The name of the last stop? The closing of the doors? Or was it just the spoiler instinct? A jumpcut in the nerves? One moment I was the Billy Strayhorn figure, the close-cropped head behind dark glasses making thoughtful music from my passage across Amsterdam. The next I was myself, twitchy, white in the face and looking, as Anke said, as if I had just come out of prison.

'Funny that you went to Barcarès!' That was her only response to my despatch from the bicycle shelter in Lausanne. Though she did explain when Bryn and I finally reached Amsterdam three weeks later, vouched for by Hannah's parents when the Dutch police phoned them from the Hook of Holland, that they had only stayed in Barcarès one night. They had been disconcerted by the French boys, who did not simply couch beside them when they rolled out their sleeping bags on the beach but started to take their trousers off in expectation.

Amsterdam apartments had a lumber room up in the roof and it was there that Hannah's parents housed us, in a spirit of the utmost tolerance. We could descend to the shower and help ourselves from the fridge in the kitchen. Come and go like thieves in the night.

The days we could spend in Anke's mother's flat, where Anke was living while her mother was in hospital. Up on the second floor at the end of an old apartment block, it ran from light into shadow, from the high kitchen window through a little salon with a chaise longue to the brown-washed recess where a bed was tucked, almost out of sight, against the wall. There was another room beyond the salon whose window looked across a canal to the railway tracks of Central Station but that modest light was displaced by the tall cupboard beside it and an earlier life in storage behind the armchairs. We always sat in the light from the kitchen window and we could understand why Anke's mother had made her bed where she had, in its furthest reach.

Anke had promised her social worker I would not stay in the flat overnight, which was why I was to be found hunched among the early commuters on the tram. Four hours. That is what I had told myself on the first night in the lumber room. Only four hours until the first tram. Bryn was rolled into his sleeping bag on the other side of the double mattress but I was still travelling, all my senses open and hoovering up the dark.

I remembered the big bowl in the fridge we had been invited to dip into, blackberries in double cream. Crept down to the kitchen and became a wild-dog pack, hunting down the threads of sweetness until the bowl was empty. Then a convulsion in the shower, vomiting the rich cream back up.

I fled out into the street, the tramlines curving quietly away at the end of it. Why not simply follow them? All the way back to the city centre.

Not that I stopped to read the interlacing of the lines. My appetite now was for movement, the pulse hammering until the next street succumbed to my stride. A milkman was working ahead of me and I snatched a little bottle off a doorstep, no bigger than a medicine bottle, small enough to slip up my sleeve. I imagined disclosing it in my palm, *hey presto!* and presenting Anke with the milk for breakfast.

Was it just the exhilaration of the stride that flashed up the defiant look of a girl I had noticed in Oxford the week before? As if one conquest triggered another, no limit to the energy once it started to run. I came to a canal bridge and set Anke's bottle carefully down on a girder so that I could leap up on to it. My feet hit the steel and the bottle shattered where it stood.

I ended up in a bar, dancing to the music from the jukebox. Silence as a fresh 45 swung into place, hiss of the needle and then the opening chords I would hear as the voice of the oracle, the dark power I had to outpace as I drew Anke out of the shadows in the glass door where my reflection pleaded, such yearning in the steps I might still have been in Barcarès and not just a taxi ride away.

But it was not a shadow who came to the door of the flat, it was a sleepwalker, head bowed, long blond hair fallen over the long flannel nightdress that sealed her into her separate self, and the room behind her still disposed for sleep, a glass of water on the bedside table. An illumination came to me then, a moment of pure glee, and I folded myself below the table. As she shuffled back towards the bed, I threw the water over her.

She didn't say anything for a long time. Lifted off the wet night-dress and lay on the chaise longue, covered in a towel: 'I hate you sometimes.'

It was five o'clock in the morning.

I was quiet after that. Sunk in self-doubt as Anke made a pot of coffee. Barely lifted as the first car started in the street below and the sound of a radio came from next door's kitchen. Indifferent as Anke twisted the switch on the wall and our own radio moved from Mozart to the morning news to the jazz station. And then I heard something I recognised, the repeated chant of *Eat that chicken!* from one of Charles Mingus's wilder LPs.

Perhaps the sheer gusto in the voices was enough to rouse me. Perhaps there was a physiological trigger, something in the rhythmic structure of the chant that was operating below the level of aware-ness. Or perhaps I was still so stoned from the night before that any phrase would have resonated in my consciousness. Whatever the mechanism was, I grabbed the sketchpad Anke was using for her art school portfolio, selected a stick of charcoal and began, in all seriousness, to draw a chicken.

I think the first impulse was to finish the sketch before the chant ended. Then I remembered Redmond showing me Martin's drawing of a dead fox, a finely detailed pencil drawing, and remarking that was just the way the hairs lay where the shoulder slumped against the keel of the ribs. I was used to handling chickens on the farm and I was determined to emulate Martin, to show just how feather lapped over feather.

Charcoal was hardly the instrument for that and what started as a chicken's wing ended as an avalanche about to fall, nub after nub of rock slanting down the page. Misspent energy gave it a certain menace and I watched anxiously as Anke knelt on the floor and blew fixative over the propped-up page.

'You're smoking too much.'

I learned to wait for the trams. I would arrive at eight and sit at the kitchen table in the morning sun. One morning I picked up Anke's box of colours, making stray marks until I had evolved two flying dragons, one in dark green pastel and one in purple. They could hardly fly at all, they were two bumbling dragons, an apology for the way I had been when I first hit Amsterdam.

'How did you put up with me?'

'I just remembered how you were in Oxford.'

She took me to see Labberton, a painter who was a friend of her stepfather. In his early sixties then and keeping under cover while he built up a body of work that some people believed would rival Mondrian's, he looked decisive, the grey hair brushed straight back from a high forehead, and detached, as if he were the guardian of an energy expended elsewhere. He apologised for saying very little over lunch, explaining that he worked from early morning when the light was at its clearest: but then he showed me his work, setting a small watercolour in front of me and leaving me time to absorb it before he replaced it with another. They were like no water-colours I had ever seen, an exploration of light that was not so much abstraction as alchemy, distilling to a quintessence. A landscape or a city skyline was reduced to its elements, just two or three panels of colour, dark green set against a violet white and then against a much smaller panel clarifying into orange, all still in motion and only momentarily brought into balance. This was more fluid than Mondrian, a technical advance, if you like, but rooted in the Dutch landscape tradition.

One morning, as Anke was putting up her hair, she switched to the jazz station and a Charlie Parker solo came from the speaker in the wall, such a joyful flow of invention that she stepped away from the mirror and we danced out through the door, the rhythm of it carrying us into the day as if we had found our feet again, our instinctive unity. That night we went dancing in a club, a wide, low-ceilinged room with R&B coming from the speakers overhead. Anke was wearing her pierrot costume and as she spun out across the floor, long blond hair flying and the frills at ankle and wrist catching the light, the other dancers moved back and made a circle we crossed and recrossed, coming together in the centre and spinning out to the edges. She would step under my arm as we crossed and I would touch her lightly on the top of the head. That's where I was when the music stopped, in the centre of the circle with one hand raised, the riffs from the horn section so dense in the air around me, so solid to tread I had not realised they were coming to an end. A black American voice called out, 'One more time!' and I touched Anke's head and completed the step.

For his second year Redmond was going to share with Martin in a house down the Abingdon Road, a suburban semi-detached that hardly prepared you for the wilderness you entered once you stepped through the front door: rabbits' feet on the bookshelves, Martin's fox drawing on the wall and a heron he had found frozen in the winter of 1963 uncertainly stilted next to his easel. In the long coat he invariably wore, Mart was as tall as Red but thinner and altogether more finely drawn, the white skin of an Elizabethan miniature glimpsed through ringlets of long brown hair he was continually pushing to one side, only for them to fall back. He had the Marlborough equivalent of Derek's Liverpudlian 'aah', though it was more of an 'aarrh' on a rising intonation, a wordless response accelerating away from language because there was so much to be said. After which he would give a nervous laugh and deliver himself of an opinion very fast, 'Though I suppose you could say . . .'

Three weeks of the long vacation left. Three weeks in which to read the whole of Shakespeare. Nothing for it but to close the magic theatre. Bryn had stayed in Amsterdam, which made it easier. But everyone who had been sleeping on my floor ended up sleeping on Port Meadow. Every morning they would trail back along the lane and I would make them toast and coffee.

Not so easy to sit over my books with no counterbalance, without Anke's presence across the table from me. 'I have been happy these last two days,' she had said before I left Amsterdam. At the time a restless little thought had flickered across: *I found them a bit boring actually*. They had been the quietest days of all, when we had done little but read and listen to music. But now her absence was palpable. Not just the absence of a sexual charge, though that was part of it: twenty minutes before my train was due to leave, we had glanced at each other, torn into each other one last time and run for the train. But the absence of something I must have recognised when I first saw her in the street and thought: *Don't lose her!* Something that calmed and completed me, as she had after the frazzle of that first sleepless night. If she remembered how I had been in Oxford, I knew that I would remember how she had been in Amsterdam.

I had never expected to feel at a loss in Oxford. There was a quickening in the streets, sudden greetings and sounds of surprise as returning students recognised each other and stood in eager conversation on the pavement. But to me the whole place felt purposeless. It was like my earlier feeling of having to mark time but much more profound. I had fallen out of love with Oxford as irrevocably as I had fallen in love with Anke.

I cannot remember exactly where we were walking when I confided in Redmond, only the colour of an old stone wall and the heaviness of the late summer air.

'Why don't you marry her?'

This was a magical solution. I felt transformed, as if I were being changed then and there, cell by cell. Married students were rare but not unknown. Someone had come up to Merton already married. In his first year he had been obliged to live in college, with his wife visiting in the afternoons, but that would not be expected of me, not in my final year. I had a sudden vision of myself in my translated state, Anke on my arm like Wild Edric's fairy bride.

I called on my landlord to ensure that we could stay on in the flat. And then I wrote to Anke, knowing that she would accept.

Joy seemed to have its own strange clarity, in which I was one with the flow of the world. And I needed to be in that flow, not bent over a copy of Shakespeare. Suddenly I was a conversationalist, sitting over a coffee in the lounge of the Randolph and talking in French to a young diplomat who was attached to St Antony's. Or I would descend on friends from Merton and take the magic theatre with me. Naturally it had reopened to the world's flow.

One afternoon I arrived at David Jessel's room in Folly House with Lesley, who had just brought me the drawing of herself clinging to Lizzie's ankle, and Jenny, a pretty dark-haired little Mod who would have been passing through if she had not slipped over and broken her arm. Her travelling companion had to travel on, leaving Jenny in our care while her arm was in plaster.

In that heightened state it was impossible for me to sit still. I seemed to find meaning in movement, in a sycamore key twirling down, in sunlight glinting on a stone. And so I was off down the towpath from Folly Bridge, leaving the girls with David and another Mertonian, Russell Keat. I found a piece of driftwood that seemed of some moment, streamlined in its soaked brown weight. Then a twist of sweet paper. A nub of cut green glass that must have fallen from a child's bracelet. Gold foil from a cigarette packet. I arranged my finds until I had a miniature Cleopatra's barge. By the time I returned, the girls were two silhouettes from the Left Bank and the boys were looking intrigued. I laid the barge at the girls' feet and Russell said, 'It's like being in a play.'

There was innocence in that, as there was in my footling in front of the stage at the Freshers' Fair. I was helping to man the Poetry Society stall when Pat Crumly, a good local alto player, came onstage with a group from the Modern Jazz Club. Music was so immediate to me then that I started to turn in my own space, tracing the patterns of it with my feet. No one seemed to mind, they just walked round me or watched for a moment and then moved on, and I let the runs of notes carry me a little further. Rather as I had been when I started to rearrange François's stall, I was intent on something that made sense to me.

But then a photographer who was covering the Fair for *Cherwell*, the student newspaper, moved everyone back and crouched down with his camera. The space was mine, much more space than I had open to me in that little hut at Barcarès.

I made full use of it, skittering out to the edge on the alto's fast runs, crouched over feet rapid as the cymbal ride and turning under the very nose of the crowd as if I were strapped into the Whip at the funfair. The vibes came in and I had to leap back on myself, rocking from note to note. Then the trumpet, tearing off strips of notes so fast I found myself spinning, the overhead lights turning as if this were the Rotor and the floor about to drop away. Mustn't get dizzy, I thought, and changed step so that the lights were turning the other way. Then I was looking up and the lights were stationary above me. Make something of it! I moved my arms and legs into a star shape, slowly, twice, sprang up and finished the dance.

I don't remember whether there was any applause. Possibly, because later someone told me they had thrown me a coin. But I did hear someone say, 'That was really something else!' And perhaps it was there that the seeds of illusion were sown.

\*   \*   \*

Lesley was asleep beside me – innocently but in token of our implicit bond – when I heard Redmond's motorbike come into the lane. I put on the French cavalry jacket the gypsies had given me, picked up Lesley's long red silk scarf and tied it over my eyes as a blindfold. Not difficult, in a space I knew so well, to make my way down the stairs and out into the bright morning sunlight, where I veered towards Red, locating him accurately enough. 'Very good!' he said, as though I had qualified for Special Operations. There was often that element in our play, a martial instinct neither of us quite knew what to do with.

The scarf streamed out behind me as I rode pillion, a dashing sight, I thought, as we went down St Aldate's. But the lights were against us on the way back up the Cornmarket and then again by the Randolph. As the bike came to a halt for the second time, I felt a slight tug on my neck and looked down. The scarf was tangled in the back wheel. It must have dropped at the first red light, when there was no slipstream. A green light by the Randolph and I would have been throttled like Isadora Duncan.

'I think we're upsetting Roger.'

Lesley had forgiven me the loss of her scarf, which came from Biba and which I had been unable to replace in Oxford. But she could see me getting out of sync, given to little flares and misfires, and thought they must be crowding me.

What had welled up in me as joy had given me an impetus I could barely contain. Calling in on Peter in his new room in Folly House, I had found him out and lain down on the bed with my head spinning. Then I saw his fencing foil leaning in the corner, leapt up and whirled it round my head. It caught the light bulb, which scattered glass all over the bed. I knew there was nothing I could do: I was in no state to stand at arm's length on a chair and delicately detach a shattered light bulb. 'Oh, Peter!' I said to the empty room, 'this is awful.'

I had come across two American girls, sitting with their ruck-sacks on the steps of the Martyrs' Memorial, and stopped to talk to them. I told them I was on my way to draw a spider's web I had seen, high up under the ceiling of the toilets in Mob Quad. One skein crossed another with a third stretched behind, naturally cross-hatched in such an intriguing recession of angles and densities that I was sure it would be the ultimate drawing of a spider's web. 'Here!' one of them said, and gave me a rapidograph. 'You can use this. And then you can keep it,' she explained gently, 'and draw anything else you see.'

They thought I was on a trip.

'When did it start?' the other one asked. I explained and they looked at each other in some surprise: 'It's been nine days!'

Jenny had an aunt in Kidlington and Lesley went back up to James Street. I almost asked her to stay but on what basis?

Dance these days through, I thought, and went off to a party in St John's, where Ron and I hurled ourselves back and forth, collecting a covey of admiring schoolgirls. Walking the most detach-able of them home through North Oxford, I started to feel cold and put on my jacket. It did not seem to hang right, it felt oddly stiff, and there was an unfamiliar weight in the inside pocket. I drew it out and found it was a wallet, a wallet in what seemed to me, disabused old bohemian as I felt myself to be, perfect freshman order: a neatly filled-out paying-in slip, recording the safe deposit of that term's grant, twelve pounds in cash and a chequebook.

It *was* a blue corduroy jacket, the familiar blue I had taken off a peg in the cloakroom and swung over my shoulder as we left, but it was not my jacket. I had gone to the party in a black sweater.

I think it was the neatly filled-out paying-in slip that provoked me. On that evening at the farm when Anke told me I was the most beautiful person she had ever met, she had also tried to tell

289

me something else: 'Do you know what is the most important thing? That you have never done anything wrong.' She had grown up in care: her previous boyfriend had been a joyrider, adept at cornering a Citroën DS with just one finger on the wheel. But I was so taken with my outlaw glamour that I was oblivious to the most important thing. I decided to keep the jacket.

There was something in one of the side pockets, a girl's purse with some coins and a set of keys. Those at the very least I should have returned. There was an address label and a name that looked Danish. Quick off the mark, this freshman, an au pair in the first week. I held their evening in my hand, to restore or tip into anxiety.

Mine had ended like a Victorian parlour song, in a kiss at the front gate. But that hardly allayed me. I was all adrenalin. Just so much white water.

I was leaning against a garden wall when a group of town lads came up the road. The pavement was broad and they would have yomped past if I had not thrown the purse down.

One of them picked it up, a stocky lad who might have come off a butcher's stall in the market.

'Hey!' I said. 'Give it back! That belongs to my Danish dolly.'

'Might be a few quid in there,' he said and unzipped it.

'C'mon, Hambone! Give it back!'

The others heard the challenge and one of them called out, 'He means you, Jem!'

But Jem was already rising to it. Leaning hard back, he hurled the purse into the night. And turned to batter me, his fist held up like a shovel.

I could dance back as quick as I danced forward. Kicked his feet from under him and pattered back down the pavement, a jack o' lantern, always just out of reach.

\* \* \*

A long street stretching downhill. Not St Aldate's but the back street that ran parallel to it, descending past Paradise Square, then awaiting demolition. A pub in the crook of the hill, at the quiet end of a passageway. The roof slates shine and even the modest line of the gable looks freshly glossed. The paving stones glisten and the gypsies' straw hat shades my eyes as I stroll down to Redmond's at six o'clock in the morning, smoking a cheroot.

Someone has caught the sound of my footfall. Or the gleam of the straw as I descend the street. I am no longer in sole possession. He steps from the pub passageway and waits for me with his hand held out, two pennies on the open palm.

They are resplendent, new-minted as the sunlight itself. Two bronze discs, only matched by the light in the eyes above them, the amused intensity of someone who knows how to gamble on the moment. From that, as much as from the faded brown suit and the battered trilby, I assume that he must be Irish.

'It's been a good night,' I say, taking the pennies from his palm and replacing them with a crisp pound note from the freshman's wallet.

If only it had been.

I come to the neat front door of Redmond's digs and ring the bell, keeping my head down so that he will open the door on to the hat's blind brim. I am playing Death as he might be filmed by Bergman, the blank-faced visitor, blank as the clock with no hands at the start of *Wild Strawberries*.

Raise my head into Mart's intake of breath. He recovers enough to make a well-bred noise in the back of the throat and flees the kitchen, leaving Death standing beside the washing machine.

'You'd better come up.'

Red shepherds me into his room on the first floor. He sits tall as he leans back in his chair, alert as if he were out in the woods, his back against a tree, listening for the first bird calls in the dawn chorus. It is not until we hear a 'hah' from the floor below, shock expelled in a laugh that's more like a cough, that he relaxes.

It seems that Mart's not the only one I've alarmed. Peter is convinced that I showered his room with broken glass on purpose. And yes, we have been slightly at odds, ever since I turned up stoned to his last literary salon and read poem after poem by Keith Douglas.

'He thinks next time he sees you, you're going to have a bazooka.'

The door of the flat is closed as I come up the stairs. Everyone must be out. But there's a message, several stalks of a creeper roughly twisted into a wreath and pinned to the door. The creeper has black berries on it and that's the message I read, the black berries against the white gloss.

Deadly Nightshade!

Below them a note says, *And if in London* . . . and gives an address in Finchley.

A limed twig.

Or do I snare myself if I refuse the challenge? Is that the warning concealed in the black berries?

'Got to go to London,' I explain to Ron when he returns with his essential supplies, a strawberry yoghurt and a packet of Rizlas.

Another voice on the stairs. Something in the tone I recognise, the vibrant hush of a conjuror on the brink of revelation. It's Humphrey, ushering two Swedish girls into the magic theatre.

One of them is carrying a guitar and I'm not sure which gives off the sharper screech of collision, the guitar or the undeniable blond beauty. It was Anke who would tune Bryn's guitar, her head to one side, listening to the intervals as she worked string by string. But she never played it. A car crash had smashed her wrist when she was twelve. The child's hand she was left with could not stretch across the strings.

Humphrey is expecting another romance to unfold, his or possibly even mine. Something in me resists that, as verging on parody. And it's too late anyway. I have to avert the threat of the black berries.

'Give me an address in London!'

'Whereabouts in London?'

'Finchley.'

'Swiss Cottage!'

Humphrey gives me the address of a couple he knows. And then, with the smile of the storyteller who's found another twist to put in the tale, he takes something from his pocket and passes it to me: 'That's the only thing you have to bring back with you. No matter where you go, no matter what happens, that's the one thing you mustn't lose.'

Uncannily smooth. And with just a little more weight than I expect in my palm. It's a winkleshell, blue-black on the outside and grey on the inside, but not one to be probed with a pin and left on the plate. It's made of porcelain.

I tuck it into my sock, wondering who gave it to Humphrey, what was fired into it along with the glaze.

I already have my talisman. But I am still hankering after the flashlights, just as I was when I sang into the microphone at Barcarès. I commandeer the Swedish girl's guitar, as if I were still fourteen and thought there was magic in simply carrying one. She runs after me into the street, protesting and tearful.

'I'll buy it from you!' I declare and pull out the stolen cheque-book. But she will not accept my fanciful scrip, which appears to be paying her in a currency of arabesques and stars, and finally I defer to Ron's presence beside me on the pavement and return the guitar.

Ron sets off with me for the station, carrying his own talisman, a bible left over from my devotion to Christianity, which he regards as another religious text to be investigated. I am striding so fast, convinced this is a matter of life and death, that pavement and walls rush past me in one undifferentiated grey until a snake's head of rope rears from the tarmac. Thrown back it might be, to indicate that the car park is open, but that hiss along the nerves is enough to alert me. I look up the empty slope to the low line of the station buildings and everything comes into focus. This is a screen test.

I'm taking my cue from the film of *Modesty Blaise*, where the sleeping mirrors of Amsterdam's canals are shattered by the leaping prow of a speedboat. Anke in her Amazon's green kilt is merging with Monica Vitti's Modesty, her thighs branched with body paint after making love so that she is glimpsed in her full force, a Jill-in-the-Green. Which means that I have to be Terence Stamp's Willie Garvin, sardonic and irrepressible, dropping into the back of the boat as it shoots under a bridge. With my prison haircut and my monkey jacket, a short grey jacket that flares off the hips, I almost look the part.

Not that there's much call for acrobatics as we cross this car park. I've gone into character, ready to sidestep, to outwit every circumstance. But for the moment the sidesteps have to be verbal.

Ron takes his seat on the train and opens the bible. He's using it as he might use the I Ching, for clues to what's happening. Every so often he comes on a verse that has a certain ring to it and reads it out: 'Oh that one would give me drink of the water of the well of Bethlehem, which is by the gate!'

'If only it were so simple,' Willie observes. 'This is the water you never miss till the well runs dry.'

We keep this up all the way to London, the carriage around us growing completely silent as people wait for another phrase from the prophets to be capped by another phrase from the blues.

The silence is still holding as we draw into Paddington. First up and out of the train, I run down the platform and vault over the barrier. In that moment, stretched in mid-air with the concourse in front of me, I see that someone has turned to watch me. There's a pulse of sharp red as he draws on his cigarette, signalling my arrival.

I duck into a phone box and dial the Swiss Cottage number. A woman answers and I slam the phone down, to let them know that I'm on my way.

Ron stays close by me as we go down into the Tube. I have used this ever since I was a boy but it has never seemed so immediate before, each instant thrown up in so many multiples, such a conjunction of possible futures. The arrows indicate, the colour code confirms, but I am all eyes, as if I want to experience the entire system in one continuous present. Every time we stream along one tunnel, my imagination veers off into the other. And I step on to the train as if I might switch directions at any moment, looking into the faces around me as if any of them might hold the next clue.

It must be this that has unsettled the two men opposite. We're standing by the doors as the train slows for Swiss Cottage and I notice them look uneasy and then look away. I think nothing of it. Two men in their late thirties, one quite aquiline, the other a little soft in the face. But once we're off the train and walking down the platform, they suddenly step back into it.

I crash through the closing doors behind them. They turn in shock. The train rocks on towards Finchley Road, leaving Ron marooned on the platform, and they lean against the opposite wall of the carriage, one either side of the doors, shaking their heads and breathing deeply.

So that was a dead end. I look along the almost empty carriage and see an older man looking up at me, a stocky man in a black suit. His cheekbones suggest that he could well be an ex-boxer, and a handy one at that, because his nose is unbroken.

I draw the knife from my inside pocket and throw it at his feet. Impressive, had it stuck quivering in the floor. But it's the old kitchen knife from Walton Lane and it simply clatters flat and lies there, the yellowed bone handle rather giving it away.

The old bruiser turns quickly away, suppressing a smile. 'I'm getting off at the next stop anyway.'

I follow him out into the quiet of the evening. Inexorably quiet, just as I remember it from long afternoons in the suburbs, the quiet so pervasive that any other possibility is effaced.

I step into a pub and there, sitting alone at a table, is an elderly man whom I take to be Japanese. In front of him there's an ashtray, an empty white ashtray. I turn it upside down and take out one of Lesley's pastels, slipped into my pocket as I left as if I would silence my mysterious challenger with my use of colour. A tight swirl of the pastel across the white acrylic and I present the old man with a rising sun. His face creases in surprise and pleasure.

I move on to two young couples at another table. We have hardly started talking when one of the boys says, 'You've just made the girl pregnant, look!' She is staring up at me with a strained white face and a bulge under her dress is stretching the dark green paisley. I bend over it and say, 'Hello, child!'

Turning to the bar, I ask for a half of bitter, ready to play to the circle of men at the end of their working day. But I'm not getting it right and the barman starts to look hostile. I realise that I'm expected to pay for this, which seems odd to me. Then one of the older men has a word in my ear: 'You've got ten minutes' break now. Go and sit outside for ten minutes!'

For ten minutes nothing happens. Then a girl walks past and I spring up to walk beside her, confident she's taking me to a party. Surely that's all I need to clinch the part, a party where I can dance.

Not much I can amuse her with down this street of semi-detached houses. I present her with a privet leaf and she smiles but there's nothing vouchsafed in return, no answering token. Finally she turns off down a close and I realise I'm going to have to find this party on my own.

Though that's almost forgotten as it turns to dusk and I become absorbed in the sensation of stealth, moving silently along the backs of houses in the soft-soled shoes I found in the same junk shop where I found the monkey jacket. These are older houses, the detached town houses of a more select area. I slip into a mews, keeping to the shadow of the far wall, just beyond the square of light where someone is cooking a meal. They open a door to put something in the dustbin and their silhouette ducks and bobs back, back into the seclusion they think is complete.

There's a vintage sports car parked further along, the rounded bonnet so minimal that the engine is half on display, its curious metals caught in the light from a street lamp, thin copper pipes curling up over what must be the plugs. The whole assembly is so intriguing, the brake lever braced upright, the steering rods outlined as in a diagram, that for a while I stand over the open cab, wondering which wires to pull out and push together – for all the world as if I were Anke's joyrider and not the angel-maned poet she prized for his innocence.

It's as I emerge from the mews that I hear music on the air, muted it's true, but music. It's coming from a first-floor window the other side of a garden fence. I climb the fence and stand under an apple tree, looking up. A sash window, it appears to be in darkness, but there is music playing. I take off my jacket and leave it at the base of the tree. Climb the tree and reach the window. I'm just trying to push it up when someone opens it for me, a thin-faced man whose receding hair gives him a thoughtful look.

'Don't worry!' I say. 'It's only the cat' and scramble in over the sill.

'This way,' says the thoughtful man, leading me across a darkened room and into the hall. He holds the front door open, such a reasonable gesture that I run down the steps and out into the road.

There's a van starting up on the opposite kerb, a white Transit van. I have a vision of myself riding spreadeagled on the roof, pure Willie Garvin, and catch it just as it's pulling away. I spring up the back, silently enough I think, and crouch over the cab. But as I put my knee down, ready to flatten myself and take hold of the sides, the tin creaks.

The van stops and a woman gets out.

'Good Lord! There's somebody on the roof!'

'It's all right! I just landed by parachute.'

Suddenly I'm floodlit. A squad car has pulled up, fixing me in its headlights. A policeman of about my own age is standing by the back of the van, waiting for me to jump down. I reach under my shirt, worn loose in the Russian style, and pull the belt out of the loops of my cords.

'There's my parachute belt!'

I sit in the back of the squad car, entertained by the green lights running across the dashboard and the crackle of a voice on the radio. Then on a bench in West Hampstead police station, relaxed now the action's been taken out of my hands and only agitated by the need for a cigarette. The young policeman seems sympathetic but he won't give me one.

It's warm for October and he's taken his helmet off. He's dandling it in his hands and I can look up its green skirts to the rose, the silver rose that gives a policeman his final half-inch of height. Such a potent symbol of authority you would expect it to be hammered into place, sterling through and through. But it's not, it's hollow. All it has underneath is a little metal ring, like the back of a silver button. It's held in place with a matchstick.

298

'That's not a real policeman's helmet, is it? You're all just actors, aren't you?'

The walls of the holding cell are painted green, the same colour that's used for the walls of a horse's loose box, though in a darker shade. It's believed to be more calming than whitewash.

For me it's the desired dance space, the low light from the steel mesh set into the ceiling almost as conducive as a nightclub's permeable dark. I throw all my energy into performing to the steel mesh, thinking that's where the camera must be, but however far out I step on the waves of my imagined R&B, however flashy my breaks into double time on the crests, there's no response, nothing but the dim light in its hollow behind the grid.

*That's not what they want to see! Drop to the floor as if you were doing press-ups. Stretch on over the shoulder and let the spine dip. Slip back into the cat, fluent in shadow.*

The foot grips and the thigh muscles slide, just as I had visualised, only for my bottom to lift like a lust-flushed baboon. My back legs are too long for a cat.

I am learning to keep my shoulders down and twist from hip to hip, producing a kind of elongated slink, when a triangle of yellow light appears on the wall above my head. Someone has lifted the cover of the judas hole to check on me. That becomes the marker, that triangle of yellow light. If I can keep below that, I'm passing the test: I am the cat, fluent in shadow.

The eye at the judas hole must have spread the word because the triangle keeps appearing above my head. There's a miaow through the wall, repeated more slowly and rising in pitch. Someone else is perfecting his technique. Then a whole series of woofs, low down and moving from wall to wall, as if I'm being chased round the cell.

I reach down into my sock for the winkleshell, the one thing

I mustn't lose, flick it ahead of me as I crawl and then pounce so that it's back under my palm. The more the walls woof at me, the more absorbed I become in the game, letting the winkleshell roll until it's almost out of reach and I'm lying on my side, patting at it with one outstretched paw.

The hatch in the cell door opens and a face looks down at me, the skin sallow and beginning to sag on narrow bones but the eyes aquiver, the pupils flooded with a malign energy. The cat had better not become his plaything.

At once my mind switches tracks, just as it had when the police produced my jacket, recovered from the foot of the tree, and questioned me about the chequebook.

'Oh,' I said, my voice taking on a camp intonation, 'that belongs to my friend Humphrey. He lives above the poodle parlour in Oxford.'

So far, so diverting. But as if I knew there was another, more sober reality in which I couldn't sidestep, I had gone straight over to the desk sergeant and said in my normal voice, 'Get my father and my Uncle Bob!'

Bob was an honorary uncle. He had been the station inspector at Brixton when my father started work as a police typist and proceeded to reorganise his entire office. 'What a brain!' And when my father emerged from the war as an embryo barrister, but without the private income that most barristers had in those days, it was Uncle Bob who put him on the Scotland Yard list and got him his first cases.

He had been a legend all through my childhood, my uncle who was Head of the Flying Squad. And since then I have come to know him as a quiet man who keeps bees and makes parsnip wine. But when he steps into the cell and asks, 'Now what's all this about, Rodge?' I keep wrong-footing him, twisting away and answering in my camp voice, dancing past him towards the door.

I have to stay in character, even if I'm no longer sure who that character is.

My father has enlisted the help of a doctor, the wife of one of his pupils. Luckily for me, she is also a police surgeon and it is she who finally resolves things. In the early hours of the morning I am ushered into the back of a Black Maria and transferred to the psychiatric wing of a London hospital.

'Treat him gently!' the sergeant advises the young constable who is escorting me. 'His father's a barrister and his uncle used to be a commander.'

It must be late morning when I wake from the sleeping pill they gave me on admission.

'Right,' says the male nurse, 'you can put those pretty clothes on again now.'

Does he mean the Russian shirt, which Su had made from a curtain fabric, durable and dark green?

The day room is absorbed in art therapy. I take a sheet of blank paper and start writing out a short poem I had made from my night walks across Oxford, writing the lines out slowly and carefully as if the final compression would give me something to hold on to:

> In mid-winter's early dark
> from a small tree by the church's wall
> a flush of berries
> > met the sky's blue shrill.

'That's nice writing!' says a nurse over my shoulder and I put the cap back on the rapidograph. Can't get on with anything in here.

I stand under the hood of the phone in the corridor, pleading with my mother to come and fetch me.

'We're not allowed to,' she says, in a small frozen voice.

I slam down the phone in anger and another voice comes through the perforations of the soundboard, an all-encompassing male voice: 'Well, we heard all that.'

But not so encompassing that I can't see the courtyard below and the unattended side gate. I walk straight out and stop a passing taxi.

'Highgate, please. And could you stop at a phone box? I'll need to check the address.'

The taxi driver thinks I'm a dubious customer but he's prepared to wait while I pull out the first of the big directories and look up Bax, Dr Martin. Editor of *Ambit*, which had published the poem with the girl-gay mothers and the middle-aged mermaid, my one and only publication in a national magazine.

It's his wife Judy who answers the door.

'I've just escaped from a mental hospital and I've no money, I'm afraid. Could you possibly pay for the taxi?'

Judy looks after me like the nurse she once was. Scrambled eggs on toast. A long soak in a hot bath. And then a lie-down in a darkened room.

Martin gets home to find me crouched by the fire, smoking a Turkish cigarette from the little carved wooden box in the bedroom, but quiet, self-contained.

Given that he's a doctor himself, I could well be compromising him professionally. But he runs me to the nearest Tube station and gives me a handful of loose change. The ticket office at Paddington won't give me a single to Oxford on credit but I ring the lodge at Merton and the porter sends the fare down to the station by taxi.

Though not before I almost get myself arrested once more. The wait seems interminable and I'm Willie Garvinning up and down the concourse when a girl sitting on one of the benches catches my eye. 'You'd have lovely legs,' I inform her, 'if you didn't have a 'ole in your stockings.' And then I crouch down and gaze up at her earrings: '*Mais tu as des boucles d'oreilles formidables!*'

Later I see her again, walking with her boyfriend down into the Tube. She looks back and lavishes a smile on me. And then I have to spoil it all by running up and shaking her boyfriend by the shoulders.

'Get off me, you pimp!' he shouts and two Transport Police start to bear down on me with a slow, meaningful stride, in such perfect step they seem to be sliding towards me along a rail.

It's a slow train to Oxford and for the first hour I try everyone's patience, jumping up out of my seat and trying to cadge another cigarette. I would retire behind my shades but they seem to have got broken somewhere along the way. Finally I fetch a paper towel from the toilet and fold it over the broken lens. Lean back and sit the journey out, minute by minute.

Ron's relief when I reappear is tempered with outrage: 'Two hours I waited for you on that station!'

'Don't worry, old chap! We'll soon have you right.' This is what happens when you turn to your father for help. Where does he turn in his turn, in his perplexity? He turns to other father figures and the voices become deeper and deeper until you hear the rumble of the Sky God Himself.

I had woken that morning from a deep sleep to find my parents looking down at me. They were relieved to find me there, lawfully asleep, as it were, at the correct address. I was a little disconcerted to find my parents in the magic theatre.

Before the advent of the black berries I had been planning a lunch party. Friends were coming and I had to buy garlic sausage and pâté from the delicatessen in the market. But there was a policeman at the door and my father had to accompany me as my own personal bulldog.

The lunch party ran its doomed course – 'Roger, what is that awful man doing at the door?' – and my parents drove me up to the Warneford, Oxford's other mental hospital, which had a special unit for students. Seeing the consultant as the final authority, I gave him a vivid account of finding the black berries, took him through all the twists and turns of the screen test, all my sidesteps and ripostes, some of them so inspired that I expected to be discharged then and there, *summa cum laude*. He diagnosed hypomania and prescribed a narcosis: he would arrange for me to be admitted and put to sleep for three weeks on barbiturates. I must have looked so disappointed that he felt the need to reassure me as I left the consulting room. The voice descended like a hand on my shoulder: 'Don't worry, old chap! We'll soon have you right' and the hairs stiffened on the back of my neck.

Before the consultation, I had been assessed by a junior doctor who asked me if I had experienced any hallucinations. I told him of the night in Amsterdam when I looked across a canal and saw black men in white suits dancing in a club. The rhythm was so easy and their movements so fluid that I felt a sense of privilege, of initiation, as if this were somewhere we were being taken after hours. And then the dancers broke up and I saw that they were reflections of the street lights on the water, moving in the wake of a distant boat.

'Technically,' he said, 'that's not an hallucination because there was actually something there. That's called an illusion.'

Dialogue, I thought, that's what I need, not a paternal hand on the shoulder. The next day I raced round to see the Principal of Postmasters, Merton's equivalent of the Dean.

'I've been smoking marijuana,' I said, 'and got myself into trouble with the police.'

Not a word about the screen test. My mind had switched on to the other track.

'I have to go into the Warneford and the consultant there seems rather overbearing. But there is a young doctor I think I could have a dialogue with. Could I be admitted under him instead?'

Academics understand all about dialogue. Browsing along his bookshelves while he made some phone calls, I spotted a copy of *Brideshead Revisited* and asked if I could take it into the Warneford with me. It seemed the perfect antidote.

'It's a fine day,' he said. 'Why don't we take down the hood on my old Daimler and go up in style?'

But junior doctors, as I was to discover, work under consultants. All I had done was bring forward the date of my admission. And from then on there would be precious little dialogue. From then on it was chemical warfare.


The words on my pillow were lime green. They lit up before I knew it, in italics that might have been handwritten had they not been so angular, the letters formed from tiny neon tubes that kept burning out into the whiteness of the pillow.

*Crashpaddling* they said, as if I were carrying the scene with me, wrapping myself in it like a comfort blanket. They seemed to be driven by puns, incessant puns vanishing the moment I read them. *Brain in the wind* wrote itself across the pillow, followed by *Peltdown Man*.

It was like watching my own Northern Lights, flare after flare from the cerebral cortex while the head itself was dry as pumice. There was water on the bedside locker, a cup sealed like a baby's with a spout I could suck on, but I could barely part my lips, let alone reach for it.

Above me, in the animate world, I heard a door being unlocked, the sotto voce of one voice and intimations of another. I could hear gradations of tone, the young Italian male nurse gratified and then gracious, expanding into the perfect host, the girl from the female

305

wards, Yugoslav at a guess, poised and a little playful, escaping from the tedium of the night shift. I heard the rattle of coffee cups, I heard them settle at the desk – and slowly, in their borrowed English, the voices began to preen. It would be a long time yet before I heard the clink of the tray and the sweet sound of a teaspoon.

I sat at a low table, looking down into the bowl of cornflakes, my first breakfast out of bed, the first food for three weeks that wasn't soup or Complan, fed to me by a nurse at intervals of which I had no memory. I had yet to realise how thin I was under my pyjamas and dressing gown. But I knew that I was nothing compared to the radiance of these orange flakes, to the energy that I could feel pulsing from them.

It helped that Phil was sitting opposite, the junkie I had once glimpsed on Lizzie's arm – though sitting was a form of words because we were far from certain on our chairs. Neither of us said anything but we steadied ourselves and lowered our spoons into the light. It came as quite a surprise, cold milk breaking over dry lips and the sun's scales cracking under our teeth. All at once something rose through the vacancy, the frightening void that was like the dead leg some kids had been adept at giving in the playground. It was the recovery of a sensation, appetite.

'You're having visitors this afternoon,' they said and without the shadow of a doubt, as if this were the promise I had been holding to all along, a promise made to me, perhaps, under narcosis, I knew that Anke would be coming. I imagined the moment when the door was unlocked and she stepped through, her hair illumining the grey corridor and all the energy of the city entering with her. I thought she was already in Walton Lane, living the life I had envisioned for us, not the anxious guest of my parents, flown over from Amsterdam at their expense. But when I saw her walking between them, her head down and her hair strangely lustreless, falling in two straight lines over an imitation leather coat, I knew that the illness had not just been mine. She was on tranquillisers herself.

Her reply had come the day after I was taken into the Warneford. And fortunately it was, as Ron put it, a very cool letter: 'Yes, of course I will marry you. But you must remember that I am a ward of court and I have to get their permission first.' The next thing she knew, I was in trouble with the police.

It was impossible to talk in front of my parents. We just looked at each other, bereft. But there was one afternoon when Anke came rushing into the ward on her own. She had given my mother the slip in Oxford and caught the bus up. Gradually, in the twenty minutes or so it took my mother to appear, our awkwardness fell away and Anke told me how she had negotiated the long silence when I was under narcosis: 'I used to talk to you through the mirror. Each night I would sit in front of it and tell you everything I had done that day.'

Misha, the Yugoslav male nurse, could hold down the ward by his sheer presence. He would open the newspaper, gripping the page with his right thumb and giving it a little shake so that it was stretched taut across his knees. Then peer down into it, the broad forehead tightening in turn under thick black hair, and read with such concentration that for half an hour no one would move on the circle of chairs. George, the old soldier who clambered out of bed every night to move the ammunition boxes, sat in a state of blank beatitude. Father Howard, a thin, sweet-faced old man, meditated under the black shoulder cape he was allowed to wear over his dressing gown. While Stafford, like a priest bound to his own singular office, bent his domed head over a fresh translation of the New Testament. A brilliant linguist still consulted by deferential young men from the university, he had set himself to learn every language in the world by the simple device of reading successive translations of the first Gospel, the Gospel according to St Matthew. He knew it so well that he could deduce the principles of each new language from the way it rendered particular passages. Grammars might not exist, dictionaries might not exist, not for the more obscure languages, but there was almost always a translation of the New Testament.

If he had confined himself to mastering all the world's languages, he could have remained one of Oxford's eccentrics, poring over St Matthew at his desk in the Bodleian. But he had another obsession that was felt to be disruptive. The moment he was let out of the Warneford, he would go straight to Windsor Castle and announce that he was King Edward IX.

Still, he was luckier than the gaunt figure glaring over his knees on the far side of the circle. It was said that he was a Fellow of Balliol who had been admitted in 1912 to avert a homosexual scandal. That may have seemed a merciful provision at the time, compared to picking oakum in Reading Gaol. Half a century later it did not seem so merciful. Seeing him pent in his chair, I thought of Ted Hughes's Jaguar, 'hurrying enraged / Through prison darkness after the drills of his eyes . . .' If anyone came near him he snarled.

I sat in Misha's calm, rather as I had once sat in my grandfather's warm, and almost as childlike, except that my hands were trembling as if I had Parkinson's. This was the effect of the new pill, the chaser they had started to give me with my slugs of Largactil.

There had been a few days in early November when it looked as if the consultant's assurance might be justified and they would soon have me right. I was moved on to an open ward, which meant that I was free to go into Oxford during the day. I stepped out into such fires as I had never seen before. This is worth three weeks' oblivion, I thought, poring over the lemon burning in a leaf. I was so absorbed that it took me half an hour just to get to the bus stop.

Then the bus came and I was aware of the platform trembling under me, of the thin skin of steel inside which, by common consent, we were all taking our seats.

I stayed at that pitch of perception for several days, descending on Redmond and Martin and pulling the charcoal drawing from Amsterdam out of my pocket, as if there were anything to be made of those hectic strokes. I sat up all night in the little kitchen off the ward, talking to the staff on their breaks. Until the evening they administered the new pill and I broke down in tears. 'We brought you up too soon,' they said.

To be back on the locked ward was like being back in a play by Samuel Beckett after being caught up in a drawing-room comedy. The open ward had the atmosphere of an Edwardian country house party, the patients rising from their armchairs when the gong sounded for dinner. Conversation as such hardly took place on the locked ward. There was the Liverpool Irishman who talked to himself non-stop, in a companionable fashion that would admit you if you took a chair nearby and continue, quite unperturbed, when you moved away. There were the games of catch with a rolled-up sock when the old boys suddenly sharpened up and I found myself back in the playground with them, George shouting 'Good throw!' and Dougie patting the ball back to me with his big soft hands. And there was the morning Father Howard rose to his feet, possessed of a quiet determination. Ever since he was admitted, he explained, he had been meditating on the strangeness of our situation and he had been led to an understanding that he could only express in these words: we were between the upper and the lower congregations.

The lime-green words had gone from my pillow. I would wait for the night sister, Sister Simon, to process through the ward, the starched white of her headdress floating swanlike over a dark-blue

309

cloak and the soft Irish voice so unhurried in its intonation, so certain of its cadence – 'May God bless you and keep you this night!' – that I slept the sleep of the protected.

By day I squinted at paragraphs of Wilson Knight on Shakespeare, never able to read more than a few lines before they bent out of sight. I would lift the book away and scrabble at the pouch it rested on, the pouch of Captain Grant Anke had sent from Amsterdam. Roll another roll-up and try to focus on the words as they coalesced out of the phosphorescence of the page.

But whatever survival instinct had flashed up words on my pillow was still at work. One morning, prompted, I imagine, by the amusement I had felt when the dinner gong echoed along the stone corridors of the open ward, I awoke to find myself thinking a poem through, thinking it straight through as if I were writing it straight out. One or two phrases still felt sketchy but a few mornings later I awoke to find I had it complete, all the lines firmed up. Sister Simon must have seen the light in my eyes when she was walking past on her final round. She paused and I went straight up to her and said it under my breath:

### Angelus

*for Anke*

The imagined dinner gong
     – ambre solaire packed up
         handbags clicked to
            and cameras snapped
                    shut

They swooped on the debris
     cleared bottles into the fridge
        glasses into the rack
           padlocked their hut

I was sitting, writing to Red
when they gathered round
*Qu'est-ce-que ça veut dire?*
I told them
*Mais ce n'est que de bêtise!*
It might make him laugh.

They cleared off, left me to the wind
whistling through their yacht masts,
the weird cries of their tinfoil streamers

but I was at peace
          thought of writing for them all
                    an Angelus
                              to commemorate this hour

That night I stormed the beach
shouting your name
half-desperate

I went into a bar and they tried to cut my hair

I looked at the stars
they shot into my eyes

I was pursued by lights all over the beach
white horns of driftwood        rose in the wind
I was expecting the Devil

Hidden by a screen of whistling bamboo
snug from the sandshots
          – feet thudded into my sleep

In the morning they found me        bivouaced
my anorak pitched        as a sunshade

I haven't prayed

               yet

'That's beautiful!' she said.

Stafford cut a dash at the Christmas Dance, sweeping across the floor in long smooth strides as if he were someone else altogether, not King Edward IX but the young man he must have been before the obsession took hold.

The backward slides of the waltz were beyond me. But how else was I to dance with Sister Simon? I could hardly ask her to jive. I took a tentative hold of her slim shoulders and we shuffled from foot to foot, turning in small circles. Poignant, to step so close and be so aware of the years between us, the years that were and weren't there.

'One of these days,' I ventured, 'you'll be sitting in a café on your day off and I'll walk in through the door.'

'Oh!' She laughed. 'And wouldn't I just faint in my chair!'

For the rest of the evening I jived myself breathless. Danced with everyone and no one until I collapsed on to one of the chairs at the back of the hall. Someone else had collapsed a few chairs down. I glanced along the row and saw a familiar silhouette. As I bent to my tobacco pouch, he was already bent over St Matthew.

They had warned me that I was likely to fall into a depression: a high and then a low, the inevitable sequence of the cyclothyme, which was what I appeared to be. What they had not told me was that I would end up at such a distance from myself, such a hopeless distance.

It was a slow-moving creature who returned to the farm at the end of February, his face stiff with the extra weight he was carrying from a high dose of Largactil. Imprisoned in the shell of a tortoise, the hare had only the faintest memory that he had once been a hare. He had no idea how to change back.

It would soon be Easter. I was going to Amsterdam and we would have the flat, Anke's mother's flat. Our first time alone since that September afternoon when we had torn ourselves apart and run for the train. But when I stood in the gentleman's outfitters in Esher and tried on a new coat, three-quarter length in navy-blue, I felt like an imposter. Could that stolid-looking fellow really be going to Amsterdam?

We had seen each other at Christmas. Jiggly skeleton that I was, I had been allowed home for a few days and my parents had brought Anke over. It was strange, taking our seats at the long table for Christmas dinner, to think that we might be taking them for the future too. I would look up and see her face against the familiar faces, all the more finely composed as she was sitting a little shyly, looking down into herself, and feel what I had felt when I first saw her in the street: a distinct change of register, an opening of possibility beyond anything I had known. But when we first moved towards each other up in her room, my hand had trembled on her breast. Instead of suppressing the tremor, instead of pulling her to me or moving my hand away, I had stood back and let the shock of it go right through her. What did I think I was? A wounded war hero? 'No,' she said, 'don't!'

My only hope was that something might quicken in me once I was back in the flat with Anke, that she would twist the big brown switch on the wall and Charlie Parker would spring to my rescue. But when I stepped down from the train at Central Station, there seemed to be no one waiting for me. I had to cover the length of the platform before I saw the back of a small round head. She was walking slowly away from me, out of the station.

I brought the silver-topped cane gently down over her shoulder

313

but there was no cry of surprise, no greeting. I felt as if I had awoken a sleepwalker.

'I thought you weren't coming.'

'No, it was just that I was in the last carriage.'

We might never have been separated. She was talking as we walked, not on my shoulder but just under it. Talking as she did at night, the slowings as she thought something through as intimate as the little rushes of realisation. But what she was so absorbed in, what she was trying to convey to me, was the new relationship she had just formed with a boy from the orphanage. 'For him it was the first time. It was so beautiful.'

The blow over the heart. I had survived it before. But not this time. 'He's so funny,' she said, and an absence came into her voice that I recognised. It was the absence that came over her when she spoke of her little sister, the same vivid abstraction.

That night I was alone in the flat. Anke went back to the orphanage. And the next day, while she was at work, I went out and bought a serious amount of hashish, more than was usually sold over a café table. I had to wait while it was fetched from the wholesaler. Not quite a Brixton boot sole but certainly a boot heel. Easy enough to carry through Customs in the pocket of an irreproachable overcoat.

We had another conversation before I left. Seeing me at Christmas had shattered the image of me she had kept from the summer, the image she had been talking to every night through the mirror. She dwelled on a little incident I had completely forgotten, an incident on Boxing Day when one of my old school friends had taken us motor racing at Brands Hatch. He had a vintage car straight out of *Casablanca*, an Armstrong Siddeley with running boards and a long bonnet, and I thought Anke might enjoy riding in it. But when we were standing in the crowd and I got out the sandwiches, my hands shook and the sandwiches spilled on the ground.

'Everyone laughed at you,' she said, 'and in Oxford you were always so strong!'

On her return to Amsterdam, she had wept for days. But the new relationship had formed only recently and she wasn't at all sure what to do. Should she write and tell me, breaking off the engagement and cancelling my visit at the last moment? 'Why not let him come?' the new boyfriend had suggested. 'Then at least he can have two weeks in Amsterdam.'

I wondered if there hadn't been another motive, half-hidden, even from herself: the need to see what she felt when she saw me again. In which case, she must have been relieved when the cane fell across her shoulder and she looked up to see the imposter. 'You are ugly to me now,' she explained.

No one knew that I was back in England. I caught the train to Oxford, put my suitcase in Left Luggage, and went to find Phil the Junkie. All I wanted was the needle of death.

Would I have hesitated at the last moment? This was the line Red and I had agreed never to cross, the point of no return. The flash from the first fix was said to be so intense that you lost the desire for anything else. It was a sensation you would seek to recapture time and again, with rapidly diminishing returns.

I shall never know. I made my way to the benches in the Cornmarket where we used to sit, certain there would be someone there that I knew, someone with a room where we could roll a joint from the boot heel in my pocket, someone who knew someone who would know where Phil was to be found. There was no one. Only the shoppers the benches were meant for, stout ladies resting their legs.

Back at the farm I had to wait until the stable lad who shared my room was out before I could break a crumb off the boot heel and heat it in a twist of silver paper. 'It's herbal tobacco,' I assured him when he found the air heavy with the smell. But where once it would have lifted and thinned as I came alive to the night around me, now it just stayed as weight, another layer of wadding wrapped around senses that were muffled enough already. I was discovering the truth of Hopkins's line, '*Selfyeast of spirit a dull dough sours.*'

Louie and Kathy came over from Orléans with Louie's younger sister and stayed in the caravan in the garden. I was happy enough playing host, taking them to a West End musical, on a tour of East End pubs and along Carnaby Street, where Louie's sister bought herself a shift dress in a soft rose-pink that set off her deep Californian tan. We had even embarked on a light-hearted romance. On the final night we were all going to Eel Pie Island, to dance at the club where the Rolling Stones used to play and where I had actually danced to John Lee Hooker. But we never got there: I took a triple dose of my anti-depressant pills, smoked a solitary joint up in my room and collapsed as we were about to leave. It was as if I no longer trusted to the reach of ordinary happiness. As if, with enough chemicals inside me, I might turn on the dance floor and feel Anke pass under my arm.

And then pride rose up in me, the conviction that she had only taken refuge in the new boyfriend. Surely I could win her back if I clambered out of the tortoise shell and reappeared as myself?

The next day I stopped taking my medication. And as soon as I had earned enough money from private tutoring, I went back up to Carnaby Street and bought a suit. It was daffodil yellow with a faint blue pinstripe.

*Sergeant Pepper's Lonely Hearts Club Band* had just been released and it was playing in all the shops. I was completing the look of the suit, choosing an apple-green shirt and apple-green shoes that might have formed out of the phrases drifting overhead, when I heard 'A Day in the Life' and it was as if my own emptiness reverberated along the street. Strange to go up to the till under that relentless final crescendo, to hand over money with the inward look of a listener and see the assistant looking down and listening as he gave you the change, the two of you continuing with your shadow play because what else was there to do?

To me it felt almost too personal, the oscillation on *I'd love to turn you on* opening on to a space whose echo I knew only too well. But I wore the yellow suit as if I'd just stepped out of a Donovan song. 'By Christ,' said an old man as I walked down into the Underground, 'now I've seen everything!'

Through the gloom of the platform, in the mid-afternoon lull between trains, I saw a pale face behind curtains of long, straight black hair. Surely purple loons would talk to a yellow suit? I walked up to her and found a sister in my solitude. She became my guide to the other Underground, to the nights in UFO when Arthur Brown sang 'Fire' in his flaming headdress and Michael X took the stage to reflect on the coming Revolution, reassuring us that 'there were some people in this town who would be remembered, people who would share their last orange with you'.

Judy was from Bromley and one of her friends was the girl-friend of a pop singer who had just brought out his first LP. This came as a surprise because she looked so straight next to Judy, so neat in her miniskirt and pin-tucked blouse: dark-haired, petite and very pretty. But then she was very together. Her parents had even given her her own flat, separate from the main house. We were invited there one evening to watch the Beatles perform their new single on the world's first television link-up.

The second surprise came when I was introduced to her boyfriend: 'Roger Garfitt – David Bowie'. He was in a black cashmere sweater and black trousers. Whereas I had come as a complete production, the slim flowery tie I had chosen in burnt orange and primrose, to complement the apple green of the shirt and the daffodil yellow of the suit, carefully tied in a Windsor knot.

317

*The wrong one has come as the rock star*, I thought, and flushed as we shook hands. A moment's heat, then a moment's transparency, as if I were being X-rayed, or X-raying myself, so determined was I to be equal to the encounter. Was there really any poetry in me? Any dark fire in the white bones I had been so careful to invest with a firm grip?

David didn't say much. Sensitive and self-contained, he wasn't going to take any risks. They would be left to me. I should have had a card printed: *Mistakes Made for You – Every Embarrassment Catered for*. But I warmed to him during the preamble to the Beatles song, which turned out to be 'All You Need is Love', sung to what looked like a hippie revival meeting, with Mick Jagger clapping in the back row and Keith Richards processing at the end. The link man was talking about the explosion in the music industry and the number of new singles that came out across the world every year, some astonishing figure. David gave a despairing little whimper, a little cry of self-mockery, as if he would be lost in all that number.

'Why did you flip, man?' It was late summer and I was back in Amsterdam, sharing Bryn's pad in an attic lumber room. He had stayed on to be with Hannah, working long shifts in the Heineken brewery to pay the rent.

'I don't know.' It had seemed so innocent, that upsurge of joy at the thought of marrying Anke. And it had felt so natural, to give myself to the world's flow, to talk till all hours and dance the days through. Even when I started to misfire, when Lesley withdrew to James Street and Jenny went off to her aunt's, I just thought, *This will be over soon. Anke's letter will come and a great calm will descend. I'll shut the door on the magic theatre and start to make a home. That will be magical enough*.

And perhaps a calm would have descended if her letter had come before the black berries were pinned to the door, sending Willie

Garvin off on his wild odyssey. I knew now that it hadn't been a screen test. That illusion had faded, though not immediately. I was still sustained by it as I came round from the narcosis.

'Have you heard from the film company yet?' I asked my mother.

'In our experience,' she replied carefully, 'film companies usually make all the arrangements before they shoot the film.'

One day it just dawned on me, quietly, as a headache will sometimes clear before you are aware it has gone: *no, of course it wasn't a screen test*. But it would be years before I realised that the mysterious message, *And if in London* . . . hadn't been meant for me: it was meant for Jenny, left by the boyfriend who had entrusted her to us when she broke her arm. And more years still before I recognised that the black berries weren't deadly nightshade, which is not a creeper: they were black bryony, a couple of strands he must have taken from a nearby garden wall and pinned to the door as a courtship gesture. There was nothing sinister in them at all.

In the meantime, I had to catch Anke's eye. Or at least, her imagination. She would know that I was back in Amsterdam but I could hardly just drop in. I had to become a rumour, an intimation, a presence behind the mirror. I had to furnish Hannah with stories to tell.

There was a Chinese quarter in Amsterdam, which meant that it was possible to obtain opium. Bryn made some discreet enquiries and came back with a sachet of thick brown paste. I had imagined smoking it in a pipe, leaning back on cushions and drifting off into De Quinceyesque visions, but Bryn insisted that was wasteful and dissolved a little to inject with a hypodermic. There would be no flash, he reassured me: it was not like mainlining heroin.

We did drift off, but into a blankness in which we lost all sense of time. Every so often Bryn's voice percolated up from his mattress. Some inconsequential remark would hang in the air. We drifted on until another bubble rose and I heard myself speak in the voice of some distant relative, some laconic second cousin. Between remark and reply, half an hour might have passed.

Then I found myself reading a book. The title had intrigued me and I wanted to see how it began. The opening paragraph was masterly, so terse in its irony that I was conscripted from the very first sentence, charged with the book's angers and taking a fierce pleasure in its humour, which was a survivor's humour. The second paragraph was a descent into the underworld, taking me down in three long sentences, each so secure in its syntax, so inevitable in its descent that I felt no fear, no sense of the darkness deepening around me, only a strange exhilaration, as if I were in free fall. The third paragraph was different again, subtly constructed on such a frail ledge of perception that I turned the page, curious to see whether it would hold.

But it had dissolved to nothing. There had been no book there in the first place.

The word of mouth that had secured us the opium brought news of another possibility: tripping on belladonna. You boiled up ten asthma cigarettes and drank the water. Disgusting as that sounded, there was an allure in the drug's ancient lineage, in the dark eyes of all the beauties who had used it to enlarge their pupils, in the visions of the witches who had concocted it into their flying ointment. As our informant was careful to explain, 'There are three dangers: that you will go blind, or you will go mad, or you will die – but no one has yet.'

We drank the stuff down and waited. A small hole in the plaster on the wall began to move around. At last the doors of perception were creaking open. But all they let in was a draught, an existential draught. I felt colder than I had ever felt before, cold and isolated. 'Let's go to the cinema!' I said. It was the cinema as womb, the thought of sitting in the warm dark with pulses of colour sliding across our eyes, our own film playing over the film on the screen.

But it was a black-and-white film we blundered into as we made our way down to the street, the pavement coming at us at an Eisenstein tilt, wave upon wave of wintry slabs we had to step on, each step a separate determination, a push down on the thigh while our shoulders angled into the wind only we could feel. 'Can't go in, man,' muttered Bryn as we huddled in the foyer. 'Haven't got our passports. In this country you have to show your passport before they let you in to the film.'

We headed on into the arctic blast, only to be blown back on ourselves, blown so thin we seemed to be elongating with every stride like Korky the Kat. When I came to, I was on the side of a canal, just down from the little French restaurant where Hannah worked as a waitress. It was her afternoon off and she was looking at me with shining eyes. 'You were so funny,' she explained, 'you kept seeing flowers growing out of the pavement. "Look!" you kept saying, "They're so beautiful!" and you'd be pointing at a lamp post.' But I had no memory of that, no lingering sensations of warmth and colour – the earthly paradise it can be fatal to slip into if you are chilled to the bone. 'Phew!' said Bryn. 'Never been that far out before.'

*So funny*. The phrase that had been haunting me all summer. 'She keeps asking about you,' Hannah said.

And finally we did arrange to meet, one Saturday when Bryn was working a late shift and Hannah had suggested we went dancing: 'Otherwise I'll just have to sit around all night.' It was the club where the other dancers had given us the floor, where Anke had spun out across the room in her pierrot costume. Now she was waiting outside with Henk, the new boyfriend, the two of them standing quietly together in shirt and jeans.

As I walked up in the yellow suit, left arm folded to give the appearance of poise, I might have been back at Barcarès, keeping my pride intact under the eyes of the hotel balcony. Amsterdam had no equivalent of Carnaby Street and, for a moment at least, pride was assuaged. I saw Anke's eyes travel over the daffodil pinstripe, over the blue of the shirt I had chosen for the occasion, toning into the night sky as if I were an emissary of the possible and not just a daydream believer.

We moved into the club and stood a little awkwardly on the edge of the floor. Henk did not dance. The girls took a few, slow steps and I moved with them, careful never to step outside the courtly *pas de trois*.

The last fixes of opium I had taken in the veins of my feet, in case my arms were checked on my readmission to college. I need not have worried: there was no medical, just an outpatient's appointment at the Warneford. I put on the blue corduroy jacket, wound the charcoal-grey tie into a neat triangular knot, and appeared as the shadow of my former self. 'Excellent!' intoned the consultant. 'Come and see me again in three weeks.'

But it was hard to revert to being that shadow, to descend from the narrow room in the gate tower where I had been placed under the eye of Bert, the head scout, and squash on to one of the long benches in Hall as if I were a freshman all over again. Eager conversations were starting up all around me, the conversations I had had three years before. But there was no one I could tell about shrinking into the sand under the bamboo screen or spreadeagling myself on the roof of the van, no one whose laughter would kick-start as the stories unfolded and lift away the fear that had enshrouded them since. Redmond had been rusticated for a year and I knew that I was largely to blame.

'You used to talk to Dad about it while you were under narcosis.' My mother had let that slip. I had no memory of those conversations but I could imagine how they must have gone, my father leading me with a skill developed over years of cross-examination, the quiet voice creating the impression that I was talking to a friend while all the time he was preparing to abuse my trust, the lawyer's tactic of fingering someone other than his client driven by the father's need to believe that someone must have led his son astray. I came round from narcosis to find that my father had already given Red's name to the college. He would have been sent down if John Jones had not intervened, pointing out the effect that would have on my frail mental state. As it was, Redmond was rusticated for circulating the manuscript of his novel, which was deemed to be a bad influence.

I had to see the Warden and the Principal of Postmasters to request permission to attend the Poets' Workshop in London. At first the Warden seemed a little aggrieved. He talked wistfully of evidence they were unable to use and I pointed out that evidence gathered under narcosis was hardly reliable. We turned to my appearance at the Poets' Workshop and he exuded a fatherly warmth. This could only redound to the credit of the college. Then he asked rather cautiously whether I had found any dividend for my poetry in the smoking of hashish and any sense of this being a tribunal vanished. The old scholar and the young researcher leaned forward, two finely tuned brains, curious to hear of anything that might enhance their performance. I wondered what would have happened if I had been able to answer in the affirmative.

George MacBeth's reaction at the Poets' Workshop should have told me that I was getting something right: the free verse layout of 'For Lesley', which he defended in the face of Peter Porter's scepticism. My friends at the University Poetry Society had re-elected me as President, which was kind of them. Hugo Dyson was tutoring me in Shakespeare and I had done a solid piece of work for my Anglo-Saxon tutor, a don's wife who had clearly been a little nervous of me. But I could hardly bring myself to hunch down the two flights of stairs from my room. It all felt so thin, so grey, so joyless.

The image came to me of a knight kneeling in a chapel, keeping vigil. Silence mirrored him like clear water, a preparation that was almost an end in itself, and the night hours gleamed ahead of him like stepping stones. It was the vigil a knight had to keep before he was received into the order and I was still keeping it. I was still Anke's knight, pledged to her service.

More than a recognition, it felt like a purpose. I put the image into a short poem and sent it to Anke. And for the rest of the day it lost none of its clarity. Voices swirled from the arch as people returned from lectures, the usual hubbub broke over my head in Hall, but the silence stayed with me as a confirmation, a secret strength.

The next morning there was a letter from her in my pigeonhole: 'I would like to come to England but I don't have any money.' The timing was back. We were out of the courtly *pas de trois* and back into the dance.

I sent her £20, which was almost all the money I had – I had no grant for this term because of last year's confusion. And even as I walked back from the post office, the world began to brim with all the chances it had been withholding. I met Ron, who had a story straight out of the troubadours' chronicle, of a girl with Pre-Raphaelite hair, long twisting strands of a brown so light she might have been spun out of the air. He had first seen her in a dream, standing at the top of a flight of steps leading into the sanctuary of a temple. Then across the floor of a London pub, so clearly the girl from the dream that he hardly dared speak to her. He had just come off heroin and she wanted to come off. He had been with Sandy ever since she came out of rehab.

While we were talking, someone else wandered up, someone I had never met before. Fresh-faced, with long blond hair falling straight down over his shoulders, John Foster was the nearest thing the city had to a Dharma Bum. He rarely smoked and he had never used hard drugs. But by various stratagems, such as living so frugally that he could save on the dole and sign off as soon as they hassled him, he had kept an inner freedom that I found intoxicating. We sat and drank china tea in his room off St Clement's, almost unfurnished but for a couple of mattresses on the floor, a concrete poem by Dom Sylvester Houédard on the wall,

me no

you no

u

s

and the company of a white rat who had the freedom of the room.

We walked all across the city, just as I had when I first arrived. And ran across it at night, keeping a steady rhythm through the darkened avenues, a Native American trick, John said, to change the perception. And change it did, whether from the speed or the darkness or the diversion of blood from the brain. I was running with my head up and there was nothing below the level of the eyes. I might have been running in the second verse of Genesis across an earth that was without form and void. Ahead of me there was only the lit strip where paving stones turned under a street lamp and a pillar box stood in silhouette. So narrow, that lit strip, I felt I might slip back from it at any moment, back into a darkness where I was without form and void.

In the small hours John took me to meet John Bentine, nephew of the comedian Michael Bentine, and reputedly a brilliant mathematician who had dropped out of college. We climbed a narrow flight of stairs to a room over a shop and there, sitting over a paraffin stove, was someone I had seen wandering the streets in a long coat, peering through John Lennon glasses under an untidy mass of tight curls. His only furniture, other than the mattresses on the floor, was a small bookcase. Oxford was so awash with books, he explained, that he kept only the most essential: any new book had to displacc another.

We sat in the upglare from a street lamp, the window showing an empty bus stop on the pavement opposite and a glistening silence where the rush-hour traffic would stream down St Clement's to the city centre. These were John Bentine's chosen hours, the hours when he kept his own vigil, but to me, used to the backwater of Walton Lane, it felt as if we were sitting on a Tube station plat-form over the electrified rail. Perhaps I was unnerved by that, that and the bareness of the room and the realisation that I was back on the wrong side of the tracks. When a girl looked in from a neighbouring room, I simply registered a pallid, nocturnal face over a long peasant dress and flaked out on one of the mattresses.

I came round to hear myself talking, talking out of the conflict that must have arisen in me the moment I felt myself coming alive again, but alive in the wrong company. I was describing the way surfaces closed on the dead days and the city streets became obdur-ate, even the Cotswold stone turning a cold shoulder. And how the light glancing off them was the first sign that you were back up to speed, moving easily through the white water of perceptions as faces flowed past you on the street and the hemisphere moved through its hours towards the sun. I opened my eyes to find two faces looking down at me, John Bentine's and the girl's. The face I had seen as pallid was quick with amusement and interest, as if I were waking into the play of light I had just described.

With a discreet turn of his bunch of keys, Peter, the night porter, opened the great door to Hall and led me up the staircase to the Senior Common Room. It was two o'clock in the morning and I was sending

Anke a telegram at the college's expense: *Hey! We're on cigars!* I wanted her to bring some for Christoff, a German philosophy student, whose box of Coronas I had been rapidly depleting.

Christoff was worried about me. He had watched my elation unfurl and take wing. But I felt only relief. To me they were a homecoming, these stratospheric flights of what could only be pure energy, because I was not taking any drugs. Ron and I would sit in my upended armchairs, the arms enclosing us like the uprights of a stone circle, and feel ourselves on the brink of some wordless illumination. Or I would set off on an impulse, like the night I set off to read the 'Ode to Psyche' to John Foster and ended up reading it to a policeman who had stopped me in St Clement's.

No one was going to bring me down this time, not even the consultant. When the day came for my next appointment, I put on the yellow suit and tied the flowery tie in an immaculate Windsor. I was going to present him with the whole drama, Easter's shock and my recovery over the summer, everything we had never talked about. But I needed someone with me, someone whose presence would keep me calm. I thought of Sandy, of that face Millais might have painted, and asked Ron if she could go with me.

I introduced her as Columbine but the consultant did not rise to it. He was in factual mode. 'What is your Christian name?' he asked her, peñ poised over his pad. 'Colo,' she replied coolly. The pen began to race when I described the summer in Amsterdam. There were murmurs of increasing my medication, of readmitting me, both of which I refused. Then I launched my counter-attack. I reminded him how he used to bliss out during our consultations, how the room had to wait in silence, the charge nurse and the staff nurse studying their ties while he stared into his own nirvana. Rumour had it he had become hooked on one of the drugs he prescribed. I had even sent him a squib in the hospital's internal mail:

327

Lost Youth
I am high on adrenalin
Whilst you prefer amphetamine.

'It wasn't amphetamine,' he said quietly.

'But something was wrong.'

He bowed his head and said nothing. Ron had heard from the Drug Squad that he had taken time off to kick the habit and that certainly looked to be the case. He had lost the embonpoint he had gleamed in last winter.

I had struck at the father figure. And in the moment when he bowed his head, in the honesty of that silence, I felt compassion. Even a degree of affinity. But we ended on an impasse. As Sandy and I walked out of the room, his voice reached for its old resonance and shook in our ears.

'I have to look after my brother.' Rob moved over to the corner where Pete was muttering and pulling on his half-bottle. It was before midnight and no one had challenged him when he slipped in through the college gate.

Pete was a bluesman, a saturnine figure with a dark voice and a rare sense of cadence in his fingers, the notes falling with such elegance that they lifted away the pain in the voice. I had seized on the idea of creating a show with him, of dancing onstage while he was playing, rather overlooking the fact that his guitar picking would have shrugged off any such distraction. But he liked my enthusiasm and I had provided him with another port of call. One afternoon when I was out, he had simply installed himself in the room of the freshman below and made a pot of tea. 'Do come in!' he called out as I came up the stairs, reclining on his elbow and pulling on his pipe in a perfect imitation of an Oxford don.

None of that aplomb now. Only bitterness and anger. The uncle he had been lodging with was going to throw him out unless he stopped playing the blues and got a job. The very thought of that sent a shock through the room, through me and through Rob and through Paul, who was their kid sister's boyfriend and counted as family. To us Pete's playing was something holy. Unaccountable, perhaps, in that his most delicate touches came when he was playing for two people in the middle of the night. Unmanageable, even, in that he turned down as many gigs as he took on. But a flower from the true, dark root.

Paul slipped away to catch the last bus and I put *Kind of Blue* on at low volume. Through the infinities of its rise and fall I could hear Pete's vehemence, the impetus behind his phrases as he spat them out, and the allaying warmth in his younger brother's voice, his adroit turns and forays into humour, the moments of recognition when the two voices meshed and I envied them the undertones they shared, the enfoldings of the dialect, the brotherhood they had found their way back to by the early hours when we all crashed out on the floor. And then a different set of sounds took over, the shouting of a name and number and the slamming of a fist into the face, so abrupt that the face had hardly finished shouting before the fist slammed into it. Rob had just come out of an army prison. He had been a sniper in Malaya and only hit trouble when the Emergency ended, when he was brought down from the treetops and confined to camp.

We climbed out of college early in the morning, a simple step over the railing where it met the tower. Rob was going to walk with Pete out to Wolvercote and pacify the unruly uncle. I walked with them up the Cornmarket, still bending Pete's ear with my plans for the blues show. I was going to dance in my Myrmidon jacket over the yellow trousers, the Myrmidons being the college dining club and the jacket an imperious purple with wide silvery lapels of watered silk.

And dance in it I did, back down the almost empty Cornmarket. I was just taking off, just turning into a spin opposite Woolworths, when along came a bus, an ordinary, everyday bus. I led it up to Carfax as if this were May Morning, pirouetting in front of the cab while the driver sat stony-faced at the wheel.

*If I'm not careful*, I thought, *I'm going to dance myself into the Warneford*, and went round to see John Jones, ringing his doorbell as he was having breakfast.

'I think the same thing is happening as happened last year. But last year it was all crushed out of me before I could make any sense of it. This time I think I just have to follow it and see where it leads.'

Later that morning John Jones appeared at my door. 'Quick, Roger, pack up your things! Your mother's coming to fetch you. You have to be out of Oxford within two hours – it's that or go into the Warneford on a section for a year, and we don't want that, do we?'

This is what happens when you strike at a father figure. He rears up and reasserts his dominance.

John Jones must have won me those two hours' grace. 'See you in San Francisco!' I said to him as I stepped into my mother's little blue van. But loss tore at me as we drove down Merton Street and four years of my life, let alone the chance of a degree, were stripped away without warning.

At that moment I needed another mother, Frances's mother perhaps, not the pale, tight-lipped figure beside me, anxious as she always became in the presence of authority. And I certainly needed another father, not the half-grown man I would be facing at home, someone, it seemed to me, who barely knew himself.

'Your father's really dishy!' The first girl I brought home from church said that. Was it some balance in the face, the breadth of the cheekbones in proportion to the full lips? Or some emanation from a body I would have said was rather thickset, the animal presence I had to find my way past?

Whatever it was, in his mid-forties my father had come into his own, in a way that was hard on my mother, who was four years older and naturally shy. We had already shared the favours of one stable girl. 'Isn't it funny?' she said to me. 'I either like older men or . . . people my own age,' she corrected herself hastily, but she had meant to say 'boys'. My father had even laid a preliminary hand on Anke's knee when he was driving her to visit me in the Warneford.

I did not mind about the stable girl. I just considered myself lucky to have won my share. I did not even mind the hand on Anke's knee, not in itself. After all, he was left looking foolish. 'I just froze.' What I did mind was the cackhandedness of it all, the moral clumsiness. He was a successful barrister who was always away in London. Why didn't he find himself a mistress? Why didn't he show a little *savoir faire*?

Raw with shock and anger, I spoke of my father in terms I should never have used, not in my mother's hearing. She was barely able to complete the journey home. Once there, I took some money from his desk and prepared to leave. There was a core of common sense to this. We might well have come to blows if I had still been there when he came home. But my preparations were hardly sensible: instead of packing a bag, I armoured myself in peculiar ways, strapping a dog collar round the arm of my coat so that the dark-blue cloth glinted with metal studs, and throwing a sheepskin numnah, meant to go under the front of a saddle, over my shoulders, pulling it down tight so that I had a hump like a bison. Over that I put my Clyde hat – the film of *Bonny and Clyde* had just come out – and the inevitable pair of shades.

The buffet on Waterloo Station fell silent as I walked up to the chocolate machine. *Give the public what they want!* I turned as I went out of the door, gave a wild grin and flung my fingers out like a cat showing its claws. The room roared its appreciation, everyone convinced they had seen someone different.

'Hello, pelt!' said a man outside a pub in Earls Court.

'And what are you, then?' asked an older man sitting at the bar. 'Are you a rocker or what?'

'No,' I said, 'I'm something much more dangerous. I'm the hippie with a razor blade,' taking the little rectangular blade from a safety razor out of my pocket and executing a swift hand jive half an inch from his face.

He sprang off his stool, legs braced as he issued his challenge.

'Why don't you sit down and have a drink? Then we'll see if you're still quite so quick.'

'No,' I said, 'my friend'll be waiting for me.'

I was pretty sure John would be back from the bank by now and that's where I was planning to stay, in the flat he shared with two other college friends, just as I had when I read at the Poets' Workshop.

The creature who started to haunt the Poetry Society was very different from the quiet, controlled figure who had given that reading.

'Meet Red Fox somewhere groovy later!' I said to Fleur Adcock, laying a bright new penny on the table next to her glass.

'Can't do that!' she said and turned the penny over.

However hard I danced in the empty flat while my friends were at work, taking off on Lester Young's 'Indiana' with Nat King Cole on piano and trying to lay a pattern over it, a coherent pattern I could repeat, the energy still soared out of me at night as I lay on the narrow bed in the spare room.

'I was out over the North Sea last night,' I said to Fleur.

'But for how long?'

When Frances Horovitz and George Wightman came to perform *The Flower-Fed Buffaloes*, a programme of American poetry presented by an American poet resident in London, I entered in full armour and stood in the darkness at the back of the room, still wearing my shades under the Clyde hat. The shades were the first to come off as I focused on Frances Horovitz, whom I had only seen before in a shot from a modelling assignment pinned to the door of the Horovitzes' Notting Hill flat. The night that Anke and I stayed there, Frances had to leave early and it was Michael who gave us their last egg for breakfast. The long eyes had a Byzantine beauty that came as much from their inner concentration as from their outer line. She stood tall, her head slightly back, so taken up in the being of the poem that I doubt if she noticed the Clyde hat start to move to its rhythms. I kept up a slow dance for the rest of the performance, shedding first the hat and then the sheepskin and finally the jacket as I concentrated the energies coming from the stage and conducted them back to the three readers in what I was sure was an essential part of the dynamic, the visualisation of their pauses and their pacing.

At the end of the show I went up to Frances, who was talking to George Wightman. She was saying how difficult the performance had been towards the end, how she had felt herself coming under an intense heat, and I took the chance to explain:

'I was giving out a lot of heat.'

'It was the lights,' she said, glancing across at George and keeping her eyes down. 'I think it was the lights.'

Frances moved away and I stayed talking to George, whom I knew from the Poets' Workshop. I was rhapsodising about Anke when he asked what her mother's name was.

'Ah yes,' he said, 'I knew Clara in Paris.'

Something about the way he said it made me see Anke's mother in a different light. Not the woman we had seen in the grounds of the mental hospital, humbled and grateful for the visit, the woman who had dropped back as Anke and I walked on down the path with our heads together, whispering to Anke's little sister, 'Nothing must disturb this love,' but a woman in her own right, a figure on the artistic scene in Paris, someone a visiting English poet would remember. And suddenly I saw Anke's father in a different light too: that 'Belgian jazz guitarist' was not playing in an obscure basement club in Brussels, he was playing in Paris. And then I remembered Anke's real name, Marie Bernadette, and linked it to Les Saintes Maries de la Mer, the great gypsy festival in the Camargue. Anke's father must be Django Reinhardt, who was born in Belgium but rose to fame in Paris.

Finally, and most mysteriously, I thought of Anke tuning the guitar she could no longer play, of the accident that had left her with a child's hand that would not stretch across the strings. She was left-handed and it was the left hand Django had damaged when his caravan caught fire. Just as Thelonious Monk had to learn to play again, to stab with fingers the New York police had broken, one by one, when he would not give them his drug contacts, Django had to find another way to hold down chords, jumping two semi-paralysed fingers across the frets.

I was glad that I had only realised this now, that I had fallen in love with Anke before I knew who she was. But even that I managed to recast as myth: surely this was the moment of recognition, the equivalent of Arthur drawing the sword out of the stone? I had spoken her true name and all I had to wait for now was the transformation scene, the final scene of a romance, when everything comes out right.

But waiting is the hardest test of all, the most subtle and the most searching. By the early hours the tedium of another sleepless night on the narrow bed was unendurable. I crept down the stairs, slipped out of the big front door and started to walk the streets of

Earls Court. They offered nothing, not at that time of the morning. Only the sodium glare beyond the roofline, the gravitational pull of the A40. I was afraid that dawn would find me out beyond Hanger Lane, striding back to Oxford in seven-league boots. And then, just as it had in Amsterdam when I set out to follow the tramlines back to the city centre, the energy flashed up another face. It was the face I had been dancing to at the Poetry Society, the face of Frances Horovitz. I stopped a passing taxi and gave him the address of the flat in Notting Hill.

I had erased our actual conversation after the show, the way she kept her eyes down and repeated, 'It was the lights. I think it was the lights.' I was still focused on her as I had been in that slow dance, so sure of my role as the transformer at the back of the room that I never doubted she would leave with me in a taxi in the middle of the night.

The taxi driver pulled up outside the terrace of tall houses and I asked him to wait while I sprinted up the steps. I was a little surprised not to see the name *Horovitz* beside one of the bells but I pressed a bell anyway and the front door opened. I bounded up the stairs and was surprised again not to see *Horovitz* on the first landing. On up the last steep, curling flight to the top flat where a well-built man in his early thirties was standing in the open door and a dark-haired woman looking over his shoulder.

I explained that I was looking for Frances Horovitz and the powerful body relaxed under the white T-shirt that gave him the look of a sailor, a sailor on shore leave in Portobello. He assured me there was no one of that name there, not at 23. *I must have given the taxi driver the wrong number*. But like the nuclear bomber the mad Texan was piloting in *Dr Strangelove*, my co-ordinates were set: there was no recalling me now.

'Oh well,' I said, 'she'll do' and went to step past him towards the dark-haired woman.

He caught me and threw me down the stairs. And as I was picking myself up, he caught me with a kick, a perfectly aimed kick, right on the point of the jaw.

'Love you, babe!' I grinned and ran down the stairs.

A hypomaniac is hard to knock out. And even more difficult to deflect. At five in the morning I was ringing for readmission on my friends' doorbell. And at eight I was on the phone to Frances Horovitz.

'I made it last night!' I declared, still in the grip of my delusion.

'Would you like to speak to Michael?' she replied and passed him the phone.

'You were at *The Flower-Fed Buffaloes*?'

I told him of my conversation with George Wightman, of my realisation of who Anke must be.

'Django's chick? I recognised her as soon as you brought her into the room. Rises in Greece in the spring . . .'

We seemed to be rhapsodising happily . . . I might have got away with it.

'Listen! I let you twirl your girl in my flat. Now leave my wife alone!'

*Rises in Greece in the spring* . . . For a moment I wondered if Michael knew more than I did, if there was some deeper level on which the myth was still being re-enacted and the girl I had led along Walton Lane was Persephone in a wine-dark shirt and grey jeans.

If there was, I felt no sense of awe, no sense of privilege. I found the thought painful because it would mean that I had only been touched in passing. I wanted Anke in her mortality, wanted the girl who was camping in her mother's flat and preparing her submission for art school, the girl who had torn into me one last time because her need was as complete as mine.

And with that I shrank back to the boy that I was, huddled into myself from lack of sleep. The night taxi had left me almost penniless and I knew that I could not impose on my friends any longer. I phoned home and my sister's husband came to fetch me in the van, the same little blue van in which I had railed at my mother all the way from Oxford, throwing myself back in the passenger seat and kicking against the dashboard.

This time I sat quiet and let my brother-in-law be an older brother. 'Will Anke be there?' I asked him as we nudged through the traffic. 'Yes, she'll be there.' 'And will Ron and Sandy be there?' 'Yes, they'll all be there.'

He needed to get me home. And I believed what I needed to believe, that there would be a gathering where all wounds would be healed and all losses restored, as at the end of the world.

One of the older girls crossed the yard in breeches and boots, ready to take the next lesson. I had stepped out of the van into a world that had no time for my gathering, into a continuance that, had I remembered what François told me, I might have found healing in itself.

But it would take me half a lifetime to understand what he said, to realise that restoration is only to be found in the world's indifference. In the absence of a gathering I simply rewound the myth, wound it back to the moment of recognition: if Anke really was Django's chick, what did that make me? If she rose in Greece in the spring, a reincarnation of the life spirit, who would I have to be? The body sent up another pulse of warmth, its compensation for fatigue, and I was suffused with what I can only describe as a bleary terror: at the very least, I had to be a reincarnation of William Blake and Charlie Parker. This unlikely combination impelled me into my father's study to phone the news through to Michael Horovitz.

As I crossed the room, something shuffled under the antique

dining table on which all my father's papers were set out, the briefs in their red tape and the opinion he was drafting in blue-black ink. It was my father hauling himself up on to his knees. My mother must have taxed him with everything I had flung out in my bitterness and I doubt if he had slept any more than I had. Reduced to his instinctual core, the part of him that went back to his boyhood on Trenowath's farm and the part I felt closest to, he had curled up under the table like a sick animal.

Perhaps that sobered me a little because I did not tell Michael Horovitz that he was speaking to a reincarnation, not straight out. I simply told him that I had made a great breakthrough in modern poetry, equivalent to the breakthrough Charlie Parker had made when he was playing over 'Cherokee' and found that he could use the higher intervals of a chord. 'Well,' said Michael wisely, 'write it all down.'

There was nothing to write down but I was still elevated when our GP arrived with Dr Bearcroft, the consultant from Long Grove, one of the hospitals the Victorians had ranged across the slopes of Epsom Downs like so many psychiatric sanatoriums. 'None shall pass these sacred lips!' I declared when he asked if I had been taking any drugs, holding my arms out as if I were about to deliver another chapter from Blake's *The Book of Los*. I twisted through a whole series of poses, each more hieratic than the last, as he explained that he would have to section me for a month, something that even I could see was inevitable. All I wanted was an assurance that I would not be forcibly sedated: 'No needle must pierce this holy skin!'

That night the holy skin was pierced, though Dr Bearcroft was not to blame. I was duly admitted, giving my occupation as Aerial Transmitter, and shut into a side room. I was lying back on the high bed, just setting out on what I was sure were my astral travels, when the door was wrenched open, so abruptly there was barely time for the spirit, as advised in all the manuals, to slip back into

338

the body. I protested to the young doctor who had come to examine me but he was in no mood to wait on astral travellers. He proceeded to test my reflexes, tapping the sole of my foot with his rubber hammer, and got such a reaction he thought I had kicked out. Two male nurses held me down, he slammed a hypodermic into my buttock and had me thrown into the pads.

The options are rather limited in a padded cell. You can yell at the door until it dawns on you that the padding has insulated you for sound as well. You can hurl your rubber potty until it whirls off the walls and you begin to perceive yourself as a rather large infant. Or you can complete the regression and go into the foetal position, curled up under the thin sheet which is the only bedding provided.

I yelled. I hurled my potty. And finally I curled up and waited for the dawn.

'He didn't need to do that,' the charge nurse said when he released me in the morning. But it did have the effect of making me very careful how I behaved.

I was interviewed by the registrar who took down my full history, including all the details of the summer's experiments in Amsterdam. And then came a consultation with Dr Bearcroft. The registrar wanted to enter me in the records as a drug addict, a drug addict in a state of toxic confusion, but Dr Bearcroft did not agree: 'I don't think he is a drug addict, you see.' 'Well, what do you think he is, then?' Dr Bearcroft paused for a moment before he gave his diagnosis: 'I think he's a poet who's in love.'

But that has its dangers too. That evening, when a crowd formed at one end of the locked ward and the old hands directed me to the serving of cocoa, I palled up with the other new arrival, who was a couple of years older than me and very carefully dressed, right down to his suede shoes. Almost tremulous in his sensitivity and fluent in his hesitations, selecting just the right word with just the right tone, he might have been translated straight from an Oxford common room: but he was on his way to Broadmoor for attempted murder. He had phoned his girlfriend after she had broken off their relationship and asked her to meet him in the park, warning her that he would have a revolver in his pocket. She had phoned the police, who arrested him at the rendezvous. 'Would you have used the revolver?' I asked him. 'I honestly don't know,' he replied. 'But what I have to acknowledge is that I did have it in my pocket.'

He was driven away the next morning and I was left to reflect on how close the Furies can tread on anyone's heels. Keep yourself in check, I told myself, and do your time. There was a pressure just in the hours to be passed, all of us packed into one large room with the television blaring from mid-afternoon. But the atmosphere changed when the shifts changed and the Persian nurses came on. 'You would be well advised', Ron had told me, 'to buy a cigarette from old Joe, who sits by the radiator.'

'How much for a cigarette, Joe?' 'Threepence,' he said, with a slow smile, easing himself in his chair and unrolling the tobacco pouch in his lap. He was West Indian and sat at his own angle to the rest of the room.

The moment I moved away, I felt the eyes upon me. Two pairs of eyes, from different sides of the room. Eyes from thin faces a little older than me. Thin faces under short haircuts. Thin faces looking out of brown tweed jackets that must have been standard issue. I drew deeply on the little joint, if it really was a joint. Drew on it again and strolled across the room, putting it down on an ashtray on one of the little round tables. The first man darted across, drew on it a couple of times and left it for the second man, who glanced back as he left it for me.

How much was suggestion and how much was substance I don't

know, but it was just as if some great partition had been rolled back and I had space enough to sit back and watch the room from a comfortable distance, the shapes on the television dissolving and re-forming as if they were a light show at UFO. It must have been hard on my partners in that surreptitious dance when I was moved on to an open ward and could spend my days in the Art Therapy room.

Not that I produced anything. I was all talk and no paint. But there were interesting people to talk to, like Bernard, a one-armed ex-naval frogman who had once shared a chicken coop with Brendan Behan. The farmer rousted them out after three weeks, so covered in feathers and chicken shit that he had to sluice them down with a hose. 'Never mind,' said Brendan, 'I've got something hidden away that might change things.' It was *Borstal Boy*, written on sheets of toilet paper.

Or like Konstantin, who had studied at the Slade and brought intense concentration to the most delicate of pencil sketches. 'When your honour and your talent are in equal proportion,' he said, 'then your face appears on the banknotes.' Or like John Anderson, who said, 'I didn't know where I was when I woke up this morning. And then I thought, "Oh, it's all right, I'm in a mental hospital."'

There was something beguiling about John Anderson, the way he would quietly subtract himself from a situation that did not suit him and reappear somewhere else, his shadowy independence preserved. He had dropped out of art school and found a room in a converted piggery where the landlord, who was Indian, would only rent to people whose aura was clear and untroubled. But then, brought up by his mother, a devout Catholic who had had a passionate encounter with an eighty-two-year-old Breton missionary priest, he had learned to keep his sense of self from an early age.

In him I felt I had found a companion, someone who was passing through the same marginal lands and knew them better than I did.

341

He even knew of another poet, an ex-junkie, who lived just down the road from the hospital. 'He's off it now. They both are. Mary came off because she was having a baby and Nigel came off to keep her company. I go down there sometimes after Art Therapy. See if you can get permission to leave the grounds for a couple of hours.'

With John as my surety, I slipped in through the side door of what might have been a safe house in a spy film, so indistinguishable was it from any other on that suburban street. Once up a steep flight of stairs, we stepped into an apartment from another era, Mata Hari's perhaps, the windows shrouded in muslin and draped with silk shawls. John and I sat carefully in our donkey jackets, leaning back on elegant brocaded chairs like ambassadors of our own uncertainty while Mary rolled a joint in her lap, the long dark hair falling in two straight lines either side of a head so round I thought of the original Iberian inhabitants of these islands before the long-headed Celts came. And it turned out that Mary's mother was Welsh, a nurse who had come to London and become a friend of Noël Coward, which accounted for the Art Deco jewellery box Mary kept her Rizlas in and the Art Nouveau statuette a cat was winding itself around as it rubbed its neck against it. We talked against a ceaseless insinuation of cats, so many that there always seemed to be one making arabesques around the finds from junk shops and jumble sales as it slipped into another's place. Reuben, the baby who had proved to be Mary's redemption, was asleep under a cat net in the other room.

One of Mary's friends from art school had just taken over as lead guitarist of The Yardbirds and I told her of my surprise and delight when the name I had last seen slotted into the black of a signboard outside a small upstairs club in Kingston had suddenly come over the French radio when I was sitting on the beach at Barcarès. It was strange to sit there feeling so poised and so provisional, to dissolve back into our own pretensions as gates clicked in the street below and the first of the commuters came home from work, and yet to know, as we passed the joint to each other and were gently lifted up out of the street plan, that possibility might lie anywhere along the route of the 406 bus.

I did not meet Nigel on that first visit. He worked in a Ministry of Agriculture laboratory, looking after the rats on which they tested rat poison, and every so often he and his workmates had to put on waders and gauntlets and go off to a rubbish dump to catch rats from the wild to be tested for immunity. But I did express an interest in seeing his poetry and next time we called Mary had some typescripts waiting for me. I was expecting something free-form, something influenced by *The New American Poetry*, Donald Allen's anthology of the Beats and the Black Mountain poets, which I had taken into the Warneford with me, but what I found was so tightly braided in its sound patterns that it was like coming on the work of an Anglo-Saxon or an Old Welsh poet who had somehow been reborn into the outer suburbs with their paddocks and their patches of waste ground:

> Goes the berry eater
> In flurrying weather
> Starveling boned
> Through ailing grass . . .

There was more than a hint of Dylan Thomas in his creation of 'Quince' but even there the exuberance of the verses was reined in by the taut word-music of the refrains:

> And first is Quince the wonder working one
> The prayer mad in a thimble at his task
> A silly saviour blind-as-buttons man
> Blind Quince within his house

He is soft for hard
He is soothe for sore
He is foot-patter
He is hoof-print
He is a spoor

Old craftsman at his miracles
Fox-craft, Finch-love and War
Earth parent and oddjobbing god
Blind Quince's trade is love
He has earth for smell
He has fern for green
He has hedge-wonder
He has ditch-murmur
He has his ground . . .

The irony of this was not lost on me. Here was I who had found Anglo-Saxon poetry something of a chore, despite having an Anglo-Saxon tutor at Oxford and surroundings of the utmost privilege in which to study it, and here was Nigel Wells, who had left school at sixteen and stumbled on the Penguin Classic of *The Earliest English Poems* as he was coming off junk, writing as if he had the tradition at his fingertips.

This must have been an ordinary working day at the lab because John Anderson and I were still talking to Mary when there came the sound of a motorbike and sidecar pulling into the drive and an outhouse door opening somewhere below. 'That's Nigel back now.' He came up the stairs in a stiff leather greatcoat, a proper motor-cyclist's coat that strapped round the knees, another jumble sale find. He hauled that off and I saw a tall, thin young man in a hand-knitted striped sweater, ready for his mug of tea and looking a little wary of John and me as we sat there with the hair falling over our faces and workmen's scarves doubled over our open-necked shirts, two anarchists from 1905 who had yet to do a day's work in their lives.

Gradually his wariness yielded to my obvious enthusiasm and we did talk a little as Mary rolled another joint, which she did not pass to Nigel. He had had a very bad trip and that came back if ever he smoked. I could glimpse survival strategies in the poems –

> I'd join the little things
> Dumb as doubt
> And perfect in the earth,

– bleached landscapes from which imagination offered the only escape, though it had to duck down to do so:

> Making myself very small
> I slip beneath the eyelid of the horse.

Nigel's feeling for horses was another of the ironies. There were four rows of loose boxes back at the farm and in one of them was Brummel, a finely paced part-bred Arab I had been able to ride whenever I wanted. All Nigel had access to was the paddock he glimpsed on his way to work, somewhere he liked to wheel Reuben down to in his pram. But from that he had made the best of the poems I saw, a poem so individual that it could easily carry the one present participle it had lifted from Dylan Thomas, which was in any case a theft so inspired as to be more tribute than theft:

### Easter with horses

> Horse weather hangs
> Streamed and lank

Heavying the flanks
Jesuing the earth

Horse is still
Only the lips move
Blue soft wrinkling
Spluttery with prayer

Horse weather teems
Slaves the air to drips
And Christ is small and dappled
Foaled in rain

It is little enough
This place where God
Groans to the last
And the horses sniff

It is drab here
The wind
Dizzies the world
And I am thin I tell you, thin.

'Yes, I was afraid that you were moving too fast. Or not fast enough, so that they would catch you.'

Anke had heard nothing from me in over a month. Nothing since that telegram I had sent in the middle of the night.

And to come straight in like that, right on the beat . . . in a quick turn of phrase that showed me just what I was losing.

I had sent her a jubilant letter on my discharge from Long Grove, giving her Dr Bearcroft's diagnosis and saying how lucky I had been to come under his care, which largely consisted of leaving me to find my own feet. And for a while I did hold on to the final sentence of her letter: 'The money you sent is still burning a hole in my purse.' But when I received a little note of warning from Hannah, 'You know, she never will come to England,' it confirmed what I already suspected: I was never going to come out from behind the mirror, not now that I appeared to be on the same trajectory as her mother. I had flipped once too often.

I had also written to the Warden, thanking the college for their understanding and explaining that I could no longer be 'a single-fold student'. Which raised the question of what else I was going to do. My father had prevailed on one of his friends to offer me a job in the antiques business, which would have meant staying in London. And I had met a girl in Long Grove, a girl I called Princess as Willie Garvin did Modesty Blaise, for whom I might well have stayed. But I was still in thrall to those night runs with John Foster. I went back to Oxford to become a Dharma Bum.


There was the face across the room, the face of Pete's kid sister, Jo, who had exactly the downward look Rossetti had caught in his paintings of Janey Morris. And there was the face I was trying to recreate in a poem, the face of Princess, newly installed in her bedsitter off the Kingston bypass. The same straight nose, the same sharp edge to the line of the lips, a face you would have gone into battle for, though Jo had her brothers' raven hair – gypsy blood, I sometimes thought, looking at Rob's head of tight black curls, or was it simply Oxfordshire, the bloodline that had thrown up Janey Morris? – and Princess was blond.

I stole only the occasional look at Jo because she was Paul's girl-friend and it was Paul who had offered me a room, the back room of his basement flat on Walton Street, when John Foster's house proved to be full. This was the poor end of the street, just past the bookie's – the bookie was our landlord – and just before the turning down to the ironworks.

I was focusing on Princess's eyebrows. They were very wide and had a slight natural arch, which could make her look haughty, though more often she was quizzical – quizzical because she had grown up in care and was slow to trust anyone. What could I make of them, those two subtle curves either side of the straight nose that went through me like a blade? The hilt of a sword? Close enough, drawn on my writing pad. Close enough to keep me pitched back on the cushions, staring down at the pad in my lap as the shifts changed on the record player and Joe Tex took over from Percy Sledge. Paul was a soul fan.

I took the sword hilt into the spread wings of a bird of prey and then into a falcon's eyes, I intensified her in her absence – or in my absence – until she rose up like a warrior princess out of some lost sequence from *Alexander Nevsky* but, whatever I did, the words on the pad looked forced, so many diagrams for a poem. And the next weekend when I hitchhiked down to see her, I realised that she was not simply going to be waiting in her high tower. She had got her dates mixed up and she was going out with someone else. I went back into the badlands, wrapped in hurt pride as if it were Clint Eastwood's poncho.

Paul and I had become friends during my euphoric last days in college. He had been with me the evening I found a girl on a trip sitting on the benches and took her under my wing. I led her down to college and then along the corridor to the chaplain's room so that she could trip in the sylvan calm of the deep green wallpaper – rather to the surprise of the chaplain who came back from Hall to find a girl with kaleidoscope eyes sitting on his sofa, and Paul and me keeping watch from the armchairs.

Paul had seen me through my ups and now he was seeing me through my downs. After he had walked Jo to the bus station – she was still at school and only allowed to stay over on a Saturday – we would split an amp of methedrine between us, sliding the needle just under the skin in a procedure known as skinpopping, and sit up all night playing Grand Prix, a board game based on motor racing. At five we would huddle into our coats and go to the back door of the bakery, where we could buy lardie cakes just out of the oven, the hot sultanas squidging under our teeth and the rich grease giving some substance back to bodies that had become entirely theoretical.

Nothing of interest came of the methedrine, any more than it had of the belladonna, and sometimes it seemed to me that the drugs were almost irrelevant and what mattered was the expeditionary instinct that had Bryn and me angling our shoulders into the existential wind or Paul and me reconstituting ourselves around the thin spills of Old Holborn we smoked in liquorice papers, the sweetness offsetting the dark tobacco and the two together anchoring us after the night of non-being.

I tried to be away at weekends so that I was not playing gooseberry to Paul and Jo. If I hitched home, I could borrow my mother's van and go over to see Nigel and Mary. Then I could go on to see John Anderson, taking the small road over the back of the downs that led to his converted piggery.

One afternoon I glimpsed someone I thought I recognised, trailing back along the same small road, a girl whose short black hair curled back from the face, which set her apart from all the girls dwelling mysteriously behind their curtains of long straight hair. I was sure she had been in the room the day I drove John up to Oxford to meet John Foster but he made no mention of her and I thought no more about it.

The next time I descended on the piggery, a couple of weeks later, she was sitting on John's floor, her legs tucked up under a long black dress, and he was all of a quaver inside his donkey jacket, as if he were about to leave this body and assume his spiritual form. She had just told him she was having his baby.

As John sat there, pushing the hair back from his face and staring down at the concrete floor – that's all the piggery was, a raft of concrete on a bare hillside – I could see that this was a possibility that had never occurred to him. I had come of age at a time when there were certain preliminaries to be observed, certain questions to be asked that would determine whether to proceed and what precautions to take. John, for all his shadowy self-possession, his familiarity with the margins, was two or three years younger than me. When Sylvia went for that sensitive look of his and selected him as the father of her foetus, he would have assumed that she was on the pill.

'I need to get my head around this,' he said. 'There's a monastery in Scotland I can always stay at. One of the monks has taken on the role of my father confessor, which I'm a bit wary of. But I might go up there for a bit.'

Sylvia wanted to look for a place in Oxford. That *was* where I had seen her before. I knew there were no rooms going in John Foster's house but there was one in mine, the front room on the ground floor. It was a little dark, a little chill, as front rooms tended to be. It even had the piano still in there. But it was a room and that's all she needed to sign on, a room and a rent book.

'Look after her for me, won't you, Roger!'


It was almost Arthurian, this chaste intimacy, sleeping naked next to the naked woman who had been left in my charge.

Sylvia had yet to spend a night in the front room. She had taken one look at the bed, an old-fashioned single bed with a ticking mattress and a solid wood frame, and declared, 'I'm not sleeping on that!' The bookie's runner who collected the rent had promised to find her something on which fewer people might have passed away. In the meantime she was sharing my double bed.

'Seems silly to keep my pants on!' She had been modelling in art schools since she was fifteen and her thighs were sheer and faintly luminous, her breasts so at ease in their symmetry that I had to settle myself carefully, just a hand's stretch away.

In the morning there was no ceremony with the hand mirror, no ritual application of mascara. She simply took a brush through the hair that sprang back in loose waves from the puckish face, the light making mischief with the dark eyes that protruded slightly and bringing out the aubergine in the full lips. 'A touch of the tar brush!' she said, though eventually she would discover that it was Italian ancestry.

I squired her on her rounds and discovered a backstairs Oxford I had never known existed. We sat in the basement of Folly House, where Peter had once had his digs, and talked to Charlie, who was living there as caretaker while she brought up her baby. We called on Catherine, who had read English a couple of years ahead of me and was bringing up John Bentine's daughter in a flat on the Iffley Road, rather more comfortably furnished than John's eyrie in the upglare of the street lamp. I could see the life that Sylvia was imagining for herself. But so far she had only the front room, where she had yet to put up so much as a poster on the wall or light a fire in the grate.

One night when Benny, a friend of Redmond's who had dropped out of the LSE, was dossing down on our floor and we were all stoned, I settled into my usual self-contained huddle in the bed, all too aware of the body next to me, of that white skin in the dark . . . there, where it curved over the hip, taut as a meniscus . . . John was far away in his monastery, far, far away . . . And I was all appetite, just as I had been that night in Amsterdam when I lifted the big bowl of blackberries in double cream out of the fridge . . . I stretched out my hand, Sylvia turned and we had a quick bundle under the blankets, rather to the surprise of Benny, I imagine, rolled into his sleeping bag just a few feet away.

351

And greatly to the surprise of Sylvia herself, as she admitted when I apologised in the morning: 'But don't let's get hung up over it. I'm just as randy as you are.'

Was it all down to 'Sand and Foam', Donovan's evocation of an evening on the beach in Mexico? We had been tripping to *Sunshine Superman* and I had surfaced with the smell of salt in my nostrils, though I had managed to recast the sea as an English sea and set myself in a fisherman's hut that must have owed more to stories I had read as a boy than to anything I had seen with my own eyes. No fishing boats went out from the holiday beaches I knew in Norfolk, even if we did go shrimping in the shallows.

'I was in this hut,' I was telling Sylvia, 'and it was really solid. The walls weren't made of planks, they were made of beams, and the beams were set upright, thick as railway sleepers and crusted with salt, like the wood you get in breakwaters. And there were all these things around me, lobster pots and anchor chains and . . .' And there my voice broke so that 'anchors' came out as a cry.

Her eyes flooded, the oscillation of light on their dark so immediate, so unguarded that she seemed to rise from where she sat against the wall before there was time to cross the room and put her arms round me.

We had slipped into living as a couple, trudging through the freezing streets to visit other couples in the diaphanous warmth of their paraffin stoves and bundling under the blankets at night. We had exchanged stories, so that Sylvia knew why my voice broke on 'anchors' and I knew of her long-running battle with her parents in Southall and her strict Catholic upbringing, one of her points of affinity with John, and knew what an uneasy rebel she was, forthright one moment and fragile the next. But that was the moment when we decided to fall in love.

For a while it almost worked. 'Something's changed around here, hasn't it?' said Jed when next he blew in from the North. Bluff and black-bearded, Jed was driven by a bullish energy that had led him to believe he was a Beat Poet. He liked to sit in our hearth and tell us stories of his sexual encounters, which were a source of unending astonishment to him. 'Eight times I came that night! Eight times!'

But one morning I came in through the back gate to a moment of inexorable clarity. Perhaps it was the fact that I was alone, which I almost never was. Sylvia had gone to see Catherine, who was like an elder sister to her. Perhaps it was the clarity of the sunlight on one of the first fine mornings in spring. But as I opened the back door into the basement, I had the sense that I was looking into my own life. I felt happy at first, intrigued even, to have this slant on myself as I stepped in out of the sunlight. But when I opened the door of our room and saw the bed with its corners neatly turned down, I felt a sadness there was no escaping.

I knew that I had to tell Sylvia. But how? I thought about it for a couple of days and realised that I could only tell her the truth. Because she looked exotic, and because she was frank about her own sexuality in a way that was quite unusual then, men tended to treat Sylvia as an odalisque. One of her undergraduate boyfriends had even suggested that she should take all her clothes off, go downstairs and, as she put it, 'disport myself among his friends'. (Sylvia might not have been educated beyond the age of fifteen but she always used the language well.) But reckless as Sylvia was, she was a romantic. She was reckless just because she was a romantic.

And so I told her of the moment when I first saw Anke looking up at the city map, how distinct that was from anything I had known before. 'That's how love comes to me. It happens. I can't will it into being, however much I might want to.'

Sylvia understood. But before she had time to adjust, to write to John or to move up into the front room, where the deathbed had been replaced by something a little more contemporary, Jed appeared, warning me that I was about to be arrested by the Drug Squad.

He had sent a letter a couple of weeks before from the pub in Lancashire where he was working as a barman, thoroughly depressed and asking me to get him a little bit of hash, a two-quid deal. I should have ducked out of that and simply written a letter to cheer him up, elaborated a comic fantasy of some kind, an imbroglio of barmaids from which he barely escaped with his manhood. The solitary joints I had smoked in my room at the farm had only walled me up behind a thicker and thicker wall. But I didn't, I sent a quick reply, explaining that I'd have to have the two quid in advance because I was living on the dole and didn't have two quid to spare. And then a brief, friendly note with the hash itself, the little square wrapped in tissue paper in the corner of the envelope. Surely that would pass through the post unnoticed.

What I didn't know was that Jed, with his usual excess of energy, had also been sending telegrams trying to organise a large consignment. The post office had passed the telegrams on to the police, who were watching everything that went through his letter box. Jed had just been charged with possession. As soon as he was released on bail, he had caught the train down to warn me that I was about to be charged with supply.

Jed clearly expected me to run and I did consider it. Moses, a West Country hippie who used to crash on the floor in Walton Lane, had found some cheap rooms in an old manor house outside Stow-on-the-Wold and was always urging me to move out there. But then I would have been condemned to a life on the run. And crucially, I would not have been able to sit my Finals in June. Once I was settled in my basement room, it had occurred to me that, though I might have gone down from Merton of my own accord, I already had my three years' residence qualification, which entitled

354

me to sit for my degree. I had gone to see John Jones and asked if the college would enter me for Finals. He saw no reason why not. He had even asked if I would like to come back into college for the summer term but I knew how impossible that would be. I preferred to rise like a shadow from the basement.

I had been raided by the Drug Squad once before, in Walton Lane. We were always careful to burn our roaches, the stubs of the joints, rolled from the tops of Rizla packets or cigarette packets so that we could smoke them right down past the last precious grains of resin, and they found nothing. But there had been a feudal moment when the detective sergeant drew me aside after questioning Ron. 'We know what to expect from the likes of him,' he confided, 'but we don't like to see a young gentleman like yourself getting caught up in all this.' And it must have been privilege that was creating this strange delay in which I waited to be arrested: first they had to get permission from the proctors, two dons who acted as the university's disciplinary officers.

'How's the poetry going, Rog?' the detective constable asked as the squad car took me down the Cornmarket.

Ten minutes later he was having to ask me to bend over so that he could peer up my naked arse for any drugs I might have concealed there. They had found nothing when they rousted us out of bed that morning and searched the room. But they had found my Carnaby Street clothes hanging in the wardrobe, bought from the long months of private tutoring: not just the yellow suit but a burnt-orange silk shirt with a Russian collar, a replica eighteenth-century coat in silver and blue brocade and a duellist's shirt, complete with a lace ruff and lace cuffs, all of which convinced them that I must be making money from selling drugs. Plus there was a phrase in my second letter to Jed in which I said that I had 'lost my contact in London'. I had never had a contact in London. It was Bryn who knew where to score a Brixton boot sole. I was just trying to excuse my hesitation when Jed's postal order arrived, the couple of days while I debated the wisdom of this before I thought, 'What could possibly go wrong?', scored a two-quid deal from someone I trusted and put it in the post. But it was that moment of bravado the prosecuting counsel seized on, that phrase that furnished him with the headline-winning phrase all the newspapers carried the next day: *Oxford undergraduate 'runs mail order service for dangerous drugs'*.

Though they might not have picked up the story at all if it had not been for the final flourish on my letters to Jed. Ever since my first year at Merton when we used to listen over and over again to the last track on John's Dylan Thomas LP, the track where Dylan read Auden's 'As I Walked Out One Evening', I had been playing variations on the impossible declarations the lover makes when Auden hears him sing

> Under an arch of the railway:
>     'Love has no ending.

> 'I'll love you, dear, I'll love you
>     Till China and Africa meet,
> And the river jumps over the mountain
>     And the salmon sing in the street,

> 'I'll love you till the ocean
>     Is folded and hung up to dry
> And the seven stars go squawking
>     Like geese about the sky.

If I was writing to a friend, I would never sign off 'Yours sincerely', it would be 'Yours till dolphins leap in the High' or 'Yours till the buffalo roam over Radcliffe Square'. I can't remember what I put at the end of my first letter to Jed but at the end of the second I had put 'Yours till they tax the grass'. When that was read out in court, all the taxpayers chuckled and all the journalists who were there for another case picked up their pens.

This time I had not turned to my father for help. This was the path I had chosen and this was a pitfall I should have had the sense to avoid. But I did have a character witness, one of the Dominicans from Blackfriars, who had started to hold poetry readings on a Sunday evening as a way of drawing in the Oxford underground. And what kept me out of jail was the claim that I had just been offered a place on the Writers' Workshop at the University of Iowa. The magistrates hesitated to send me down 'at this crucial stage in your career' and gave me a suspended sentence.

They were not to know that I had yet to hear back from Iowa. Paul Engle had liked my work when he came over to Oxford on a recruiting mission. At least, he had picked out one of my lines as an example of what he was looking for, a finished line. But eventually he replied in tones of some regret, pointing out that the finished lines were sitting alongside too many that were far from finished. I was still a long way from being able to take Michael Hewlings's advice and cover seventy sheets of paper to get sixteen good lines.

'We are not sure whether or not you still consider yourself to be under the authority of the university.'

It was several days after the appearance of a certain small item on the front page of the broadsheets and of much lengthier reports on the inside pages of the tabloids, complete with a photograph of me holding Sylvia's cat, for which the papers' Oxford stringer had paid me the sum of £6, and I was facing the proctors in their office in the Sheldonian.

'Well, insofar as I'm entered for Finals, I suppose I must be.'

I left them to their deliberations and went back to my basement. Two days later a letter came, informing me that I must leave Oxford forthwith. I was allowed to return for the period of the exams but then I must absent myself once more, staying out of the city until the exam results were published.

That hardly came as a shock. What did come as a shock was a letter from Merton, informing me that, while I would be allowed to sit Finals, I would not be allowed to take my degree and my name would be struck from the rolls of the college.

The first penalty I took in my stride. Going through the degree ceremony was a formality that many of my generation dispensed with anyway. But to have my name struck from the rolls of the college! As freshmen we had been taken up to the Savile Room to inscribe our names into a massive leather-bound book that lay open on the table. That was the moment when I felt myself entering into a history that went back to 1264, when the college was founded. Now I imagined the great book being opened and a line struck through my spindly signature.

That image must have reverberated in the psyche because I began to have a recurring dream in which I returned to the college and had to find my way through the upper rooms into which the dons withdrew after Hall, and where they dined outside term, as I knew because, in what proved to be my last long vacation, I had once dined with them as the guest of a junior fellow. In the dream the wooden staircase opened out and turned into a wide flight of steps carved out of a stone the colour of terracotta that may have carried the memory of a ruined abbey I had visited one summer in Provence with the boys I was tutoring in English and three or four of their uncles who were priests, a space so resonant for all its ruin that, as we walked across it, the uncles broke into plainchant. Sometimes I would be coming down the flight of steps, as if there were still higher storeys where I had some legitimate business, where I would be, not an honoured guest, but someone with a recognised role, a postgraduate, perhaps, or a visiting researcher.

Whether I was scrambling up the steps or hurrying down them, at the focal point of the dream I would come to a landing, wide as a terrace and in the same terracotta stone, that the dons would be crossing on their way in to dinner. One of them would look up, never anyone that I recognised but someone with a young, friendly face who would walk with me to the table so that I felt part of the company. Other faces would look up, again not the actual faces I had known from Merton but faces that were clearly at ease in this setting and they would have expressions of interest, as if I were returning from a long exile during which they had kept in touch with my work.

A momentary sense of acceptance and I would awake, never sure whether to be amused or embarrassed. However much I might relish the freedoms of living hand-to-mouth, in my subconscious I was still my mother's son. I was amused to see how the dream adapted itself to different forms of High Table: after the poet George Buchanan had invited me to lunch at the Savile Club, the faces would be turning with their expressions of interest as I rose from the little table where we had been seated and made my way down to the bar. But though I could see through the dream, I could never quite rid myself of its comical persistence. The best I could do was to balance it with another recurring dream, in which I tumbled through a series of mishaps. The reasons for my predicament were never too clear but the sensations were of falling and twisting this way and that under a variety of blows, escaping each time by a hair's breadth. I would land among other scapegraces, so laid back that they would just look up and nod, as if it came as no surprise to them that I had suddenly tumbled in among them.

Rob glances at me from under his tight black curls. Or I

glimpse the gingery moss of Ron's beard and feel a different kind of acceptance. How did James K. Baxter put it?

> Despair is the only gift;
> When it is shared, it becomes a different thing . . .

But this dream absorbs new material too and in recent years the faces have begun to change. Trevor glances out of the thin shoulders that range over his drum kit, whether he is playing or not. Dick nips out his fag and picks up the flugelhorn, raising it towards a face Picasso might have imagined in his Blue Period. And I think, *Oh, it's all right, I made it to the rehearsal after all. In a moment the banter will start to fly.*

'How's John?'

'Still up there,' Sylvia said. 'Still being chased around the room by his father confessor.'

We were sitting in the buffet at Euston. Sylvia had just come back from Scotland and I had arranged with Trixie to meet her off the train. Trixie was her oldest friend and a member of the Exploding Galaxy, a dance group that had evolved into a continual happening, an arts lab that had no need of a lab. They took their metaphors from geology and eschewed anything *centriclinal*. They were interested only in *quaquaversals*.

We had guessed that Sylvia would be travelling back from a disappointment, for which I could hardly blame John. Sylvia really should have asked him before she conceived his child. And I could only have added to the confusion. But whatever she felt, she seemed to be outwitting it, the cynic covering for the romantic. I was quite relaxed by the time the three of us got up from the table and I asked her where she was going next.

'Home, I suppose.'

At once I was shocked back into a state of alarm. Home was the last place she should be going. She shouldn't be putting herself at the mercy of her parents, not with that downcast tone in her voice.

'No, you mustn't do that! Come back to the farm with me.'

Sylvia liked the farm. I had taken her there when she was first entrusted to my care. And in the morning she could go back to Oxford, where she had taken over my basement room.

The proctors' letter had required me to leave within twenty-four hours, which had left me with little choice but to pile everything into the back of my mother's van. At least this time I was driving it myself, not railing at my mother from the passenger seat. My parents were so relieved to find me still sane that they had taken my criminal conviction remarkably well. But suspicion surrounded me now when I took my place at the long table. No one spoke of it openly, because I was still the boss's son. But I felt like the prodigal for whom no party was going to be thrown. I sat up in my room, rereading the books that were supposed to secure me a degree, and hardly went out. I had no friends locally except Koki, who was working from home, making enamelled jewellery. The only plan I had for my future was to go from town to town like a medieval pedlar, selling her earrings and cuff links. Where did I think I was living, in a Donovan LP?

Perhaps that sense of isolation explains what happened that evening at the farm. Or perhaps some navigational instinct in the back of the head had already discounted the pedlar plan and taken account of the fact that my grandmother had just had a stroke and gone into an old people's home, leaving the house in Norfolk empty. Whatever the subconscious processes were, as Sylvia and I sat up in my room after dinner I felt my mouth opening, slowly and with difficulty, as if its strings were being worked by an inept puppeteer, and heard words on the air I could hardly believe my lips were forming: 'Why don't you marry me, then?'

'Well, if you still mean that in the morning, of course I will!'

In the morning I did still mean it, though I could see the dismay on my mother's face when I told her after breakfast. I still meant it that evening when I phoned Redmond and asked him to be my best man, though I could hear his misgivings in the initial silence over which he was quick to throw his congratulations. But by the time I had a letter from Father Paulinus, who had acted as my character witness, telling me that Sylvia had returned to Oxford walking three feet off the ground, I knew that I had made a terrible mistake. And by the time I had a letter from Sylvia herself, describing the amethyst in the engagement ring she had found in a second-hand shop, just the right shade for her colouring, and how the man was sending it to be altered because her ring finger took a K – K for King, she said happily – I knew I could never take back those words, not if I wanted her to live and the child she was carrying to be born.

It's strange how strongly I felt my responsibility to that unborn child. I might be a chancer who had seized on the idea of a life in Norfolk, a life that my father, who owned the house in Caley Street, would never have sanctioned if I were not getting married. And Sylvia might trade on her vulnerability – if I edged towards voicing my doubts over the phone, she would be quick to say, 'I don't think I can take any more' – but the vulnerability was real. Just before she met John, she had been gang-raped by a vanload of Irish labourers from whom she had been unwise enough to accept a lift. And none of it was the fault of the child that was growing in her womb.

# PART FOUR

## Norfolk

### 1968

Down on my springs
I barely bounce, but do
Just bounce

Nigel Wells, 'The Dumps'

N o one except the postman used the front door of the house in Caley Street. Everyone walked round the corner into Joyce's Lane and came in through the back gate, set into a low carrstone wall that ran on for a few yards further to mark off the backyard where the privy had been and where a stout wooden shed now held my grandfather's finishing machine and a cut-down work-bench on which Ruth still did small repairs for the family. A clothes line ran diagonally across it and a coal bunker stood against another low wall that marked it off from next door's yard. Small as our yard was, it felt spacious because it opened on to the width of the lane.

My grandmother had died a few days after we arrived in Heacham. We had gone to visit her but she was taken with a choking fit and all I saw of her was one last apologetic glance as the staff rushed in to help. She died as I had always known her, humbly. It was only when my mother let something slip on the way to the funeral that I began to glimpse the irrepressible young woman my grandfather had married in the spring of 1918.

Sylvia and I were in the back of the car when I heard my mother ask my father, 'Has anyone let Jack know?'

She must mean Uncle Jack. Father of the other Sylvia, the one I had idolised as a boy. Uncle Jack whose beach hut was the size of a villa. I remembered being invited there for tea and wondering why my parents came away muttering whereas I had simply been delighted with the generous helpings of Neapolitan ice cream. It suddenly struck me that I had no idea where Uncle Jack fitted into the family.

'Exactly what was Uncle Jack's relationship to Grandma?'

I was merely puzzled but my question must have sounded unnervingly precise. The car rolled on its wheels for some time before my father said, 'Well, if you must know, he was her son.'

Immediately I thought of Frank. Frank in his RAF uniform, standing under the Lockheed Hudson. The oldest of my uncles, or so I had always been told.

'And what about Uncle Frank? Was he born out of wedlock too?'

'I think he may have been,' my father conceded uneasily. 'It was all part of that upheaval brought on by the war.'

Not just in my imagination, then, the uncertainties I had read into the books in the little bookcase in the front room.

'The one who must never know is Frank,' my father stressed. 'It would take away his sense of himself to discover that he wasn't the eldest.'

Frank who was gentle and always seemed a little anxious, who had never quite found his niche once he had come out of the air force. And Jack who was a detective sergeant in the Special Branch, a big man with enough swagger for even my father to feel challenged.

When I had asked about Frank, 'Was he born out of wedlock too?' I had just been imagining that my grandparents might have been a little previous. But no, said Ruth when I went to talk to her the next day, my grandfather had brought up Frank as his own son and they certainly shared a gift for music – Frank only had to hear a piece once and he could play it by ear – but my grandfather had told his family back in Yorkshire that he was marrying a widow with two young children. And Frank didn't have a birth certificate, something my father had to sort out from his desk in Brixton police station when Frank was posted abroad and needed a passport.

'She was too easygoing,' Ruth said, 'that was her trouble,' but I didn't think it was that at all. In the first photo she showed me of my grandmother as a young woman, she looks striking, with a head of fine curls that I knew to be ginger, and thoroughly independent. She is standing with her bicycle, ready to cycle out unchaperoned, the mere thought of which scandalised her parents: 'Florrie shouldn't be going all over the countryside like that, without a man to look after her.' Her family were rigidly conservative, 'just like the Forsytes, but without the money'. Her father, a tram driver in Norwich, was 'a sweet old boy' but his wife was a martinet: 'If she didn't like the look of the coal in the scuttle, she'd send him back down to the cellar to change it.'

Florrie had made her escape when she went into service at the age of thirteen. She worked for a doctor in Norwich, then found a place at Cawston, near her mother's people, the Lees, who were farmers. There she was no longer the eldest daughter, bearing the brunt of her mother's discipline. She was just one of a tribe of cousins. It was there she bought the bicycle and established her independence. And it was there I imagined her riding the lanes, rebellious, high-spirited, her hair firing the hedges with a beech's clear flame.

In the second photo her hair is up, gathered into a double wave that is flying off the forehead, and she is sitting posed in a photographer's studio, which has clearly made her self-conscious. But she looks as if something had already made her thoughtful, thoughtful and even a little troubled. Perhaps Jack had been born by then. What is striking in this photo is the intensity in the eyes, which are as full and dark as any belladonna-using beauty could wish for, so flooded with feeling that they look almost aggrieved.

All that feeling, that hurt pride, must have passed into Jack. He would never ask who his father was, not even when he was in the police and in a position to make enquiries. If he had treated his mother like that, he declared, he didn't want to know him. And Jack would have needed all the pride he could muster. He was brought up by the martinet herself, Great-granny Edwards, into whose presence I had once been ushered as she sat bolt upright on her chair. But he did come to stay with his mother in the holidays. 'We never asked where he came from,' my father explained. 'To us he was just Cousin Jack.'

Ruth seemed in two minds as to who Frank's father might be. 'He does have a look of the Lees,' the farming cousins. But then she remembered a mysterious cousin from Bristol who would phone whenever he was holidaying with his family in Norfolk. Each time, it seemed, they would come as close as King's Lynn, only for something to prevent them driving the last few miles to Sedgeford.

The third photo Ruth showed me is the wedding photo. Rush and Florrie are sitting outside a cottage in Sedgeford, Rush in a forage cap and the uniform of the Royal Flying Corps, the jacket buttoned across to one shoulder and puttees wound tightly below the knee, and Florrie in a well-cut uniform that she had tailored herself. One of two WAACs sent to Sedgeford aerodrome when the Corps was formed in 1917, she was given a man's army jacket, issued with an army blanket and told to make herself a skirt. According to villagers Ruth had talked to, 'All the men beau'd her a bit because she was the first woman they had ever seen in uniform.'

In the wedding photo Florrie is in her late twenties. She has had two children, and the face has broadened and softened, the intensity in the eyes steadied to a look of quiet determination, as if, now that she has found a safe haven in Rush, whose arm she has taken, motherhood can come to the fore. There is determination in Rush's face too, a steady gaze levelled at the camera. I found that impressive because Rush was only twenty-three when he took on Florrie and her boys, which must have taken some courage in 1918. But then his own mother had been widowed, forcing him into an early maturity. His father was a 'beerkeeper', according to the marriage certificate, and his mother had kept the pub on because it provided a living while she raised the children. Rush had grown up behind the bar of the Rising Sun in Scholes and would never drink himself: 'The things I've seen come crawling out of a pub door . . .' He had served his time as a bootmaker with the Cleckheaton Co-op and must have given a wry smile when he was sent to Sedgeford aerodrome to mend the officers' boots.

Bit by bit, Ruth filled in the story for me. But only when her husband Harold wasn't around. She knew just how he would taunt her if he ever found out. I only wished that I had found out sooner. Not that I would have been able to talk to my grandmother about it, not directly. Convention would surely have run too deep for that. But I might have taken a hint from Percy Sledge and taken the time to know her.

We had only been alone together once, the Easter after my grandfather died. She had been staying at the farm and I was deputed to drive her home. Nosing my way round the North Circular, navigating by the ominous names that had been stages in my carsickness as a child – Hanger Lane, Staples Corner, Apex Corner – I was as cautious as my grandfather had been in the Maggot. Once through Hatfield, Baldock and Royston, I increased speed and she began to grumble, 'You're going too fast!'

We were hopelessly out of sync. Ahead of us was the Cold War zone, the roads I remembered being full of American convoys. As a small boy my heart would quicken. From being a queasy passenger in the back, I would become an intent pair of eyes at the window. If we stopped at a transport café, I would hunt along the verge for Lucky Strike packets. Now I was retracing the route at the wheel of a car. All I wanted was to put my foot down and exult in my coming of age. But the old lady beside me was feeling as queasy as any child. For the first time since her husband's death, she was going home to an empty house.

I slowed down. But I was just twenty-two, burning my high octanes, and slowness oppressed me. It felt as if the brakes were being applied to me. I let the speed creep up to fifty, so smoothly she would never notice. 'It's still too fast!' she complained and I slowed once more. The road surface stretched. I felt I was seeing every hairline crack as it passed under the wheels. 'At this rate we'll never get there!' I protested and let the speed creep up again. She clenched herself against the passenger door and the rest of the journey passed in silence.

I knew I was failing her. And knew I could not help myself. I gave her a poor homecoming. She went almost straight to bed, saying she was not feeling well. Next morning she was still aggrieved. My father's idea had been that I should stay for a few days and take her out for drives. There seemed little chance of that now. I took a solitary walk around the lavender fields, wondering what the herb was for repentance, and left in the afternoon.

I thought how different that drive might have been if I had realised who my passenger was. Not someone I had known only as one half of an inseparable pair, Grandma and Grandad, but a young girl who had ridden out unchaperoned, the impassioned young woman in the studio photograph. But I was aware, too, of how different I was from the lad who had driven her home, still blithe in his self-belief. Perhaps I only felt her close to me now because I had met with difficulty myself. And could see in her eyes an impetus I had yet to harness.

Quarter to eight in the morning. I stood at the end of Woodend Road, waiting for the works bus as it came down from the bypass.

I had been taken on at Donald Cook's, a factory on the outskirts of King's Lynn that canned fruit and vegetables for Dewhurst's, a chain of butcher's shops owned by Vestey's, which shipped in frozen meat from Australia. My first job was to pull a trolley to the end of the strawberry lines and collect bins of rejected strawberries for my mate to put through the pulping machine. A wide plastic tray sat on a pallet under the pulper's nozzle. Once it was full, we would put on our store coats, push down the iron lever and open the heavy door of the cold store, into which we were only allowed two at a time in case one of us succumbed to the cold and his heart stopped. I would guide the forked bars of the trolley into the pallet, lift it gently and manoeuvre it into the strawberry mausoleum, where tray upon tray lay purpling under swirls of rime, ready to be shipped out to Australia to make ice-lollies. Lord Vestey came to inspect the factory one day, a thin white-haired old man in a suit, accompanied by his son, who was dressed as he might have been for a day's shooting. I stood by the pulping machine while they were shown the cold store, feeling rather as my Uncle Peter must have felt when he stood by the railway line cap in hand and the King's funeral train glided past.

The women on the bus had their hair up under factory head-scarves so that no stray hairs ended up in the cans. Some got on singly and sat silent by the window, as if working a day-long penance. Others climbed on in two and threes, their banter reaching to the back of the bus. These were the women from the field gangs, who came into the factory when there was nothing to be picked in the flat fields that stretched beyond the window as the bus got closer to Lynn. A couple of them were ahead of me one afternoon on the steps up to the wages office and too intent on their story to break off. I heard, 'He caught her by the quaint' and realised that I was hearing the Chaucerian *queynte*, which lost its lilt and all its mischievous possibilities when it descended into *cunt*.

371

When the season ended, the Spotted Lady from the fairground came into the factory too. She had spent the summer behind glass, long blond hair falling over her shoulders and framing what the black spots did not cover. In previous summers she had been the Snake Girl and then the Rat Girl. I talked to her one lunchtime and she seemed to me sweet and completely guileless. In the fairground she worked for her keep 'and whatever I want for Christmas and my birthday'. She was oblivious to her reputation and the mistreatment it brought: one of the men from the factory had taken her down to Wootton Marsh, stripped her and left her. All she wanted was a little attention. 'Just take me out!' she said. Which would have been like taking out a child.

The men shifted back and forth too, even the supervisor on the pea line becoming a ganger out in the fields when it paid better. Some of the older men had come into the factory from a lifetime's farm labouring because the work was easier. I used to chat to one of them, a small, fine-boned old man called Eddie who had a thin line of white moustache. The moustache reminded me of my grandfather and I had invested him with the same steady glow until I glimpsed him in Lynn one Saturday lunchtime. Sylvia and I were waiting to cross a busy street when I saw Eddie standing just down the kerb from us. I sang out, 'Hello, Eddie!' and turned to introduce him to Sylvia. He blinked up at me out of watery eyes, barely afloat in a storm force of ale, and a woman standing the other side of him glared down at us out of her corsetry. The last thing she wanted was some young couple distracting him at this late stage.

I did step back into the warm in another kitchen. One of the cleaners from the factory lived in Heacham. I had first noticed her when I was trundling the bins on my trolley, a bent figure in a headscarf mopping around the feet of the students who were brought in over the summer to work twelve-hour shifts. Some of them saw her as the very image of Mrs Mop and laughed behind

372

her back. When I clocked off at the end of my eight hours, she was waiting in the queue for the bus. And when the bus pulled up opposite the school, she pulled herself up on to her feet, ready to step down ahead of me.

It was easy to retreat into my donkey jacket and stride past. But we both turned down Broadway and I would glimpse the head-scarf over the line of the fence as I turned. One evening I decided to be sociable and walk down into the village with her. She and her husband were Londoners, I discovered, part of the overspill the area was keen to attract. They had bought a small house down an entry off the High Street and weren't too impressed: 'There's nothing here for working-class people.'

I can't remember why Sylvia and I called on them one Saturday afternoon. Did they have something for sale, something we might need when the baby came, like a clothes horse or a fireguard? What I do remember is stepping into the kitchen and meeting someone I would never have recognised from the hunched figure under the headscarf. She was standing by a table filled with the day's baking, trays of scones and sausage rolls sending out their sheen as if they had just this moment come out of the oven. But that was as nothing to the sheen that was coming off the baker herself, the shoulders plumped back and the eyes bright under the bob of grey hair.

'You look rather different from the woman I see at work!'

Her husband laughed.

'She comes off with the overall. And she doesn't go on again until Monday morning.'

Harold had a gleam in his eye as he came through the back gate: 'Did you know there's a bit of Gypsy Rose Lee in the family?' I knew that Great-granny Edwards's maiden name was Lee but I had never made the connection. It was hard to imagine the martinet as a gypsy.

But Great-aunt Jesse, Florrie's younger sister, had been looking into the family history and found that the Lees were indeed gypsies.

If the family in Norwich were 'just like the Forsytes, but without the money', Jesse had grown up to become Lady Bracknell without the title, an imposing woman whose underlying kindliness had to contend with her strict sense of propriety. She had made a good marriage to an older man, a dispensing chemist, and still lived over the shop in Unthank Road. If she said there were gypsies somewhere back along the line, there probably were.

My father refused to believe it. 'There was nothing of the gypsy', he said, 'about Farmer Lee,' according him the same respect he had accorded to Farmer Trenowath. But in the early nineteenth century a number of gypsy families, seeing that the nomadic life was becoming impossible, had bought land and settled to farming. And I had only to look at my father, always so much more at ease talking to Shep or to Charlie Chambers, the dealer who drove such a hard bargain over the pigs from the farm, than he was among his fellow lawyers, to think there might be something in it.

Difficult in his case to tell the gypsy from the countryman, to separate an instinct dormant under the years of settlement from the informal trading that had always held the countryside together, particularly in hard times, and which I could see continuing in Harold, who was making no claims for himself, being an in-law, a Hudson from Snettisham. Harold was a bus driver but in his spare time he was a fisherman, a cockle picker, a samphire gatherer, a chimney sweep and a bicycle repairer. The house was called Scandiscopist, from the Latin for 'Climbing Brush', and he ran the bicycle business from the garage. It was on a bus route and a bus would drop off a couple of crabs if one of Harold's mates had had a good haul. It seemed to me that the factory cleaner and her husband were mistaken and the area had rather a lot to offer working-class people once you linked into the networks that ran alongside work.

As for me, with my grandmother's rounded cheekbones and the pommel of her chin, features that were clearly Anglo-Saxon, what was I to make of it? Not too much, I thought. I had already woven one myth around Anke and I was not about to weave another. If there were a thread of gypsy ancestry, it would show of itself.

In the meantime, I had to find something a little more enlivening than working in the canning factory. My exam results had come. For one paper I had sat up all night reading some notes Redmond had lent me and stayed awake through the exam itself by dipping into my pocket for crumbs of methedrine. Otherwise I had given straight answers and got a straight Second. John Jones would give me references for teaching jobs, provided I went into Further Education and not into schools. And Robert Levens, who had been my Classics tutor, had taken the trouble to send me a little note: '*Allegro ma non troppo* is my prescription for you. By which I mean that I hope you will continue to be subversive but with sufficient control to be usefully so.'

There was no rush. I had been taken on to the permanent staff in the factory and assigned as assistant to the stock controller, which meant that I spent my days scaling roof-high stacks in the warehouse in search of pallets of forgotten produce that were suddenly in demand. And at the end of the day the works bus would return me to the width of the margin, dipping down towards the south beach and running along the back of the village before it set me down on what must once have been a ridge of shingle and was now the slope up to the bypass.

The school playground was deserted in the early evening and I always stepped down into quiet. One evening in September, after an unusually warm day, the sunlight was still so strong that it was like stepping down into the shine off a lake. The cleaner was on holiday and, as I turned into Broadway, all I could hear were my own tentative steps, trespassing on the light, and birds singing from gardens either side of the road and other gardens beyond, singing from as far down as the recreation ground and the road to the north beach. Nothing but curls of sound that were shavings of light, as if the houses were translucent and the village given over to the last long hour of the sun.

For the first time since that morning on the locked ward when the lines about storming the beach at Barcarès had begun to form in the back of my head, I felt the possibility of a poem, not one that I was willing into being, like the paean to Princess's eyebrows, but one that I was being given, and I started work on it that evening.

It seems to me now that I muffed it at the end. What looks like lyric is really just a fit of impatience. I should have stuck with the long line and the quieter language and seen what I could get out of that. But somewhere between the *planes of silence* and the *ringing trines*, whatever they might be, I was up and awake and on the move, and that was enough to be going on with.

### Walking Home

Summer has slammed its last car door,
given the engine its last superfluous rev,
shouted this year's last 'Bye till next year'
and lurched off, twisting the final plume of exhaust
down High Street and Broadway
round, out on to the bypass.
Yes, September has put the shutters up and closed the till,
leaving the villagers to think of carrot-topping,
going on the sugar beet, spud-picking in the snow,
or sitting watching the summer's hoard
shrink through till spring.

The afternoon has shot its bolt,
sent its brief explosion of schoolchildren

out through the gates,
spattering into their homes,
into their fishfinger teas, three-minute chips
and tinfoil squares of country-style pie.

The clocked-in hours have ticked to a close
and we've streamed out, dunking our cards
in the machine, to the works buses,
lit up the longest cigarette of the day.
The stop-go lurch between traffic lights and traffic jams,
the long blank stretch between town and the villages,
the trundle all round everywhere dropping people off,
they're over again, and I'm dropped off too, back at my spot,
back on the edge of this urbanised, spilt village,
this creeping motley of summer pickings and casual winters:

but it's strange, walking home through the village this evening;
today's rare sun has hung daylong over it,
one ounce of balm in a torn Indian Summer,
and all is still – no one on the streets save me,
and even I am walking almost without footfall;
only the birds are making any sound, a mere scatter of them,
singing quietly – but their song cuts over the landscape,
piercing the village:

                              down a street of glass
                    between transparent walls
                              and roofs of crystal

                    a joyously empty man, my centre
                    a circle of nothing
                    through which anything may pass,
                    aware only of one identity,
                    a pair of ears moving on a surface,

I walk a new landscape
limpid as geometry, of space
resolved into planes of silence
or ringing trines, of time
refined to the pulse of surprise,
a flicker of notes through stillness.